Modern Growth Theory

To

Professor Lionel W. McKenzie

With Love, Admiration, and Respect

Preface

This book has grown out of an earlier one by the author, *Growth Theory: Solow and his Modern Exponents* (Dasgupta 2005). The earlier book attempted to cover the seven-year period (1986-92) during which a number of classic papers on New Growth Economics appeared in journals. In the process, however, the book neglected certain issues which gained prominence after this period. A major omission was Charles Jones' (1995) critique of the scale effects in Romer (1990), Aghion and Howitt (1992), and Grossman and Helpman (1991a and 1991b). A second important lacuna concerned the literature on growth and inequality. The latter is vast and it is beyond the scope of a small book such as the present one to address it satisfactorily. However, given the importance of the problem, especially for developing economies, Chapter 8 presents a summary of two important works in the area due to Alesina and Rodrik (1994), and Galor and Zeira (1993).

These were not the only reasons that gave rise to the need for a new book. The Indian data used in the first chapter to motivate the study of Growth Theory called for updating. This task has been accomplished in the present version of the book. The treatment of the Leontief production function model needed extensive changes as a result of the publication of Dasgupta (2008). The exposition of the model is clearer in this new book and clarifies the link between the fixed coefficients Leontief structure and the AK model of endogenous growth. Chapter 3 deals with these problems. The chapter also summarizes the growth models of Harrod and Domar in an attempt to distinguish them from each other as well as from the fixed coefficient model. The earlier book had ignored the Harrod and Domar exercises except for a cursory reference in the Preface.

Chapters 3 and 4 have undergone substantial modification. The Barro and Sala-i-Martin models (1990 and 2003) for flow infrastructure (public input) had been included under Chapter 3 of the earlier book, while the Dasgupta (1999 and 2004) models of stock infrastructure found a place in Chapter 4. The present edition lifts these works out of Chapters 3 and 4 and presents them, in search of a unification of ideas, in Chapter 5 which deals exclusively with growth and infrastructure. Also, the treatment of Dasgupta (1999) has been substantially simplified. Besides, the model is reinterpreted to allow for growth with unemployment, as is the case for developing economies like India. This introduces a policy question relating to maximization of employment vis-à-vis maximization of the welfare integral. Two other important additions in this book are summaries and problem sets that advanced Master's level students, research scholars and teachers might find useful.

As with the previous book, the present one too travels both backward and forward in time. To the extent that all the authors focused on the Solow (1956) scaffolding to build up their ideas, the book starts off with a detailed discussion of the relevant tenets of that seminal work. This constitutes the backward journey. As far as the forward trip goes, it outlines important attempts to tackle new questions about the old classics. It is prudent to point out that, given the phenomenal speed of research in the area, articles published even as late as the closing years of the twentieth century should probably be considered dated. Consequently, some of the works included in the book may not qualify as recent. In fact, many of them have already made their way into standard textbooks.

The decision to set out on a fresh voyage to excavate trodden areas is motivated by two considerations. First, the works addressed by the book do not receive uniform treatment in existing references. In matters of details, the student is often compelled to seek help from other sources, which in turn depend on alternative notational structures as well as conceptual frameworks. These can lead to unforeseen difficulties, especially for the beginner. The book hopefully resolves some of these problems by presenting a self-contained development of the subject matter, including an exposition of the basic mathematics (viz. Control Theory) needed to study the subject. The treatment of Control Theory should prove useful for first year graduate students studying macroeconomics also.

At the same time, the different authors' contributions are presented with reference to a common platform, consisting of viewing a state of dynamic equilibrium for the economy as a simple supply-demand cross, where the notions of supply and demand apply to the rate of growth itself. Since students of economics are exposed to the tools of supply and demand starting from the most elementary of courses, it is expected that they will readily grasp the messages of Modern Growth Theory when presented in this familiar language.[1]

In this connection, Mausumi Das'(2006) review of the first book in the *Indian Economic Review* raised an important question about the concept of a balanced growth *equilibrium* path. Das' review pointed

---

[1]The diagrammatic device that this viewpoint leads to was used, probably for the first time, by Romer (1990), but later on by Barro and Sala-i-Martin (1992), and Rivera-Batiz and Romer (1991) also. However, the identification of the diagram as a supply-demand apparatus is an original contribution of this book.

out, however, that the question had not been adequately dealt with. Accordingly, the present book attempts to explain the qualification of an *equilbrium* more clearly. To re-emphasize, the book depends crucially on the separation of demand and supply factors affecting the notion of a rate of endogenous growth and views balanced growth itself as an instance of a demand supply equilibrium. Consequently, this book, motivated by Das' review, attempts to improve over the exposition of the first book. These matters are dealt with in Chapter 2.

An important consideration that led to both books was the emphasis they accord to the role played by externalities in most of the recent literature. The externality arises from the fact that the subject derives its fundamental motivation from a need to grapple with the force of technical progress in a market environment. By its very nature, knowledge regarding improvements in productive technology often assumes the form of a public good. As in the case of most public goods, technological changes generate non-internalizable externalities, that constitute one of the primary reasons for the failure of the competitive market system. The failure led to a natural quest for policies to sustain efficient solutions with minimal interventions by the government. A pervading theme pursued by the book consists of the market failure characteristic. For many of the models presented, the failure is linked to the non-marketability of technical change. However, the book also brings into focus a class of models that bear formal similarity with the models of technical change, though the market failure they suffer from may be traced back to other forms of externalities, such as the ones associated with public infrasturcture mentioned above.

Neither this Preface nor the book itself is concerned with history of thought. Hence, only a cursory treatment of the events that led to the evolution of ideas would suffice. Formal Growth Theory began with Harrod (1939), who looked into the possibility of economic growth with full employment of resources. His analysis depended on the Keynesian multiplier theory of aggregate demand. At the same time he postulated that the path of capital accumulation was guided by entrepreneurs' expectations regarding change in demand over time. He found that a dynamic equilibrium path with these features would not be consistent with the requirement of full employment of resources. In fact, he demonstrated that an attempt to follow such a path in a free enterprise society would be self-defeating, leading to chronic unemployment or inflation. Thus, Harrod believed that a free enterprise system would more likely than not be characterized by cyclical fluctuations rather than steady growth. Chapter 3 below contains more details on the issue.

Harrod was not so much concerned with capacity improvement over time. It was Domar (1946) who looked into this issue explicitly for the first time. He linked any steadily maintained growth path of investment to a well-defined rate of capacity creation. On the other hand, like Harrod, Domar too visualized a path of output demand by appealing to Keynesian multiplier theory. His major concern was to ensure if the path of demand would match the capacity at each instant of time. Somewhat in Harrod's fashion, he concluded on a negative note that such a path was implausible. In addition, he pointed out that capacity improvement brought about by investment programmes often relates to the advent of new technologies. Such technological change renders existing technologies obsolete. Consequently, the economic costs of unutilized capacity might be aggravated further by capital scrapping in the face of competition, leading to inadequate returns to investment. Along with Harrod's work, Chapter 3 looks into the Domar exercise too.

A number of authors wrote on the Harrodian instability problem, suggesting the existence of inbuilt mechanisms in the free competitive system that might correct it towards full employment growth. Notable amongst them was Kaldor (1956), who suggested a Keynesian theory of distribution that could affect the savings rate of the economy in a stabilizing fashion and keep the economy rolling along an equilibrium growth path with full employment. Nonetheless, the Harrodian scepticism continued to dominate the profession for a long time. It is in this context that Solow (1956) occupies a truly revolutionary position in growth economics. It was Solow's neoclassical model of growth that argued for the first time that the unbridled process of competitive capital accumulation leads to a stable long run path of economic growth. The Solow exercise not only presented an example of a competitive growth model that was free of fluctuations in the long run. In addition, it incorporated the Domarian emphasis on capacity creation by allowing for explicit growth in the productivity of technology over time. (See Chapters 1 and 2 below.)

Of the multifarious directions in which Solow's work provoked new research,[2] there were none so important as the attempts made to capture the nature of technological progress itself. Like Domar, Solow was content to point out the possibility of productivity growth associated with investment. However, the precise link between investment and productivity was left unclear. Future researchers, including Solow (1960) himself, Drandakis and Phelps (1966), and others, devoted considerable energy towards clarifying the role of investment in productivity

---

[2]One recalls in particular the Uzawa (1961a, 1963) exercises aimed at generalizing Solow's stability result to multi-sector growth models.

improvements. However, the credit for first success in this quest goes perhaps to Arrow's model (Arrow 1962) of 'Learning by Doing'. Arrow's explanation of the force of technical change led first of all to a logical determination of the productivity growth rate of an economic system. Secondly, it offered a clear explanation of the reasons underlying technological progress. (See Chapter 3 below.) Uzawa's (Uzawa 1965) work on the effect of education on growth constituted another instance of a breakthrough, though it received less attention at the time it initially appeared than the Arrow's work. (See Chapter 4 below.)

Despite the Arrow and Uzawa successes, however, Growth Theory stood at a standstill for a little over two decades. Indeed, interest in economic growth dwindled considerably (though a parallel literature in economic development flourished) till the mid-1980s when Romer (1986) rekindled interest in economic growth problems by generalizing the scope of the Arrow paradigm. Around the same time, Lucas (1988) broadened Uzawa's framework to study the links between human capital formation and economic growth. (See Chapter 3 below for a discussion of Romer, 1986 and Chapter 4 for Lucas, 1988.) These works were only the beginning of a long line of papers on the subject. In particular, Romer's multi-sector model (Romer 1990) opened up a new horizon by explaining productivity improvements in terms of specialization. Further, it broadened the scope of Growth Theory by introducing non-competitive market structures to accommodate the problem of patent protection. The richness of Romer's exercise has lent to it the aura of a classic paper in the area of what is now commonly referred to as *Endogenous* Growth Theory. (See Chapter 6 below for a discussion of Romer's model as well as a similar exercise due to Grossman and Helpman, 1991b).

An echo of Domar's concern for obsolescence is heard in the work of Aghion and Howitt (1992), though these authors themselves trace their lineage further back to Schumpeter (1934). One comes across forces of uncertainty in this work, connected to the success date for research endeavours. The corresponding equilibrium turns out to be stochastic in nature and captures clearly the losses arising from obsolescence. Once again, Grossman and Helpman (1991a, 1991b) carry out a similar investigation and arrive at comparable conclusions. (See Chapter 7 for a discussion of these models.)

While the main line of the literature on Endogenous Growth Theory is concerned with explaining technical progress, Barro (1990) initiated a research programme by attempting to capture the need for infrastructure in economic growth. Barro's work was pursued further by Barro and Sala-i-Martin (1992, 2003), Futagami *et al.* (1993), Dasgupta (1999,

2001, 2004, and 2006), and others. (See Chapter 5 for a report on these exercises.)

A particularly interesting piece of analysis goes back to Rebelo (1991) who succeeded in providing a comprehensive view of the essential components of any exercise in Endogenous Growth Theory. This book owes its overall point of view largely to the Rebelo contribution. (See Chapter 4 below for a discussion of this model.) As already noted, some of the above ideas find place here in a unified framework to help connect common analytical themes running through them. Details are worked out as far as practicable to help the student. These have added to the size of the book, to compensate for which, the book abstracts from the details of certain other analytical issues. One such issue is the problem of stability of dynamic paths. An obvious reason for this neglect lies in the fact that existing text-books (such as Barro and Sala-i-Martin 2003) cover the material adequately. There is a second reason, however, why the book avoids stability issues. Almost all stability results proved so far in endogenous growth theory are local in nature. Given that theory is concerned almost entirely with problems of long term growth, a stability property in the local neighbourhood of the long run equilibrium values of relevant variables, though not entirely irrelevant in nature, points out a grey area surrounding the models. Nonetheless, Chapter 5 introduces a simplified model of local stability of the balanced growth path for the Dasgupta (1999) model to give the student a feel for the nature of local stability properties. Besides, Chapter 2 of the book discusses in detail the global stability of the Solow-Ramsey-Cass-Koopmans model.[3]

Certain other omissions in the book deserve special mention. First, the book does not present the *convergence* problem. This literature has both theoretical as well as empirical components, connected to the hypothesis that economies in their initial stages of development grow faster than when they turn mature. The convergence-related investigations generated controversies as well as a large volume of empirical literature. Barro and Sala-i-Martin (2003) consider these results in extensive detail.[4] Covering the convergence problem in this book would be space consuming, given the attention the book pays to details. Moreover, convergence analysis does not fit naturally into the flow of ideas pursued by this book. Its exclusion therefore does not constitute a serious shortcoming.

---

[3]Bond *et al.* (1996) and Mino (1996) represent non-trivial examples of stability analysis for Endogenous Growth models.

[4]See also, Galor (1996), Quah (1996) and other articles in the symposium issue of *Economic Journal*, Vol. 106, 1996.

There is very little that the book has to offer on open economies, except for a hint in the form of a problem in Chapter 5. Grossman and Helpman (1991b) did pioneering work on the topic. The presentation in this book does cover parts of the Grossman-Helpman contribution on growth in a closed economy. Students who master the relevant chapters (Chapters 6 and 7) of this book, should find it relatively simple to familiarize themselves with the rest of the Grossman-Helpman contribution. The literature on trade and growth, however, is yet to reach a conclusive state. This, along with space considerations, guided the decision to restrict attention to closed economies alone. Interested readers are referred to contributions by Feenstra (1996), Bond *et al.* (2002), Dinopoulos and Segerstrom (2004), Grossman and Helpman (1991b), Rivera-Batiz and Romer (1991), Stokey (1996) and others.

Finally, the book is devoted almost entirely to the dynastic household genre of Endogenous Growth Theory.[5] While this may be described as the mainstream approach of Growth Economics, there has been a parallel development based on the overlapping generations model. There is an interesting body of results that needs reporting in this context. However, given the limited scope of the present work, this has been avoided. Readers who wish to pursue these models are referred to de la Croix and Michel (2002).

The book has depended almost entirely on the author's experiences in the classroom.[6] Thus, student inputs have been vital to its final emergence. The author has taught regular courses on the subject at the Delhi and Kolkata campuses of the Indian Statistical Institute and at the Jawaharlal Nehru University. He has also had the opportunity of addressing research scholars (as well as the faculty) at the Delhi School of Economics.

Amongst students, he acknowledges fondly the help received from Ranajoy Basu, Kaushik Gangopadhyay, Sambuddha Ghosh, Raman Khaddaria, and Gurbachan Singh. Further, he owes a special note of thanks to Vidya Atal and Arpita Chatterjee for their comments on sev-

---

[5]The only exception occurs in Chapter 8 in the presentation of Galor and Zeira (1993).

[6]Every teacher has his unique set of experiences to respond to as he strives to communicate and his originality is largely traceable to such fortuitous events. Nonetheless, no teacher can possibly disown the impact of other pedagogic works on his train of thoughts. It is best, therefore, to record here the additional help received by the author from the celebrated books by Grossman and Helpman (1991), Aghion and Howitt (1998) and Barro and Sala-i-Martin (2003). The author's exposition, both in the courses he offered as well as in the present book, has been significantly influenced by these works.

eral versions of the manuscript. He is also deeply indebted to Bikrama-ditya Datta for meticulously checking through the latest book for typos as well as errors of omission and commission. It is his painstaking effort that has brought about, in the author's opinion, significant improvements in the second book compared to the first. Despite the care taken to remove errors, however, one cannot rule out the possibility that typos still exist in the book. Interested readers are encouraged to bring these and other questions to the author's attention through email addressed to *dasguptadipankar@yahoo.com*.

As far as professional colleagues go, Kaushik Basu, Amitava Bose, Satya P. Das, Pradip Maiti, Sugata Marjit, Anjan Mukherji, Deepak Nayyar, Prabhat Patnaik, and Abhirup Sarkar have contributed directly and indirectly to this project. Professor Koji Shimomura had made it possible for the first book to be produced by providing a congenial atmosphere at Kobe University, Japan. More recently, Professor Partha Basu invited the author to teach a course on Growth Economics for the Five-Year Integrated Course in Economics at the Indian Institute of Technology, Kharagpur during the spring semester of 2009–10. But for Professor Basu's invitation, this new book would almost certainly not been written.

And finally, as was the case with the first edition, Sankari's encouragement and patience played a vital role in creating the pages that follow. I know that she will welcome the appearance of the book most happily, but I do not think that she will ever end up reading it.

Kolkata
September, 2010.

Contents

Part I: The Solow Model and Optimal Control Theory

Part II: Selected Models of New Growth Theory

Part I: The Solow Model and Optimal Control Theory

Chapter 1

Long Run Growth:
Objectives and Received Theory

1.1 Introduction

A rise in the annual growth rate of an economy's real per capita GDP signals, to a large extent, an improvement in the standard of living enjoyed by the inhabitants of the society. Per capita GDP growth, by itself, is of course an imperfect indicator of welfare improvement. Distribution of the GDP across the population matters a great deal also. A large value of per capita GDP, accompanied by severe inequality of distribution, may even signify a deterioration of human well-being rather than advancement. Nonetheless, most nations which are reasonably advanced in terms of a wide variety of social indicators do exhibit significantly large values of real per capita GDP also. Consequently, attempts to maintain, and if possible raise, the growth rate of an economy's per capita GDP continue to occupy policy planners, economists and governments in power.[1]

---

[1] Lucas (2002) has pointed out that, as opposed to the modern interest in a growing per capita GDP, scholars such as Malthus (1798) and Ricardo (1817) were mostly concerned with a stationary per capita GDP. A reason underlying this preoccupation, according to Lucas, might have been the historically stable level of per capita world GDP spanning the period 1000 AD through as late as 1800 AD. The Malthusian theory of population and Ricardo's use of the iron law of wages were examples of early attempts at explaining the constancy of per capita GDP. A theory of growth for Malthus and Ricardo was a theory of population growth. As we shall see, Modern Growth Theory, by contrast, is a theory of per head productivity growth.

It is helpful in this context to quote some numbers. According to the *Human Development Report 2003*, the US per capita GDP was $ 35,277.00 in 2001. Norway enjoyed a per capita GDP of $ 36,815.00. Japan's per capita GDP was $ 32,601.00, Switzerland's $ 34,171.00. At the other end of the spectrum, the per capita GDP for Ethiopia was a mere $ 95.00. In terms of PPP US $, the Ethiopian GDP translated into the somewhat higher figure of $ 810.00 of course, but this fact should offer us cold comfort, since even graduate students in an average US university receive scholarships in the range of $ 15,000.00–$ 20,000.00 per academic year. Similarly, Sierra Leone had a per capita GDP of $ 146.00, the Democratic Republic of Congo's per capita GDP was $ 99.00.

The differences in the numbers at the two extremes are disconcerting to say the least. As one studies these figures, it becomes impossible to resist asking questions like: 'Why? What explains the difference?' 'How did the US economy manage to reach this level of GDP, while Ethiopia lagged so far behind, along with a large number of sub Saharan African countries?' Will it be possible for the per capita GDP of Ethiopia to ever reach the US figure? In other words, what makes the real GDP of a society rise significantly over time? As the Nobel Laureate Robert E. Lucas observed, 'The consequences for human welfare involved in questions like these are simply staggering: Once one starts to think about them, it is hard to think about anything else.(Lucas 1988.)

Some would seek answers to these questions in the political histories of the countries, the exploitation that today's poor societies suffered during the colonial age at the hands of today's rich. To an extent, there would be an element of truth in this perception. However, it would not offer us a clue about what the poor societies ought to do *now*, in this postcolonial age, to cure themselves of the economic illness of acute poverty and the associated human suffering.

The problem is serious enough to exercise the minds of a large number of economists. Growth economics is mostly an outgrowth of the efforts of these economists to explain the factors that boost or inhibit growth in particular societies. As with most of economics, the explanations offered by the economists centre around two of the most basic tools of economic analysis, supply and demand. If demand could be stimulated to rise over time, producers will produce more, the supply of goods and services will go up and along with it the GDP. Moreover, if the population does not grow faster than the GDP, then per capita GDP will register an increase also. On the other hand, if demand keeps growing without commensurate increase in supply, then GDP can rise at best in nominal terms without a matching rise in real goods and services. Consequently, to explain the growth or decay of economies over time, economists are led to study the causes underlying the growth of demand as well as supply over time.

Further, a temporary rise in demand cannot be the object of analysis if one is concerned with growth over time. Growth over time must refer at the least to a positive growth rate sustained over several years. And this means that demand growth must be accompanied by a corresponding increase in supply. Also, when demand induced GDP grows steadily over time, it is not adequate to view the corresponding supply responses as movements along a supply curve. Indeed, sooner or later, it would be infeasible for supply to respond to demand rises unless the production capacity is also raised. This means that a study of sustainable growth of per capita real GDP calls for an inquiry into the factors responsible for a growth in the *capacity* to produce, or *shifts* in the supply curve.

The book is devoted to studying alternative theoretical explanations of these factors. Before plunging into these explanations, however, it is of interest to present a few more figures to convince ourselves that it will be worth our while to spend the time in pursuing the subject. We do this by looking into the magnitude of change in per capita GDP brought about by sustained growth over several years. To begin with, we present the findings of Barro and Sala-i-Martin (2003) in their discussion of inter-country growth performance data. The US economy grew at an approximate trend rate of 1.8 per cent over the period 1870 through 2000. Measured in 1996 US dollars, it had a per capita GDP of $ 3340.00 in 1870 and its per capita GDP in 2000 was 10 times higher at $ 33,330.00. The last figure demonstrates that the US economy had achieved a very high standard of living by 2000. Moreover, the fact that this level of per capita GDP was reached through steady growth over a long period of time lends to it an element of robustness. It represents a level of GDP from which the economy cannot be dislodged (either upwards or downwards) in a significant manner by short run changes. It is impossible that the US GDP could fall anywhere near the Ethiopian level quoted earlier or vice versa at short notice. In other words, the level of per capita GDP achieved on the basis of steady long-term growth has an element of *firmness* about it. It indicates a standard of living that has *come to stay*, that the populace has gotten used to. One cannot make a similar statement about a rise in per capita GDP that is brought about by an abrupt rise in the annual rate of growth. Thus, if we have to understand why an average American is substantially better off than an average Ethiopian, we must be prepared to undertake a comparative study of the trend rates of growth of the two societies over a number of years.

Needless to say, the long-term rate of growth alone cannot explain the entire difference between the wealthiness of two economies. There are other factors, such as the initial per capita GDP in the two economies for the period under consideration. Yet other explanations could be based on political factors, as already noted. Despite these possibilities, however, the fact remains that the trend rate of growth is one of the most important explanatory variables of the standard of living that a society has grown accustomed to. It is hard in fact to overestimate its importance, for even small changes in the long run rate of growth lead to substantial changes in the level of living. As Barro and Sala-i-Martin observe, had the US economy, starting from the same level of $ 3340.00 in 1870, grown at the trend rate of 0.8 per cent (instead of 1.8 per cent), its per capita GDP in 2000 would have been $ 9450.00, which is only 2.8 times higher than where it started. As opposed to this, if it had grown at the rate 2.8 per cent, it would have reached the level of $ 127,000.00 in 2000, which is 38 times higher than that in 1870. Thus, small changes in the long run growth rate can lead to significant changes in a society's established way of life, whereas even large changes in the short run growth rate may lead to transitory improvements at best.

It is hard to replicate the Barro and Sala-i-Martin exercise for most developing countries. Fortunately, however, the Reserve Bank of India has made available a data series for the Indian Economy at 1999-2000 prices, spanning the 58-year period (1950-51) through (2008-09). Based on these figures, the trend rate of growth for the entire period of per capita GDP at factor cost turns out to be 2.31 per cent, which is higher than the growth rate of the US economy over the 130 year period indicated above, though it falls short of the Japanese long-term growth rate of 2.95 per cent calculated over the 100 year period (1890-1990). In 1950-51, India's per capita GDP (at factor cost) was Rs. 6261.45 (1999-00 prices). The rupee-US dollar exchange rate was around Rs. 45.00 per dollar in 1999-2000. Using this figure, the US dollar equivalent of the Indian per capita GDP was $ 139.13. As opposed to this, the Indian per capita GDP in (2008-09) was $ 643.1. Thus, over the 58 year period (1950-1) through (2008-9), the trend growth rate of 2.31 per cent helped to raise India's per capita GDP by a factor of 4.6. In absolute terms though, the per capita GDP attained over the 58 year period compares poorly with some of the fast growing nations of Southeast Asia, such as South Korea, Taiwan, Singapore, etc. These economies displayed trend rates of growth lying between 5 per cent and 6.3 per cent during the years 1960-90. Such sustained levels of high growth had, amongst other factors, caused the per capita GDP of Singapore to rise to as high a level as \$ 20,733.00 in 2001 and that of South Korea to reach the level of \$ 8,917.00 (at current prices).

India lags far behind these figures, its per capita GDP at current prices having been only around US \$ 396.6 in 1999-2000. Using 1999-2000 prices and the rupee-US dollar exchange rate, where would India be in 2069-70 (say), had its 2.31 per cent trend rate of growth continued? In other words, where should we have landed in 120 years, beginning 1950-51? This is found by solving the equation $x = 396.6 \times e^{\{0.0231 \times 70\}}$. The figure turns out to be US \$ 1998.9 approximately. It is nowhere near India's intended goal of catching up with the developed economies. The only way therefore that India can do better is to try and raise its trend rate of growth substantially.

What should be its desired rate of growth? The answer depends on two factors: the per capita GDP level it wishes to achieve and the number of years it allows itself to reach the goal. Suppose that starting from the 1999-2000 figure quoted above, India were to decide to reach a per capita GDP of \$ 3000.00, which is around a 7.6 fold increase. How long should it allow itself to achieve the target? Following the example of the Southeast Asian miracle during the period (1960–90), suppose the policymakers were to set a 30-year target. It is a simple exercise to calculate that the required growth rate would be 6.7 per cent. On the other hand, if the growth rate were to be 8 per cent, the required number of years to reach the goal would be around 25.

Obviously, even at a growth rate as high as 8 per cent, India's performance would be somewhat unimpressive in terms of the per capita GDP achievable over periods as long as 25-30 years. One of the reasons underlying the problem is the size of its population. In the year 2001-2, the Indian population had already crossed 1 billion, while the population of Singapore was a paltry 4.1 million, with an average growth rate of 2.2 per cent over a 25 year period. Interestingly enough, India's population growth rate during the same period was also around 2 per cent, but whereas the population of Singapore was 2.3 million in 1975, India's population stood at 620 million.

It is no wonder therefore that even with a significantly high growth rate, India cannot reach the standard of living prevailing in Singapore or other developed nations in the foreseeable future. Nonetheless, while controlling the rate of population growth is essential for per capita GDP growth enhancement to have a significant impact on the level of living of a nation, it is clear that raising the standard of living calls for other important steps also. This is clearly demonstrated by China, which had a population of 1,285 million in 2001, but a per capita GDP that was

nearly twice as large as India's. Accordingly, growth theorists look for
other important reasons underlying a nation's success or failure in improving its standard of living. The most important of these consists
of discovering ways of pushing forward the boundary of an economy's
production frontier. Throughout the book we will be concerned with
this technological problem alone. To emphasize this fact, we shall often assume a constant labour force over time. This is not to say that
the demographic problem is unimportant. It is merely an admission of
the fact that finding solutions to the problem of population growth is
beyond the scope of this exercise.

1.2   A Suitable Model of Long-term Growth

As with the numbers quoted above, we shall be concerned in our theoretical models mostly with the trend rate of growth of GDP. In order
to concentrate on factors which explain the long-term trend, it is best
to abstract from problems of short run fluctuations, caused, say, by
Keynesian effective demand inadequacies. This procedure helps a clear
identification of the analytical framework required to study long-term
trends.[2]   The time-worn neoclassical model of economic growth due
to Solow (1956) turns out to be a convenient tool for the purpose.[3]
The present section describes the major technological features of the
Solow economy.[4]

At each instant of time t, the economy produces a single aggregative
commodity Y by means of capital and labour. Denoting the capital
stock at t by $K(t)$, the economy faces an instantaneous constraint on
aggregate consumption, $C(t)$, and capital accumulation or investment,
$Z(t)$, given by

$$C(t) + Z(t) = Y(t), \tag{1.1}$$

---

[2]The Real Business Cycle theorists do not recognize such a separation of issues.
According to this school of thought, the analytical underpinnings of short run fluctuations are indistinguishable from those of long run growth. See Long and Plosser
(1983).

[3]Swan (1956) represents an alternative analysis of the neoclassical model with
implications similar to the Solow model.

[4]The discussion of the Solow model in this chapter and the next expands on
Dasgupta (2005).

where $Y(t)$ stands for the flow of output at t.[5] No borrowing against future is permitted to enhance current expenditure. It is standard practice to refer to $Z(t)$ as gross investment. A fraction $\delta > 0$ of the capital stock depreciates through use per instant of time. (The depreciation parameter does not play any important role from the analytical point of view and will be dropped from Chapter 3 onwards.) Hence, $Z(t)$ leads to a *net* addition of

$$\dot{K}(t) = Z(t) - \delta K(t) \tag{1.2}$$

to the capital stock at each t. Accordingly, $\dot{K}(t)$ stands for net investment. Equation (1.1) is rewritten as

$$C(t) + \dot{K}(t) = Y(t) - \delta K(t). \tag{1.3}$$

The population at time t, assumed to be identical with the labour force, is denoted $L(t)$. Both K and L are fully employed and the labour force grows according to[6]

Assumption **L** $\dot{L}(t)/L(t) = n > 0$, where n is an exogenously specified demographic constant.

The technology for producing Y is represented by an aggregate production function

$$Y(t) = F(K(t), A(t)L(t)), \tag{1.4}$$

where $K(t)$ and $L(t)$ are the flows of capital and labour services entering the production process at t. Observe that the use of the same notations for capital stock and services as well as for population size and labour services implies that the stock-flow ratios for both factors are assumed to be constants (normalized to unity). The coefficient $A(t)$ of $L(t)$ represents technological progress and satisfies

---

[5]Strictly speaking, we should write (1.1) as

$$C(t) + Z(t) \leq Y(t).$$

Chapter 2 will clarify, however, that so long as the marginal utility of consumption is positive, no output will be wasted. Hence, (1.1) will always hold with a strict equality.

[6]As already indicated, we shall soon dispense with the labour growth assumption. In fact, from Chapter 3 onwards, this assumption will be dropped. We shall abstract away from labour growth and concern ourselves with ways of improving the growth in efficiency of the labour force alone and not with the growth of sheer numbers.

Assumption **T** $\dot{A}(t)/A(t) = \mu > 0$, where μ is an exogenously specified constant.

There are different ways in which the notion of technical progress may be formalized. Equation (1.4) in particular captures it by introducing a distinction between the apparent size of the labour force and its effective size. An improvement in work efficiency is tantamount to a reduction in the time taken to complete a given job. Alternatively, a worker finishes two jobs (say) as opposed to one during any fixed interval of time as her/his efficiency improves. Consequently, from the point of view of work performed, the efficient worker may be treated as two less efficient ones. Viewed this way, technical progress is referred to as labour augmenting. When labour augmentation assumes the form $A(t)L(t)$, technical progress is called Harrod-neutral. Assumption **T** says that the labour force is effectively augmented at the rate μ on account of a rise in work efficiency generated by technological change.[7]

Particular values attained by variables at a time point such as t_0 will be represented by C_{t_0}, K_{t_0} etc. Nonetheless, the time index will often be dropped to achieve notational simplicity, unless essential for the argument. The function $F(.,.)$ satisfies the standard neoclassical properties, viz.

Assumption **F1:** $F(.,.)$ is continuous and differentiable. $F(0, AL) = F(K, 0) = 0$ and F displays constant returns to scale in K and AL.

Assumption **F2:** $F_1 > 0, F_2 > 0, F_{11} < 0, F_{22} < 0$.

In a static environment, Assumption **F2** predicts diminishing marginal product of a factor as increasing doses of the factor are combined with constant quantities of the other factor. For a growing economy, however, the factor services K and AL would be increasing simultaneously. In this case, what diminishing returns implies is that the marginal product of capital (say) will rise if AL grows faster than K. In particular, a faster growth in A relative to that in K (as of given L) causes the marginal product of K to increase. In other words, it is the direction of change in K/AL that will determine how marginal products of factors respond

---

[7]Technical progress is neutral when the share of wages and profits in national income are unaffected by improved productivity of factors(s). Under Harrod-neutrality, the shares are unchanging along growth paths which leave the capital-output ratio unaffected. Such paths will be called balanced growth paths in the sequel. Appendix 1.2 provides a brief introduction to the notion of technical progress. For a useful discussion of technical change, see Burmeister and Dobell (1970), Chapter 3. See also Barro and Sala-i-Martin (2003).

to improvements in the size of labour augmenting technical change.[8]

We shall denote per capita variables by small case letters. Thus, $y = Y/L$, $c = C/L$, $k = K/L$ and $z = Z/L$. Also, it will be useful to rewrite (1.4) in terms of quantities per unit of *effective labour* (i.e., AL). Thus, denoting Y/AL and K/AL by $\hat{y}$ and $\hat{k}$ respectively and using Assumption **F1**, we obtain $\hat{y} = F(\hat{k}, 1)$. In what follows, $F(\hat{k}, 1)$ will be re-written as $f(\hat{k})$. Hence, according to **F1** again,

$$f(0) = 0, \ f \text{ is continuous and differentiable} . \tag{1.5}$$

It is easy to verify (using the assumption of constant returns to scale) that $\partial F/\partial K = f'(\hat{k})$ and $\partial F/\partial(AL) = f(\hat{k}) - \hat{k} \ f'(\hat{k})$. Assumption **F2** implies

Property **f1:** f is a strictly concave function with $f'(\hat{k}) > 0$.

In addition to Assumptions **F1** and **F2**, we will impose

Assumption **F3:** $f'(\hat{k}) \to \infty$ as $\hat{k} \to 0$ and $f'(\hat{k}) \to 0$ as $\hat{k} \to \infty$.

Thus, Assumption **F3** implies that the marginal product of capital increases without bound as capital becomes indefinitely scarce relative to the factor AL. On the other hand, using Euler's theorem, we see that

$$\frac{\hat{k} \ f'(\hat{k})}{\hat{y}} + \frac{f(\hat{k}) - \hat{k} \ f'(\hat{k})}{\hat{y}} = 1.$$

This means that $0 \le (f(\hat{k}) - \hat{k} \ f'(\hat{k}))/\hat{y} = 1 - \hat{k} \ f'(\hat{k})/\hat{y} \le 1$. Hence, $\partial F/\partial(AL) = f(\hat{k}) - \hat{k} \ f'(\hat{k}) = f(\hat{k})\{1 - \hat{k} \ f'(\hat{k})/\hat{y}\} \to 0$ as $\hat{k} \to 0$. In

---

[8]Assumptions **F1** and **F2** imply together that the isoquants relating K and AL are strictly convex to the origin. To see this, note that under CRS,

$$F_{11} K + F_{12}(AL) = 0$$
$$F_{21} K + F_{22}(AL) = 0.$$

Hence, $F_{12} = F_{21} > 0$. Thus,

$$\frac{d^2(AL)}{dK^2}|_{\bar{Y}} = -\frac{1}{F_2^3} \left[F_{11}F_2^2 - 2F_{12}F_1F_2 + F_{22}F_1^2 \right] > 0.$$

other words, the marginal product of effective labour approaches zero and that of capital rises boundlessly as K *relative to* AL becomes indefinitely scarce (irrespective of the *absolute* values of K and AL).

Assumption **F3** is referred to as an Inada condition and constitutes a regularity requirement. It guarantees that the model has mathematically meaningful solutions. Using (1.4), we rewrite (1.1) as[9]

$$C(t) + Z(t) = F(K(t), A_t L_t). \tag{1.6}$$

At each t, this equation can be viewed as the transformation frontier between $C(t)$ and $Z(t)$ given $K(t)$. Deflating both sides by $A_t L_t$, (1.6) reduces to

$$\frac{c(t)}{A_t} + \hat{z}(t) = f(\hat{k}(t)), \tag{1.7}$$

where $\hat{z}(t) = Z(t)/A_t L_t$. Since

$$
\begin{aligned}
\hat{z} &= \frac{\dot{K} + \delta\, K}{A\, L} \\
&= \frac{\dot{K}}{K}\,\frac{K}{A\,L} + \delta\, \hat{k} \\
&= \left(\frac{\dot{K}}{K} - (\mu + n)\right)\hat{k} + (\mu + \delta + n)\hat{k} \\
&= \frac{\dot{\hat{k}}}{\hat{k}}\,\hat{k} + (\mu + n + \delta)\hat{k} \\
&= \dot{\hat{k}} + (\mu + n + \delta)\hat{k}, \tag{1.8}
\end{aligned}
$$

an alternative representation of (1.7) is

$$\frac{c(t)}{A_t} + \dot{\hat{k}}(t) + (\mu + n + \delta)\hat{k}(t) = f(\hat{k}(t)),$$

---

[9]Notice that according to the convention we have adopted, particular values of variables at t are being denoted by subscripts. Since A and L are exogenously known, A_t and L_t have fixed, unchangeable values. However, $K(t)$, $C(t)$ and $Z(t)$ are chosen over time and each can assume different values at any t.

or,

$$c(t) + A_t \, \dot{\hat{k}}(t) \;=\; A_t \{ f(\hat{k}(t)) - (\mu + n + \delta) \hat{k}(t) \}, \tag{1.9}$$

$$\text{or} \qquad \dot{\hat{k}}(t) \;=\; -(1/A_t) \, c(t) + \{ f(\hat{k}(t)) - (\mu + n + \delta) \hat{k}(t) \} \tag{1.10}$$

where, according to (1.8), $(\mu + n + \delta) \, \hat{k}(t)$ represents the minimum level of gross investment per unit of effective labour, (i.e., $\hat{z}$), that prevents $\hat{k}(t)$ from falling. In other words, when $\hat{z} = (\mu + n + \delta) \, \hat{k}(t)$, the value of $\dot{\hat{k}}(t)$ is zero. Equation (1.10) shows the slope of the frontier to be $(-1/A_t)$. (See Problem 1 below.)

It is convenient at this stage to consider two cases depending on whether investment is reversible or irreversible. When investment is irreversible, installed capital cannot be 'eaten into' except through depreciation. The maximum fall in capital stock permitted under irreversible investment equals $-\delta K$.[10] In this case, $\dot{K} = -\delta K$ and $Z = \dot{K} + \delta K = 0$. Thus, Z can hit a lower bound and corner solutions can create special problems. Reversible investment, by contrast, permits direct capital consumption.[11] The literature on Growth Theory with which this book is concerned has developed mostly under the assumption of reversible investment. Accordingly, the book will not present the case of irreversible investment in any depth. However, in the interest of students who wish to follow through the technicalities of irreversible investment, the appendices to the present chapter and the next one will prove a few results on optimal growth with irreversible investment. The transformation locus between c and $\dot{\hat{k}}$ is illustrated in Figure 1.1.

Under reversible investment, it is possible to have $\dot{K} < -\delta K$, $Z < 0$. Since δK stands for physical depreciation of capital, the maximum amount of the capital stock that can be directly consumed by the household is $(1 - \delta)K$. Hence, the maximum possible net disinvestment equals $\dot{K} = -[(1 - \delta)K + \delta K] = -K$. Consequently, $Z = \dot{K} + \delta K = -(1 - \delta)K$. Alternatively, $\hat{z} = -(1 - \delta)\hat{k}$ and $\dot{\hat{k}} = -(1 + \mu + n)\hat{k}$, using (1.8).

---

[10]We are assuming of course that the economy is closed, so that there are no international capital movements.

[11]In a single macro-good model, since the same good satisfies consumption and capital accumulation needs, capital consumption is not difficult to visualize. One could, for example, compare the process of capital accumulation with growing trees. A tree is a capital good that can be consumed up in different ways.

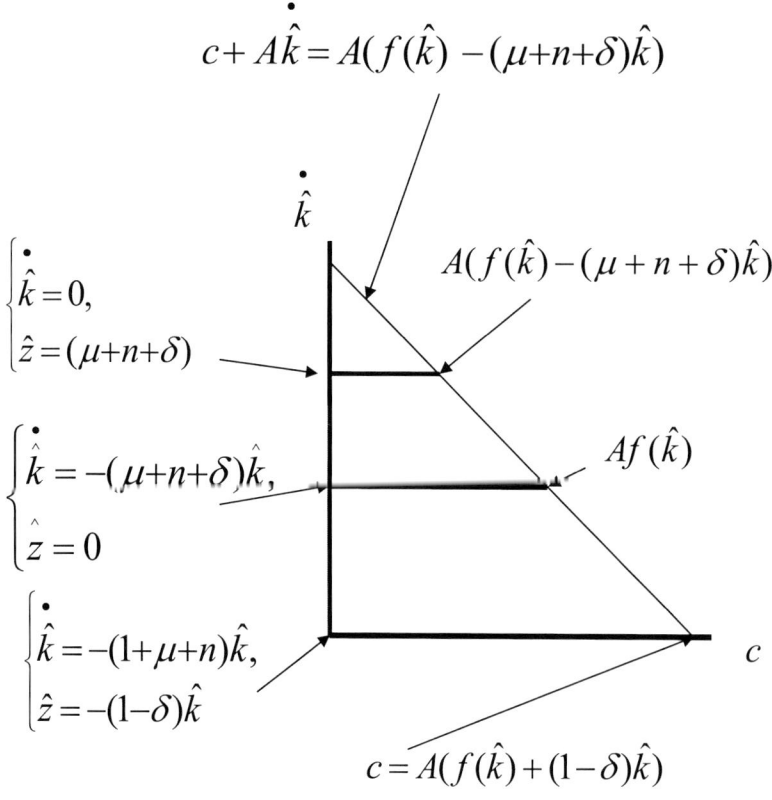

Equation of transformation frontier

$$c + A\dot{\hat{k}} = A(f(\hat{k}) - (\mu+n+\delta)\hat{k})$$

$$\dot{\hat{k}}$$

$$A(f(\hat{k}) - (\mu+n+\delta)\hat{k})$$

$$\begin{cases} \dot{\hat{k}} = 0, \\ \hat{z} = (\mu+n+\delta) \end{cases}$$

$$\begin{cases} \dot{\hat{k}} = -(\mu+n+\delta)\hat{k}, \\ \hat{z} = 0 \end{cases}$$

$$Af(\hat{k})$$

$$\begin{cases} \dot{\hat{k}} = -(1+\mu+n)\hat{k}, \\ \hat{z} = -(1-\delta)\hat{k} \end{cases}$$

$$c$$

$$c = A(f(\hat{k}) + (1-\delta)\hat{k})$$

Figure 1.1: The Transformation Locus between c and $\dot{\hat{k}}$

The corresponding maximum possible level of per capita consumption is $c = A(f(\hat{k}) + (1 - \delta)\hat{k})$. A consumption path c must satisfy the condition

$$0 \le c \le A(f(\hat{k}) + (1 - \delta)\hat{k}), \tag{1.11}$$

if investment is reversible. We end this section by deriving an important restriction on the path of $\hat{k}$.

PROPOSITION **1.1** *Any   feasible   path $\hat{k}(t)$ satisfying   (1.9)   is* *bounded above.*

Proof: Referring back to (1.9), the maximum value of $\hat{k}(t)$, hence $\dot{\hat{k}}(t)$, possible at each t is found by equating c to zero for all t. This may be called the path of pure capital accumulation. Denote the path by $\hat{k}_p(t)$. It satisfies the equation

$$\dot{\hat{k}}_p(t) = f(\hat{k}_p(t)) - \lambda \hat{k}_p(t).$$

where $\lambda = \mu + n + \delta$. By virtue of Assumption **F3**, $\exists$ a $\bar{\hat{k}}$ such that $\hat{k}_p(t) > \bar{\hat{k}} \Rightarrow \dot{\hat{k}}_p(t) < 0$. Thus, max $\{\hat{k}(0), \bar{\hat{k}}\}$ is the claimed upper bound on $\hat{k}(t)$.

The intuitive argument underlying Proposition 1.1 is as follows. If $\hat{k}(t)$ is not bounded above, then $f'(\hat{k}) \to 0$ according to the Inada conditions. A marginal unit of $\hat{k}$ adds $f'(\hat{k})$, but to maintain that extra unit, the required amount of $\hat{z}$ is λ, a positive constant. Since for $\hat{k}$ large enough, $f'(\hat{k}) < \lambda$, an extra $\hat{k}$ cannot be maintained from some $\hat{k}$ onwards. Consequently, $\hat{k}$ must be bounded above.

1.2.1 Economic Organization

Command Economy

Throughout the book, we shall be referring to two alternative economic set ups, called the Command Economy and the Private Economy. The Command Economy presumes a single decision-maker, to be called the planner, who allocates all resources at each point of time as well as across time. It does not recognize private claim to economic property. To the extent that the omnipotent planner is in a position to achieve all possible allocations of existing resources, he may attain the best one amongst these according to some criterion or the other (to be specified in Chapter 2). In fact, one may view the Command Economy to be a theoretical device for locating the best possible allocation of resources in a growing economy.

Private Economy

The alternative to the Command Economy is the Private Economy where resources are privately owned and allocated by private incentive driven forces. A large part of these forces will assume the shape of competitive markets, though, as we shall see (in Chapter 5), the assumption of perfect competition will not always be tenable. The Private Economy will represent the way an economy is actually likely to function. The Private Economy evolves over time through the interaction of the agents constituting it, viz. the households and the firms. As in most macro models, we shall abstract completely from interactions between households alone or those between producers alone at any point of time. Consequently, we will pretend that there is a single aggregative or representative household (H). As far as the Solow exercise goes, there will be a single representative business firm (B) in the economy. [12] The behaviour of H will be taken up in the next chapter.

The business firm is assumed to choose $L(t)$ and $K(t)$ to maximize net profit

$$\Pi(t) \;=\; F(K(t), A_t L(t)) - w(t)L(t) - r(t)K(t) - \delta K(t)$$

(1.12)

at all t. The *FOC*'s for this exercise are

$$r(t) \;=\; \frac{\partial F}{\partial K(t)} - \delta$$

$$\;=\; f'(\hat{k}(t)) - \delta,$$

$$w(t) \;=\; \frac{\partial F}{\partial L_t}$$

$$\;=\; A_t\{f(\hat{k}(t)) - \hat{k}(t)f'(\hat{k}(t))\}.$$ (1.13)

Equations (1.13) represent the competitive demands for capital and labour services on the part of B as functions of the market rate of interest r and the wage rate w. Factor market equilibrium requires

Demand for factor services $=$ supply of factor

services at each t.

(1.14)

---

[12]However, later on in the book, we shall incorporate into the model more than one aggregative firm, each one representing a different market structure.

As far as supply functions go, we assume that both factors are supplied perfectly inelastically at each point of time. Thus, the household supplies $L(t)$ at t irrespective of the real wage rate. Capital services too will be assumed to be so supplied. However, the household's endowment of capital at each point of time will not be exogenously given as in the case of labour. It will instead be determined by the household's consumption-savings decision over time. The decision requires solving an optimization exercise involving the choice of a consumption and saving *path* for the household's planning horizon. The next chapter will be concerned with solving this problem. In the process, it will introduce the reader to elements of Control Theory, an important tool for analysing problems involving optimal choice over time.

Factor market equilibrium (1.14) determines, under **F3** and the assumption of perfect wage-price flexibility, strictly positive equilibrium values of r and w at each t. The equilibrium time path of market returns, viz. $\{r_t^*, w_t^*\}$, has associated with it a time path of $\hat{k}_t^*$ and $\hat{y}_t^*$. Since the economy starts with exogenously given values of L_0 and A_0 and AL grows at an exogenously given rate $\mu + n$, the above paths of $\hat{k}_t^*$ and $\hat{y}_t^*$ imply corresponding paths of K_t^* and Y_t^*, where $K_0^* = K_0$, the exogenously given level of $K(0)$. These paths capture the equilibrium behaviour of the economy over time.

Appendix 1.1   Irreversible Investment

Irreversible investment refers to the case where installed capital cannot be 'eaten into' except through depreciation. The smallest possible value $\dot{K}$ can assume is $-\delta K$. At this corner value of net investment, gross investment Z equals zero. This means that $z = 0$ and $\dot{\hat{k}} = -(\mu + n + \delta)\hat{k}$. Consequently, from (1.9), the maximum possible per capita consumption is $c = Af(\hat{k})$. In this case, the consumption path will satisfy the condition

$$0 \leq c \leq Af(\hat{k}). \tag{A1.1}$$

Figure 1.1 indicates the maximum possible value of c corresponding to $\dot{\hat{k}} = -(\mu + n + \delta)\hat{k}$. The analytical consequences of C hitting its upper bound will be discussed further in Appendix 2.1.

Appendix 1.2   Technological Progress

This appendix provides a short introduction to the formalities of technological progress. The treatment is not self-complete and the reader is urged to follow up the references cited. The particular form of technical progress assumed in the text is best understood with reference to 'stylized facts' from economic history concerning the *long-term* behaviour of an economy. Some of these were noted by Kaldor (1957) and may be listed as follows:

(i) The investment-output ratio remains constant.
(ii) The capital-output ratio remains constant.
(iii) The capital-labour and output-labour ratio rise over time.
(iv) The rate of interest is a constant.
(v) The real wage rate is rising.
(vi) The shares of capital and labour in national income are constants.

Growth theorists have been motivated by the above features in modelling technological change. It is easy to check that in the absence of technical progress, i.e., in the absence of the term $A(t)$ in (1.4), the growth model outlined by the chapter will not satisfy (iii) and (iv) simultaneously, a rise in k implies r falls. In the presence of $A(t)$, however, the capital-labour ratio can increase in the face of a constant value of $\hat{k} = K/A\ L$ and hence, as per (1.13), a constant rate of interest. The form of the aggregate production function (1.4) is a special case of the function

$$
\begin{aligned}
Y(t) \ &= \ F(K(t), L(t); t), \ \frac{\partial F}{\partial t} > 0, \\
&= \ L(t)f(k(t); t), && \text{(A1.2)}
\end{aligned}
$$

assuming constant returns to scale with respect to capital and labour. The explicit appearance of t in F indicates that the function shifts 'upwards' over time. In other words, application of the same flows of capital and labour services yield larger flows of output with the progress of time. This general form of production function can also accommodate a constant k/y in the face of a growing k, because the fall in f' caused by k can be arrested by a rising t. In particular, $\pi = k\ f'(k; t)/y$ can remain constant, thus satisfying condition (vi). When the latter is guaranteed, technological progress is neutral (as opposed to being 'biased'), since the gains in productivity are being shared equally by the

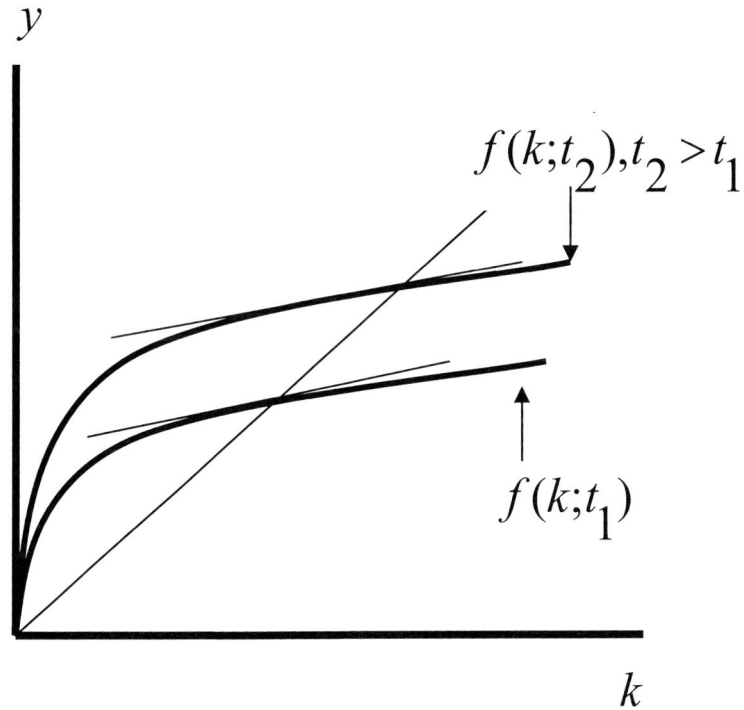

Figure 1.2: Harrod-neutral Technical Progress

two factors of production in the long run. If this happens along a path that leaves k/y unaffected, the associated technical progress is referred to as Harrod-neutral (Harrod 1948). Figure 1.2 illustrates the notion of Harrod-neutrality.

Harrod-neutrality calls for rising labour efficiency over time. Consequently, while k increases, the ratio of K to 'effective' labour remains unaltered in some sense, thus keeping the rate of interest unaffected. Since factor returns are linked to the slopes of isoquants, the last observation suggests that we try and capture the notion of technical change with reference to the basic isoquant map. Thus, technical change is said to be 'factor augmenting' if the isoquants may be drawn with respect to the 'effective' factor uses. Given any *fixed* pair (K, L), let us denote effective capital and labour by $(\tilde{A}(t)K, A(t)L)$, where $\tilde{A}(t)$ and $A(t)$ are increasing functions of time. Thus, any given point on the isoquant plane will be associated over time with different quantities of raw factors. See

Figure 1.3. In this case, (A1.2) reduces to[13]

$$
\begin{aligned}
Y(t) &= F(K(t), L(t); t), \\
&= G(\tilde{A}(t)K, A(t)L), \tag{A1.3}
\end{aligned}
$$

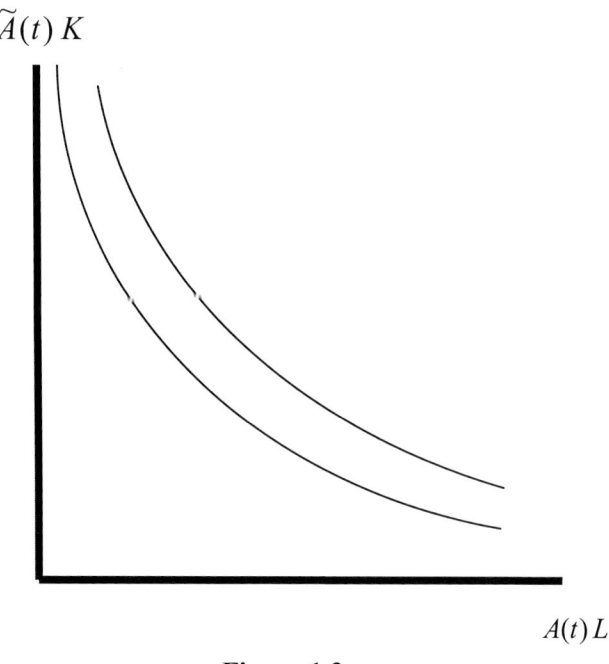

Figure 1.3

Figure 1.3: Technical Change in the Isoquant Plane

Robinson (1938) conjectured and Uzawa (1961a) proved that technical progress is Harrod-neutral *iff* it is labour-augmenting, i.e., it has the form (1.4).[14]

---

[13]A notable feature of (A1.3) is that technical progress affects the productivity of capital and labour irrespective of their vintages. A new idea improves the efficiency of all pieces of machinery (say), whether they were commissioned recently or in the distant past. The same observation holds true for labour. When technical progress has this characteristic, it is called 'disembodied' (as opposed to 'embodied').

[14]The reader may refer to Uzawa (1961a) for a proof.

An alternative notion of neutrality has its origin in Hicks (1963). Since π is a constant *iff* $(1 - \pi)$ is a constant, it follows that π is a constant *iff* rK/wL is a constant. On the other hand, $rK/wL = k/(w/r)$. The share π will be a constant if the form of technical change is such that for given k, the ratio of factor returns w/r is a constant. When technical change satisfies this property, it is referred to as Hicks-neutral. Going back to (A1.3), Hicks-neutrality occurs when $\tilde{A}(t) = A(t) \; \forall \; t$.

Let e denote the elasticity of substitution for the two factors. Using the methods of Diamond (1965) and Burmeister and Dobell (1970), it is possible to show that if property (ii) holds along a growth path, then for a production function to incorporate Hicks-neutrality, the following differential equation must be satisfied:

$$\frac{\dot{\pi}}{\pi} = \frac{\dot{A}}{A}\left(1 - \frac{1}{e}\right). \tag{A1.4}$$

Let us restrict attention to a CES production function and consider two alternative cases, $e < 1$ and $e > 1$. The solution to (A1.4) is

$$\pi(t) = \pi_0 \, e^{\,\mu \, \epsilon \, t},$$

where $\epsilon = (1 - 1/e)$. In the first case, $\epsilon < 0$. Hence, $\pi(t) \rightarrow 0$ as $t \rightarrow \infty$. Consequently, technical progress is not neutral and property (vi) above is violated. In the second case, $\epsilon > 0$ and $\pi \rightarrow \infty$ as $t \rightarrow \infty$. In other words, the share of labour in output reaches zero at some finite $t = \bar{t}$ and the model breaks down beyond that point of time, unless (ii) is dispensed with. Thus, (vi) and (ii) cannot hold together under Hicks-neutral technical progress if $e \neq 1$.

This suggests that a Hicks-neutral production function can lead to growth paths consistent with the stylized facts *only if* the elasticity of substitution $e = 1$, i.e., if the production function is Cobb-Douglas. In fact, Uzawa (1961a) proved the stronger result that a production function is both Hicks and Harrod-neutral *iff* it is Cobb-Douglas.

In view of these observations, it should be apparent that for the model of this chapter to successfully fit the stylized facts, it should have the form (1.4).[15]

---

[15]See Barro and Sala-i-Martin (2003), Chapter 1, Appendix for an elementary proof of this result.

Summary

1. Growth Theory is concerned with the long run rate of growth of per capita GDP of an economy under the assumption that resources are fully employed. It tries to identify the best possible path to be followed by an economy over time. A small rate of growth maintained over a long period of time can make a country economically powerful. A short run rise in the rate of growth may not signify sustainable economic performance. Also, successful growth accompanied by rising income inequality could cause problems.

2. Solow (1956) represents one of the earliest attempts to study the behaviour of per capita income under the assumption of full employment of resources. He views the economy as being presented with a choice between consumption and savings at each point in time. The menu of choices can be viewed as a transformation locus between per capita consumption and capital accumulation. The transformation locus shifts over time as savings are invested for capital formation.

3. A Command Economy is a planned economy where resources are allocated by an omniscient planner. A Private Economy is governed by freely functioning markets for final goods as well as factors of production. Producers maximize profits at each point of time.

4. Investment is reversible when invested capital can be dismantled and consumed in the form of consumer goods. Investment is irreversible when invested capital cannot be transformed back to consumer goods. Normally, invested capital depreciates over time through wear and tear.

5. Technological progress refers to growth in output brought about by a rise in productivity of capital or labour. Technological progress is neutral, as opposed to biased, when the growth in productivity is shared equally by labour and capital.

6. Factor augmenting technical progress refers to effective augmentation of existing capital and labour without any actual change in their sizes. Harrod-neutral technical change involves effective augmentation of labour alone. Hicks-neutral technical change considers effective augmentation of both labour and capital. Production functions characterized by Hicks-neutral technical change are not suitable for studying long run growth paths.

Problems

1. Prove that under the Inada conditions,

$$w(t) = \frac{\partial F}{\partial L_t}$$

$$= A_t\{f(\hat{k}(t)) - \hat{k}(t)f'(\hat{k}(t))\}$$

leads to a well-defined positive value of $\hat{k}(t)$ for each positive value of $w(t)$.

2. Consider the transformation locus between c and $\hat{k}$ in Figure 1.1.

(i) How does the frontier behave with respect to a rise in t given $\hat{k}$? Interpret your answer.
(ii) How does the frontier behave with respect to a rise in $\hat{k}$ given t? Interpret your answer.
(iii) With reference to Proposition 1.1, draw the frontier for the case where $\hat{k}_0 > \bar{k}$}.

3. Assume that the production function has the form $Y = min(\tilde{A}K, AL)$.

(i) Which of the assumptions of the Solow model does this production function violate?
(ii) Derive equation (1.9) using this production function. (This problem is discussed in detail in Chapter 3 below.)

4. Consider the constant elasticity of substitution production function

$$Y = F(K, L)$$

$$= \{a(bK)^\psi + (1-a)((1-b)L)^\psi\}^{1/\psi},$$

where $0 < a < 1$, $0 < b < 1$, and $\psi < 1$. Note that the production function does not involve technological change.

(i) Calculate the elasticity of substitution between capital and labour for this production function.
(ii) Does this production function satisfy Assumption **F1**?
(iii) Does it satisfy Assumption **F3**?
(iv) Derive equation (1.9) using this production function.

5. Consider the production function $Y = K^{\alpha(t)} L^{1-\alpha(t)}$, where $0 < \alpha(t) < 1$ and $\dot{\alpha} > 0$.

(i) Verify that the elasticity of substitution between capital and labour is unity.
(ii) Prove that the production function cannot be written in the form $Y = F(\tilde{A}(t)K, A(t)L)$.

6. Prove that for the Solow production function technical progress is both Harrod and Hicks-neutral *iff* the production function is Cobb-Douglas. (Result due to Uzawa 1961a).

7. Prove the following result due to Burmeister and Dobell (1969). Consider the neoclassical production function $Y = F(K, L; t)$. There exist (i) positive functions $a(t)$ and $b(t)$ of time alone with $a(0) = 1 = b(0)$, having continuous first derivatives and (ii) a function G homogeneous of degree one in all its arguments such that F may be represented by

$$
\begin{aligned}
Y &= F(K, L; t) \\
&= G(b(t)K, a(t)L)
\end{aligned}
$$

iff there exists a positive function $h(t)$ of time alone ($h(0) = 1$) such that when the expression $h(t)k$ is constant then the relative share π is a constant.

Chapter 2

Growth in Private and Command Economies

2.1 Optimal Growth in a Command Economy

The previous chapter discussed some of the salient features of a Private Economy. In this chapter, however, we shall start off with a fully planned economy and look for a characterization of the optimal path a planner will choose. In the process, we shall introduce the reader to elements of Control Theory, an important mathematical tool employed by Modern Growth Theory. In addition, we shall discuss the notion of a dynamic equilibrium over time and try and understand the concept of an *equilibrium balanced growth* path for an economy, an idea that will play an all important role in the rest of the book.[1] Our discussion of the planned economy will be followed up by an analysis of the Private Economy and a comparison of the planned and private paths.

The planner is concerned with the optimal choice of an accumulation path of $\hat{k}$ and c over time. The exercise we shall engage in goes back to Cass (1965), Koopmans (1965) and Ramsey (1928), who assumed that a consumption (hence, saving) plan is chosen by maximizing a welfare integral over a time domain. The economy, being infinitely lived in principle, the planner too will be assumed to have infinite life. The planner at $t = 0$ derives the optimal path for the entire future of the economy. In other words, he decides about an optimal path $C(t)$ enjoyed by $L(t)$

---

[1]Harrod (1939) was the first economist to distinguish between the concept of a static equilibrium at each instant of time and a dynamic equilibrium path.

persons, $t \in [0, \infty)$. Optimality of the path is judged with reference to (2.1), since the planner is supposed to act in the best interest of H.[2]

The planner cares (in a limited way) for all subsequent generations. Thus, its welfare function is assumed to be

$$U = \int_o^\infty u(c(t)) \cdot e^{nt} \cdot e^{-\rho t} dt$$

$$= \int_o^\infty u(c(t)) \ e^{-(\rho - n)t} dt, \tag{2.1}$$

which is a weighted sum of instantaneous (cardinal) utilities, $u(c(t))$ derived from $c(t)$. The weights reflect two facts. First, e^{nt} shows that utilities from per capita consumption receive exponentially higher weights with time to take account of the fact that the economy's size (which is identically the same as the household's size) increases at the rate n.[3] Secondly, $\rho > 0$ stands for the rate of time preference arising out of the fact that utilities further down in time are valued less than utilities enjoyed earlier on. As noted above therefore, the planner is less than altruistic in his attitude towards future generations. This leads to an exponentially decaying weight $e^{-\rho t}$ on utilities with the passage of time. The arguments of the function U in (2.1) are restricted as follows:

Assumption u1 $u'(c) > 0$, $u''(c) < 0$,

Assumption u2 $u'(c) \to \infty$ as $c \to 0$ and $u'(c) \to 0$

as $c \to \infty$,

Assumption u3 $\rho > n$.

In other words, instantaneous utility is a strictly concave function of c, the marginal utility is unboundedly high for small values of c, while it is as close to zero as possible for large c. The first part of **Assumption u2** rules out corner solutions at each point of time. **Assumption u3** ensures that U is well defined.[4] In view of **Assumption T**, the convergence of (2.1) will generally call for a strengthening of **Assumption u3**.[5]

---

[2]Assumptions regarding the technology used by the planner and its properties are stated in Chapter 1.

[3]We are normalizing $L_0 = 1$ in writing $L_t = L_0 \ e^{nt}$.

[4]When $\rho < n$, the function U could be unbounded.

[5]See the discussion in Section 2.3.1.

We saw in Chapter 1 that equation (1.9) can be viewed as the transformation frontier between $c(t)$ and $\dot{\hat{k}}(t)$ given $\hat{k}(t)$ at each t. Thus, the **Planner's Optimisation Exercise** is stated as follows:

Optimisation under Reversible Investment:

Find $\{c^*(t)\}_0^\infty$ to maximize (2.1) subject to (1.9) and $\hat{k}(0) = \hat{k}_0$.

In standard terminology, $c(t)$ is referred to as a control variable and $\hat{k}(t)$ as a state variable.

2.1.1 Necessary Conditions for Optimum: An Intuitive Discussion

This section assumes that the planner has chosen an optimum path $\{c_t^*, \hat{k}_t^*\}_0^\infty$ of per capita consumption and capital per unit of effective labour over time and derives intuitively the properties to be satisfied by that path.

Let us note first that with reversible investment,[6] the optimal value of c must necessarily be an interior point of the transformation frontier. To see this, note first that it is impossible for the equation

$$c = A(f(\hat{k}) + (1 - \delta)\hat{k}) \tag{2.2}$$

to hold at any t for which $\hat{k}(t) > 0$. (In fact, $\hat{k}_0 = \hat{k}(0) > 0$ by assumption.) Equation (2.2) implies all capital gets exhausted at t and the economy cannot produce positive output beyond t. Hence, $c = 0$, $\hat{k} = 0$ at all time points subsequent to t. However, a marginal reduction in consumption with an equivalent increase in investment at t makes it feasible to raise c at any chosen point of time $s > t$. **Assumption u2** implies that the gain in utility at s is larger than the loss at t.

Next, suppose $c = 0$ for some t. Then, from the preceding agrument,

$$\dot{\hat{k}}(t) = \{f(\hat{k}(t)) - (\mu + n + \delta)\hat{k}(t)\}$$

---

[6]The discussion will be restricted to the case of reversible investment in the main body of the chapter. Problems raised by irreversible investment are covered by the Appendix.

using (1.10). Now a small increase in consumption at t brought about by a simultaneous reduction in investment (and possibly an accompanying decrease in consumption at a later point of time) must be welfare improving by virtue of **Assumption u2**. Hence, $c(t) > 0$. Consequently, any optimal consumption path c must satisfy the condition

$$0 < c < A(f(\hat{k}) + (1 - \delta)\hat{k}). \tag{2.3}$$

Let us now fix any time point t. From his own past decisions, the planner has inherited an unalterable level of $\hat{k}(t) = \hat{k}_t^*$. This determines the size of net resources (viz., the RHS of (1.9)) the planner must allocate between $c(t)$ and $\dot{\hat{k}}(t)$. For this purpose, we define a reduced form welfare function governing the planner's behaviour at t. The function, commonly called the Hamiltonian, is written[7]

$$\mathcal{H}(c(t), \hat{k}(t), q_t) = u(c(t)) + q_t \dot{\hat{k}}(t), \tag{2.4}$$

where $\hat{k}$ enters the function $\mathcal{H}$ as an argument, since $\dot{\hat{k}}$ is a function of $\hat{k}$ and c on account of (1.9). The variable q_t is called a co-state variable and represents the *shadow price* of $\hat{k}$ at t. The shadow price measures the best possible value of welfare, measured in utils, obtainable from a marginal rise in $\hat{k}$.

Thus, consider any path $\{c_t, \hat{k}_t\}_0^\infty$. We imagine that the best possible value of aggregate utility across growth paths starting from $\hat{k}_t$ is given by the function $V(\hat{k}_t)$. Then, q_t is the optimal marginal social productivity of $\hat{k}$ at t, i.e., $q_t = d\, V(\hat{k}_t)/d\, \hat{k}_t$.[8] In what follows, we shall loosely refer to $\dot{\hat{k}}$ as investment in $\hat{k}$. Thus, $\mathcal{H}$ stands for the utility derived by the planner at t from the choice $(c(t), \dot{\hat{k}}(t))$, *under the assumption that the path from t onwards brought about by the investment is optimal*. As defined therefore, $\mathcal{H}$ already incorporates an element of optimality as far as the future is concerned. It says, even if $c(t)$ and $\dot{\hat{k}}$ are not optimally chosen, subsequent to t, the economy behaves optimally at each instant of time.

---

[7]Appendix 2.1 presents a rigorous treatment of this function as well as the following intuitive discussion.

[8]It is natural to ask if V is differentiable. This is not an easy question to answer and we shall not be concerned with the problem in this book. However, readers interested in the problem may refer to Benveniste and Scheinkman (1979).

Different choices of the value of investment, however, will give rise to different optimal values for the future. Which of these should the planner pick up? To answer this question, we have to compare the social productivity of a marginal change in $\dot{\hat{k}}$ with the marginal utility of c at t. This boils down to computing the marginal rate of substitution (MRS) along level curves generated by the Hamiltonian. Equating the total derivative of $\mathcal{H}$ to zero, we conclude that

$$\frac{d\ c(t)}{d\ \dot{\hat{k}}(t)} = -\frac{q_t}{u'(c(t))} < 0.$$

Next, differentiating again,

$$\frac{d^2\ c(t)}{d\ \dot{\hat{k}}(t)^2} = q_t\ \frac{1}{u'(c(t))^2}\ u''(c(t))\ \frac{d\ c(t)}{d\ \dot{\hat{k}}(t)} > 0.$$

Thus, the level curves corresponding to $\mathcal{H}$ are downward falling and strictly convex to the origin. As in any constrained optimization problem, optimum choice implies equating the MRS with the slope of the constraint. The slope of the linear constraint (1.10) is $(-1/A_t)$. Alternatively, along the transformation frontier, $d\ c(t)/d\ \dot{\hat{k}}(t) = -A_t$. Hence, using the fact that the optimal value of c is an interior point, a necessary FOC to be satisfied by the optimal path $\{c_t^*, \hat{k}_t^*\}_0^\infty$ is

$$\frac{q_t^*}{u'(c_t^*)} = A_t,$$

$$\text{or,} \quad u'(c_t^*) = \frac{q_t^*}{A_t}, \tag{2.5}$$

where $q_t^* = d\ V(\hat{k}_t^*)/d\ \hat{k}(t)$. Equation (2.5) may also be written as

$$\frac{\partial \mathcal{H}(c_t^*, \hat{k}_t^*, q_t^*)}{\partial c(t)} = 0 \quad \text{at each } t. \tag{2.6}$$

In view of the shape of the level curves of $\mathcal{H}$, (2.6) implies that $\mathcal{H}$ is maximized subject to (1.9) at each t. The equilibrium is described in

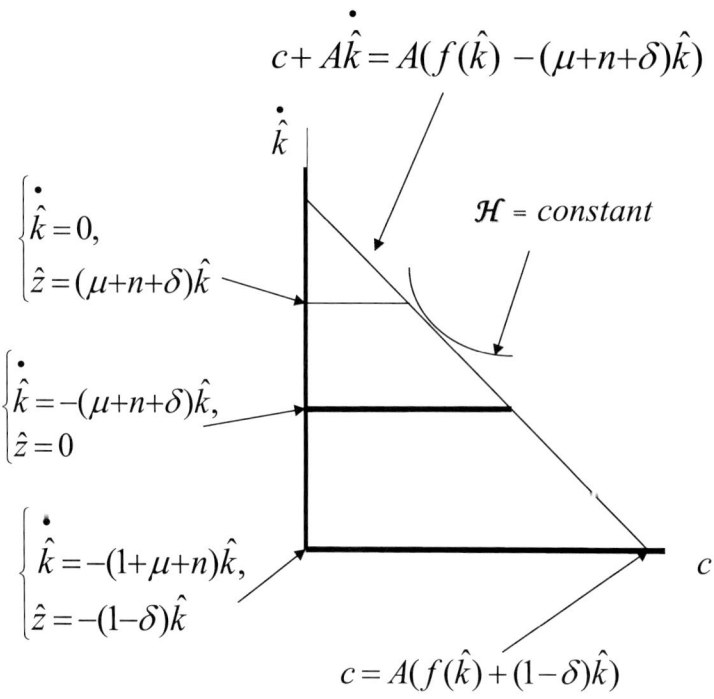

$$c + A\dot{\hat{k}} = A(f(\hat{k}) - (\mu + n + \delta)\hat{k})$$

$$\begin{cases} \dot{\hat{k}} = 0, \\ \hat{z} = (\mu + n + \delta)\hat{k} \end{cases}$$

$$\mathcal{H} = constant$$

$$\begin{cases} \dot{\hat{k}} = -(\mu + n + \delta)\hat{k}, \\ \hat{z} = 0 \end{cases}$$

$$\begin{cases} \dot{\hat{k}} = -(1 + \mu + n)\hat{k}, \\ \hat{z} = -(1 - \delta)\hat{k} \end{cases}$$

$$c = A(f(\hat{k}) + (1 - \delta)\hat{k})$$

Figure 2.1: Optimum Choice of c and $\dot{\hat{k}}$ at each t

Figure 2.1. For later use we also observe that the maximum in question is unique.[9] Note that the Hamiltonian $\mathcal{H}$ can be interpreted approximately as the value in utils imputed to per capita net national product at t.[10] Thus, an optimal path $\{c_t^*, \hat{k}_t^*\}_0^\infty$ has associated with it a path of $\{q^*(t)\}_0^\infty$ such that the corresponding imputed value of per capita net national product is maximized with respect to $c(t)$ at each point of time. In view of this implication, (2.6) is often referred to as the *Maximal Principle*.

---

[9]Appendix 2.2 will address the uniqueness question. It will show, in particular, that $\{c_t^*, \hat{k}_{*t}\}_0^\infty$ is a unique optimal path if the optimality conditions derived in this section are satisfied. This would imply from (2.5) that the associated path $\{q_t^*\}$ is also unique.

[10]The qualification 'approximate' is needed since $\dot{\hat{k}}$ is investment per unit of effective labour AL, rather than per capita investment.

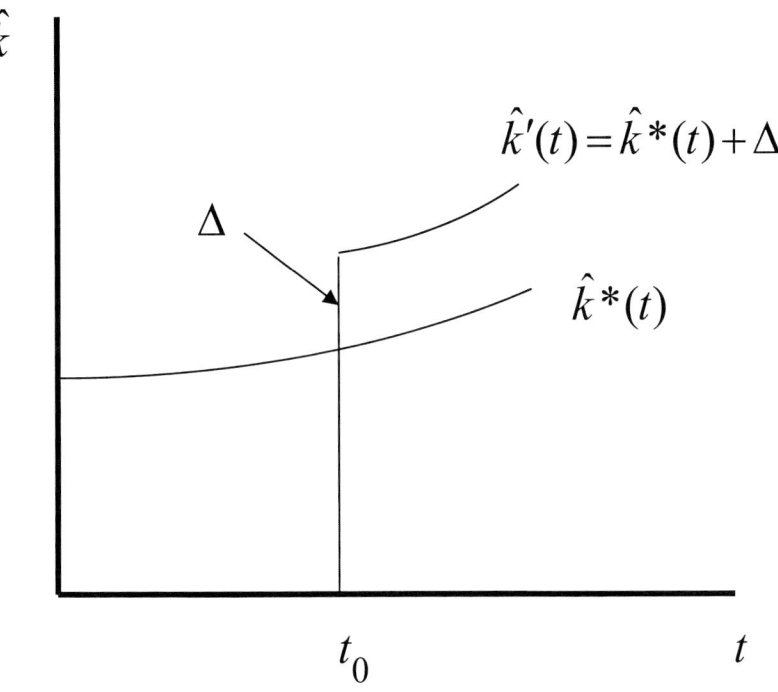

$$\hat{k}'(t) = \hat{k}*(t) + \Delta$$

$$\hat{k}*(t)$$

Figure 2.2: Comparison Paths

Equation (2.6) can be viewed as a condition of static optimality, a condition that needs to be satisfied at each instant of time. We now move on to a dynamic condition of optimality, one that connects the present to the future. Towards this end, consider a small perturbation along the transformation frontier around the point of tangency described by (2.6). For concreteness, let us assume that $\hat{k}$ rises and c falls at some t_0. Suppose moreover that the marginal increase Δ in $\hat{k}$ brought about at t_0 is maintained ever afterwards. The cost of bringing about this permanent increase is an initial fall in c. Optimality of (c_t^*, k_t^*) implies that the gain from this infinitesimal change must equal the cost. The initial rise in $\hat{k} = \Delta$ (say) implies a fall in per capita c at t_0 equal to $A_{t_0} \Delta$. The utility cost of this fall in c is $u'(c_{t_0}^*) \times A_{t_0} \Delta$. However, (2.5) implies $u'(c_{t_0}^*) = q_{t_0}^*/A_{t_0}$. Thus, the cost of the extra investment at t_0 is $u'(c_{t_0}^*) \times A_{t_0} \Delta = q_{t_0}^*/A_{t_0} \times A_{t_0} \Delta = q_{t_0}^* \Delta$.

As opposed to this cost, what is the permanent benefit? The extra *per capita* output produced by Δ at any $t > t_0$ is $A_t \ f'(\hat{k}_t^*) \ \Delta$, whereas the *per capita* investment necessary to maintain Δ is $A_t \ (\mu + n + \delta) \ \Delta$. Hence, the *per capita* extra output produced by the additional Δ at each $t > t_0$, net of maintenance, is $A_t \ (f'(\hat{k}_t^*) - (\mu + n + \delta)) \ \Delta$. Suppose now that this entire extra output is consumed. So, the initial fall in per capita consumption produces an infinite stream of extra per capita consumptions. The extra utility this gives rise to at each t is $u'(c_t^*) \ A_t \ (f'(\hat{k}_t^*) - (\mu + n + \delta)) \ \Delta = q_t^* \ \{f'(\hat{k}_t^*) - (\mu + n + \delta)\} \ \Delta$. The discounted present value of the stream of utilities is $\int_{t_0}^{\infty} e^{-(\rho - n)(t - t_0)} \ q_t^* \ \{f'(\hat{k}_t^*) - (\mu + n + \delta)\} \ \Delta \ dt$.

For optimality, the cost of an infinitesimally small investment must equal the discounted present value of the stream of returns. Thus,

$$q_{t_0}^* = \int_{t_0}^{\infty} e^{-(\rho - n)(t - t_0)} \ q_t^* \ \{f'(\hat{k}_t^*) - (\mu + n + \delta)\} \ dt.$$

Simplifying notation, let us write this as

$$q_t^* = \int_{t}^{\infty} e^{-(\rho - n)(s - t)} \ q_s^* \ \{f'(\hat{k}_s^*) - (\mu + n + \delta)\} \ ds. \qquad (2.7)$$

For q_t^* to be well-defined in (2.7), the integral on the RHS must exist for each t. We shall demonstrate later that the optimality of $\{c_t^*, \hat{k}_t^*\}_0^{\infty}$ implies that $f'(\hat{k}_s^*) - (\mu + n + \delta)$ is positive and bounded strictly away from zero for s sufficiently large. Anticipating this result, the integral can exist $\forall \ t$ only if

$$e^{-(\rho - n)t} q_t^* \rightarrow 0 \text{ as } t \rightarrow \infty. \qquad (2.8)$$

Equation (2.8) is called the *transversality condition* and constitutes a restriction on an optimal path. Intuitively, (2.8) implies that efficient paths view capital stocks far out in the future to be increasingly useless relative to present stocks. (Most authors, in particular Barro & Sala-i-Martin, seem to miss this point.)

An alternative version of (2.7) can be found by differentiating[11] the condition *wrt* t.

---

[11]The formula for differentiating a definite integral of the form

$$K(x) = \int_{a}^{b(x)} F(t, x) dt$$

$$\dot{q}_t^* = -q_t^*\{f'(\hat{k}_t^*) - (\mu + n + \delta)\}$$
$$+(\rho - n)\int_t^\infty e^{-(\rho-n)(s-t)} q_s^*\{f'(\hat{k}_s^*)$$
$$-(\mu + n + \delta)\}ds.$$

Substituting from (2.7), the last equation reduces to

$$\dot{q}_t^* = -q_t^*\{f'(\hat{k}_t^*) - (\mu + n + \delta)\} + (\rho - n)q_t^*. \qquad (2.9)$$

We shall try to find an economic interpretation for (2.9). Consider a different scenario where p is the money price of a unit of the commodity that acts both as a consumption and a capital good.[12] For simplicity, the capital good is assumed to be non-depreciating. Suppose further that there exists, alongside the capital good, an alternative monetary asset, a long term bond, yielding a nominal rate of interest $i(t)$ for each t. An infinitely lived agent is engaged in evaluating a chosen path of capital accumulation $\{k(t)\}_0^\infty$. When p units of money are invested in a unit of the capital good at time t, the marginal product is $f'(k(s))$ $\forall\ s \geq t$, assuming as before that the agent maintains the extra unit of capital for all $s \geq t$ and consumes any residual output brought forth by the extra capital. Then, the agent's return from maintaining an extra unit of k forever from s onwards is $f'(k(s))$ $\forall\ s \geq t$. In nominal terms, the return equals $p(s)f'(k(s))$ at each s. For the agent to be indifferent between investing in the physical capital and the bond, the two investments must yield the same rate of return per instant of time. The rate of return from the physical capital investment, $r(s)$, must solve the equation

$$p(t) = \int_t^\infty p(s)f'(k(s))e^{-\int_t^s r(x)dx}ds.$$

If the two rates of return are equal, then $r(s) = i(s)$ $\forall\ s$. Hence,

$$p(t) = \int_t^\infty p(s)f'(k(s))e^{-\int_t^s i(x)dx}ds. \qquad (2.10)$$

---

is

$$\frac{dK(x)}{dx} = \int_a^{b(x)} F_x(t,x)dt + F(b(x),x)b'(x).$$

See Chiang (1992), (2.11), p.31.

[12]This interpretation is based on Solow (1956).

Differentiation of (2.10) with respect to t gives

$$\dot{p}(t) = -p(t)f'(k(t)) + i(t)p(t),$$

or,

$$p(t)f'(k(t)) + \dot{p}(t) = i(t)p(t). \tag{2.11}$$

The first term on the LHS of (2.11) stands for the value of the instantaneous marginal product of investment in k in nominal terms, while the second term represents capital gain (or loss) on account of price change. The LHS then gives the *net* instantaneous nominal return from investing in k. The RHS, on the other hand, is the nominal return at t from holding the bond. The equality implies that the agent is indifferent between the two ways of investing.[13]

The logic underlying (2.11) may be applied to (2.9), which we rewrite as

$$q_t^* \{f'(\hat{k}_t^*) - (\mu + n + \delta)\} + \dot{q}_t^* = (\rho - n)\, q_t^*. \tag{2.12}$$

The LHS now gives the instantaneous net return in utils of a unit of investment in $\hat{k}(t)$, where $\dot{q}_t^*$ is the capital gain or loss measured in utils. On the RHS, the term $\rho - n$ is the rate at which utils *ought to grow* in the planner's judgement. It is the counterpart of $i(t)$ in (2.11). This rate applied to the shadow price of capital yields the instantaneous return that the planner finds acceptable, the imputed opportunity cost of investment in physical capital. Hence, (2.12) says that the rate of return from investment along the optimal path equals the household's minimum acceptable return. When (2.9) or (2.12) holds therefore, the planner has no incentive to divert away from the chosen path of asset accumulation.

2.1.2   Necessary Conditions in Terms of the Hamiltonian

We present in this section a compact version of the necessary conditions in terms of the Hamiltonian function. Equation (2.6) has already used the Hamiltonian to restate (2.5). Going over to (2.7), we note that

$$\frac{\partial \mathcal{H}(c_s^*, \hat{k}_s^*, q_s^*)}{\partial \hat{k}(s)} = u'(c_s^*)\frac{\partial c_s^*}{\partial \hat{k}(s)} + q_s^* \{f'(\hat{k}_s^*) - (\mu + n + \delta)$$

$$-\frac{1}{A_s}\frac{\partial c_s^*}{\partial \hat{k}(s)}\}$$

---

[13]A more common way of writing (2.11) is $f'(k(t)) + \dot{p}(t)/p(t) = i(t)$, usually called the Fisher equation, after Irving Fisher.

$$= q_s^* \{f'(\hat{k}_s^*) - (\mu + n + \delta)\}, \tag{2.13}$$

using (1.9) and (2.5).

Consequently, (2.7) reduces to

$$q_t^* = \int_t^\infty \partial \mathcal{H}(c_s^*, \hat{k}_s^*, q_s^*)/\partial \hat{k}(s) \; e^{-(\rho-n)(s-t)} ds. \tag{2.14}$$

Using (2.14) and (2.13) in succession, (2.9) may be expressed as

$$
\begin{aligned}
\dot{q}_t^* &= \frac{d(\int_t^\infty \partial \mathcal{H}(c_s^*, \hat{k}_s^*, q_s^*)/\partial \hat{k}(s) \; e^{-(\rho-n)(s-t)} ds)}{dt} \\[2mm]
&= -\frac{\partial \mathcal{H}(c_t^*, \hat{k}_t^*, q_t^*)}{\partial \hat{k}(t)} + (\rho - n) \; q_t^* \\[2mm]
&= -f'(\hat{k}_t^*) \; q_t^* + (\mu + \rho + \delta) \; q_t^*, \tag{2.15}
\end{aligned}
$$

Finally, since (1.9) is given by the equation

$$\dot{\hat{k}}_t^* = f(\hat{k}_t^*) - \frac{c_t^*}{A_t} - (\mu + n + \delta)\hat{k}_t^*, \tag{2.16}$$

it is reproduced by writing

$$\frac{\partial \mathcal{H}(c_t^*, \hat{k}_t^*, q_t^*)}{\partial q(t)} = \dot{\hat{k}}_t^*. \tag{2.17}$$

Let us collect the necessary conditions stated in terms of the Hamiltonian function as[14]

---

[14]The conditions resemble standard representations of the necessary conditions, except for (2.15). Equation (2.15) is borrowed from Cass (1965 and 1966). The advantage of choosing the form (2.15) is that it makes direct reference to the economic interpretation of a co-state variable. Also (See Appendix 2.1), it will allow us to use a single differential equation to describe the evolution of the co-state variable for both reversible and irreversible investment. Also, the reader should note once again that this book derives (2.8) of Proposition 2.1 for a special class of utility functions.

PROPOSITION **2.1** *Suppose* $\{c_t^*, \hat{k}_t^*\}_0^\infty$ *solves the* **Planner's Optimization Exercise**. *Then, there exists a path of co-state variables* q_t^* *such that* (2.6), (2.17), (2.15) *and* (2.8) *are satisfied.*

Proposition A2.2 (in Appendix 2.2) proves that a path satisfying the conditions of Proposition 2.1 is the unique solution to the planner's problem.

2.2   The Optimal Time Path

The ideas developed till now may be utilized to study the optimal path of capital accumulation for the Command Economy. From here onwards, however, the instantaneous utility function will be restricted till the rest of the book to the form

$$u(c) = \frac{c^{1-\theta} - 1}{1 - \theta}, \tag{2.18}$$

where θ is a positive constant. It is easy to check that θ stands for the elasticity of marginal utility, or, alternatively, $1/\theta$ the elasticity of intertemporal substitution, and that $(c^{1-\theta} - 1)/(1 - \theta) \rightarrow \log c$ as $\theta \rightarrow 1$.[15] Most of the exercises below will be carried out under the assumption that $\theta \neq 1$. The results for the case $\theta = 1$ can usually be derived by substituting $\theta = 1$ in the equations for the general case. Hence, we do not explicitly discuss this special case. However, in parts of Chapters 5 and 6, we will need to part company with the more general formulation and restrict ourselves to the log c case alone.

The analysis will be broken up into two parts to be identified as a balanced growth equilibrium path and an out of balanced growth.

---

[15]Elasticity of intertemporal substitution measures the reciprocal of the proportionate change in the slope of an indifference curve connecting per capita consumption at two points of time, $c(t_1)$ and $c(t_2)$ relative to a proportionate change in the consumption ratio $c(t_1)/c(t_2)$. Symbolically, if *els* measures the elasticity of substitution, then

$$1/els = -\left[\frac{d\{u'[c(t_1)]/u'[c(t_2)]\}}{u'[c(t_1)]/u'[c(t_2)]}\right] \div \left[\frac{d\{[c(t_1)/c(t_2)]\}}{c(t_1)/c(t_2)}\right].$$

The need to restrict ourselves to the class of such utility functions will be explained below.

2.2.1 The Optimal Balanced Growth Path

We shall start with a

Definition: An economy is said to display balanced growth if aggregate output, the aggregate capital stock and aggregate consumption grow at constant rates over time.

Notice that, for the model under consideration, the definition implies that the rates of growth of the per capita variables y, k and c as well as the variables $\hat{y}$, $\hat{k}$ and $\hat{c}$ must also be constants under balanced growth.

In what follows, we shall try to find out if the optimally chosen paths of the Command Economy variables can be consistent with balanced growth. To appreciate the point, differentiate (2.5) subject to (2.18) to obtain

$$-\theta\,\frac{\dot{c}}{c} = \frac{\dot{q}}{q} - \mu, \qquad (2.19)$$

dropping the superscript '*' for simplicity. Similarly, (2.15) gives

$$
\begin{aligned}
\frac{\dot{q}}{q} - \mu &= -\{f'(\hat{k}) - (\mu + \rho + \delta)\} - \mu \\
&= -\{f'(\hat{k}) - (\rho + \delta)\}. \qquad (2.20)
\end{aligned}
$$

Combining (2.19) and (2.20),

$$\frac{\dot{c}}{c} = \frac{1}{\theta}\,\{f'(\hat{k}) - (\rho + \delta)\}. \qquad (2.21)$$

Equation (2.21)[16] describes the behaviour of $\dot{c}/c$ along an optimal path. It says that the economy's desire to grow is positively linked to the difference between the net marginal productivity of capital and the rate of

---

[16]The economic intuition underlying (2.21) may also be understood as follows. Assume the following perturbation in the optimal growth path $\{c^*, \hat{k}^*\}$. There is a marginal increase in $\hat{k}$ at t_0, thus causing a reduction of A_{t_0} in $c^*_{t_0}$. The loss in utility is $A_{t_0}\,u'(c^*_{t_0})$. The extra $\hat{k}$ yields a marginal net return of $f'(\hat{k}^*) - (\mu + n + \delta)$ along the optimal balanced growth path. As opposed to the procedure followed in deriving (2.7), i.e., consuming the extra yield, the latter is assumed to be reinvested now, producing (approximately) the same net return per unit as above, viz.

discounting. A rise in the former raises the desired rate of growth. On the other hand, a rise in the discount rate implies a shift of preference towards current consumption. This causes the desired rate of growth to fall. Let us consider a special case of an optimal path by restricting attention to balanced growth paths only. Then, $\dot{c}/c$ and hence $\hat{k}$ are positive constants, thus implying that the set of feasible paths is restricted to those for which k displays balanced growth at the rate μ. We may appeal to (1.9) and $\hat{y} = f(\hat{k})$ to conclude that $\dot{c}/c = \dot{y}/y = \mu$ also. Hence, (2.21) may be rewritten

$$f'(\hat{k}) = \rho + \delta + \mu\theta, \qquad (2.22)$$

which solves for the value of $\hat{k} = \hat{k}^*$ associated with the optimal balanced growth path for a Command Economy. Thus, $\hat{k}^*$ stands for the value of $\hat{k}$ the planner would wish to be endowed with at $t = 0$ if he is to restrict himself to an optimal balanced growth path [17] The accompanying value of $\hat{c}$ will be denoted by $\hat{c}^*$. We have accordingly[18]

$f'(\hat{k}^*) - (\mu + n + \delta)$, if the invested amount is arbitrarily small. This procedure is followed till $t_1 > t_0$, so that an extra amount of per capita output equal to $A_{t_1} e^{(f'(\hat{k}^*)-(\mu+n+\delta))(t_1-t_0)} = A_{t_0} e^{\mu(t_1-t_0)} e^{(f'(\hat{k}^*)-(\mu+n+\delta))(t_1-t_0)}$ is available at t_1 over and above what the original optimal path produced. The extra utility this yields is $A_{t_0} e^{\mu(t_1-t_0)} e^{(f'(\hat{k}^*)-(\mu+n+\delta))(t_1-t_0)} u'(c_{t_1}^*)$. Discounted back to t_0, this gives $e^{-(\rho-n)(t_1-t_0)} A_{t_0} e^{\mu(t_1-t_0)} e^{(f'(\hat{k}^*)-(\mu+n+\delta))(t_1-t_0)} u'(c_{t_1}^*)$. Suppose now that the consumption path is growing at a balanced rate g. For optimality, the perturbation, being small, leaves the planner indifferent. Thus, using (2.18),

$$
\begin{aligned}
A_{t_0} c^*(t_0)^{-\theta} &= e^{-(\rho-n)(t_1-t_0)} A_{t_0} e^{\mu(t_1-t_0)} \\
&\quad \times e^{(f'(\hat{k}^*)-(\mu+n+\delta))(t_1-t_0)} c^*(t_1)^{-\theta} \\
&= e^{-(\rho-n)(t_1-t_0)} A_{t_0} e^{\mu(t_1-t_0)} \\
&\quad \times e^{(f'(\hat{k}^*)-(\mu+n+\delta))(t_1-t_0)} \\
&\quad \times c^*(t_0)^{-\theta} e^{-\theta g(t_1-t_0)}.
\end{aligned}
$$

Cancelling out terms and solving, (2.21) follows. The argument goes back to Ramsey (1928), who in turn quoted Keynes as its inventor.

[17]A solution must exist according to **Property f1** and **Assumption F3**.

[18]The need to restrict the analysis to a special class of utility functions for balanced growth to be possible is ultimately related to the presence of technical progress in the model. To appreciate this fact, assume that $\mu = 0$. As Cass (1965) shows, balanced growth for this case would imply constant values of k and c. Consequently, (2.21) may be replaced by the more general condition

$$\frac{cu''(c)}{u'(c)} \frac{\dot{c}}{c} = -\{f'(\hat{k}) - (\rho + \delta)\}.$$

PROPOSITION **2.2** *When restricted to balanced growth paths, the Command Economy allocates resources so that c as well as y and k grow at the rate $G_c^* = \mu$. Along the optimal balanced growth path $\hat{k}$ satisfies* (2.22).

In the class of balanced growth paths then, Proposition 2.2 ensures that the planner will choose to start at $\hat{k}^*$ and stay there forever, provided that initial values of K and L allow the planner the choice of $\hat{k}^*$. To appreciate the nature of the choice, note that the requirement of optimal balanced growth reduces equation (1.9) to

$$\hat{c} = f(\hat{k}) - (\mu + n + \delta)\, \hat{k}. \tag{2.23}$$

With reference to Figure 2.3, we see that the maximum value of $\hat{c}$ occurs when[19]

$$f'(\hat{k}) = \mu + n + \delta. \tag{2.24}$$

The solution $\hat{k}^{**}$ to (2.24) is referred to as the Golden Rule (GR) value of the effective capital-labour ratio. The corresponding solution $\hat{k}^*$ to (2.22) is called the Modified Golden Rule (MGR).[20] The value of $\hat{c}$ associated with $\hat{k}^{**}$ is denoted $\hat{c}^{**}$. Since $\hat{c}^{**}$ is the maximum possible value of $\hat{c}$ consistent with balanced growth, the reader will wonder why the planner chooses $\hat{c}^*$, a value that is obviously smaller than $\hat{c}^{**}$. Indeed, $\hat{c}^* < \hat{c}^{**}$ implies that $\hat{c}^{**}$ corresponds to a larger value of c than the value of c associated with $\hat{c}^*$ for all time.

We will argue that $\hat{k}^* < \hat{k}^{**}$.[21] The chosen form (2.18) of the utility function imposes a restriction on the exogenously specified rate of technical progress μ. To see this, observe that aggregate utility along the balanced growth equilibrium path is given by

$$U = \int_0^\infty \frac{(c_0^*\, e^{\mu t})^{1-\theta} - 1}{1 - \theta}\, e^{-(\rho - n)t}\, dt$$

A constant c reduces the LHS of the above equation to zero quite independent of the form of the utility function. In this case, the value of $\hat{k} = k$ under optimal balanced growth is found by solving the equation $f'(k) = \rho + \delta$. See Cass (1965).

[19] The reader should be able to verify quite easily that the strict concavity of f along with the Inada conditions guarantees that a maximum exists.

[20] The nomenclature GR goes back to Phelps (1961 and 1965), while MGR can be traced back to Cass 1965, Koopmans 1965.

[21] Intuitively, this is straightforward. From Figure 2.3, it should be possible to maintain $\hat{c}^*$ by choosing a value of $\hat{k} > \hat{k}^{**}$ too. Since, $(\hat{c}^*, \hat{k}^*)$ is an optimal pair, it would involve capital wastage and hence be suboptimality if $(\hat{c}^*$ were to be maintained with the help of $\hat{k} > \hat{k}^*$.

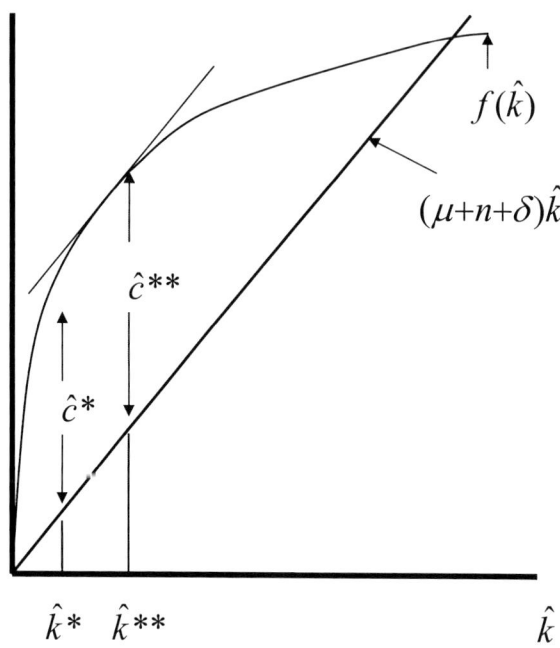

Figure 2.3: Golden Rule and Modified Golden Rule

$$= -\frac{1}{1-\theta} \int_0^\infty e^{-(\rho-n)t} dt \qquad (2.25)$$

$$+ \frac{(c_0^*)^{1-\theta}}{1-\theta} \int_0^\infty e^{(1-\theta)\mu t} e^{-(\rho-n)t} dt.$$

$$(2.26)$$

For the integral to be well-defined, it is necessary and sufficient that

$$\rho - n > (1-\theta)\,\mu. \qquad (2.27)$$

If $\theta < 1$, (2.27) leads to a nontrivial bound on the allowable rate of technical change. Thus, $\mu + n + \delta < \rho + \mu\,\theta + \delta$. Hence, comparing (2.22) with (2.24) and using the concavity of $f(\hat{k})$, it follows that $\hat{k}^* < \hat{k}^{**}$.

Why does the planner prefer $\hat{c}^*$ over $\hat{c}^{**}$? To answer the question, consider the form of the planner's objective function, a *discounted* sum of utilities. Intuitively speaking, the planner can construct an alternative and better path by (i) consuming a part of the capital associated with $\hat{c}^{**}$, thus bringing the capital stock down to a level consistent with $\hat{c}^*$ and (ii) maintaining the lower value of $\hat{k}^*$ thereafter forever. The capital so consumed will constitute an initial gain in consumption, but it will also lead to a subsequent loss (viz. the lower consumption corresponding to $\hat{k}^*$). However, the discounted sum of future losses will be more than compensated by the initial gain.[22]

In this connection, it should be obvious that, in the absence of discounting, the planner would in fact choose $\{\hat{c}^{**}, \hat{k}^{**}\}$ as the best balanced growth path. The only problem in that case turns out to be that the associated welfare function would not be a simple generalization of (2.1), because the infinite integral would be unbounded for any balanced growth path. It is worth noting here that Ramsey (1928) considered an undiscounted version of the planner's aggregate welfare function, since he viewed discounting of future utilities to be unethical. Consequently, he had to address the question of the existence of the infinite integral. He had an ingenious idea to circumvent the non-existence problem, for which interested students are referred to his paper. Much later, undiscounted future utilities were once again the centre of attraction in connection with an alternative version of the planner's utility function, the so-called *overtaking criterion*, introduced by Atsumi (1965) and von Weizäcker (1965). In the undiscounted case, the transversality condition is not expected to hold. The best way to appreciate this is to note that the value of the co-state variable corresponding to the optimal *GR* solution c^{**} equals $q^{**} = u'(c^{**}) > 0$, which stays bounded away from zero. Appendix 2.4 discusses another infinite horizon, undiscounted problem (constructed by Halkin 1974), for which the transversality condition fails. Contrary to the problem we have discussed so far, Halkin's objective function assigned a disproportionately high weight on capital in the distant future.

---

[22]See Appendix 2.3 for a rigorous proof of this claim.

2.2.2   Out of Optimal Balanced Growth Path

Pinning down a variable like $\hat{k}$ at $\hat{k}^*$ brings up another problem. Since, K_0 and $(A_0\, L_0)$ are exogenously given, $\hat{k}_0$ is fixed at the outset. Except by accident, $\hat{k}_0$ will not be identical with the optimal choice of $\hat{k}$. Consequently, the economy will not follow the optimal balanced growthpath all through. This being the case, we must discover what constitutes out of balanced growth behaviour and how it relates to the balanced growth path. The objective of this section is to demonstrate that optimal behaviour leads the planner to guide the economy over time towards the MGR pair $(\hat{k}^*, \hat{c}^*)$.

To establish this result, let us subtract μ from both sides of (2.21) to write

$$\frac{\dot{\hat{c}}}{\hat{c}} = \frac{1}{\theta}\, \{f'(\hat{k}) - (\rho + \delta + \mu\theta)\}, \qquad (2.28)$$

where the superscript '*' has been dropped for all the variables for simplicity (as in Section 2.2.1). Using (2.19), we see that

$$\frac{\dot{\hat{c}}}{\hat{c}} = -\frac{1}{\theta}\left(\frac{\dot{q}}{q} - (1-\theta)\mu\right) = -\frac{1}{\theta}\frac{\dot{\hat{q}}}{\hat{q}}, \qquad (2.29)$$

where $\hat{q} = q/A^{1-\theta}$. Given the definition of $\hat{q}$ and (2.29), equation (2.28) reduces to

$$\frac{\dot{\hat{q}}}{\hat{q}} = -\{f'(\hat{k}) - (\rho + \delta + \mu\theta)\}. \qquad (2.30)$$

Next, use (2.5), (2.18) and (1.9) to write

$$\hat{q}(t) = \frac{1}{(f(\hat{k}(t)) - \lambda\, \hat{k}(t) - \dot{\hat{k}}(t))^{\theta}}, \qquad (2.31)$$

recalling $\lambda = \mu + n + \delta$. The study of optimal path reduces now to a study of the pair of differential equations (2.30) and (2.31). The method of analysis to follow will identify the qualitative properties of this path, especially its behaviour in the long run. This is best done with the help of

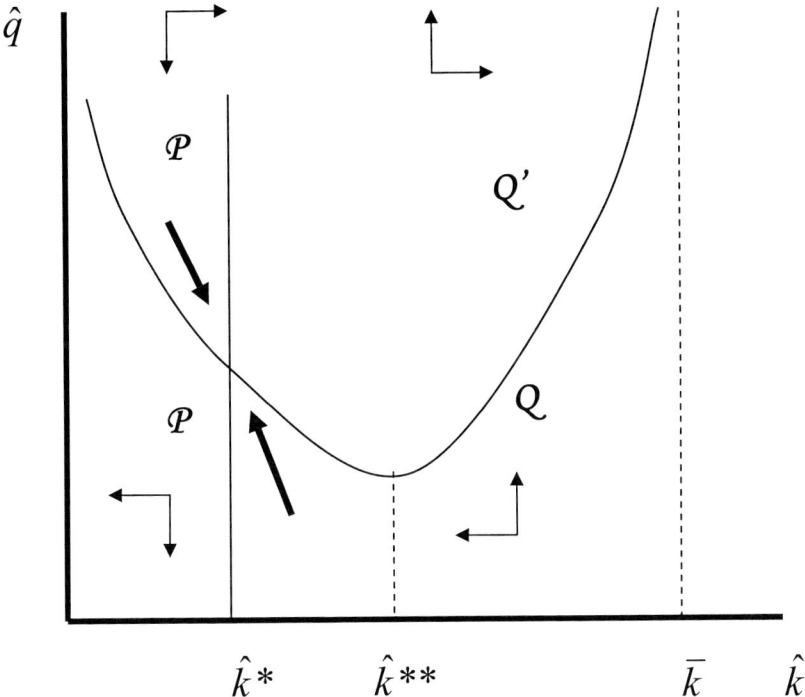

Figure 2.4: Behaviour of the Optimal Path

what is known as a phase diagram in the $(\hat{k}, \hat{q})$ plane. See Figure 2.4. The phase diagram displays two curves. One of these, the U-shaped curve, plots the equation (2.31) by putting $\dot{\hat{k}} = 0$. Along this curve, $\hat{k}$ remains unchanged over time. Recalling the definition of $\hat{k}$ in Proposition 1.1, we note that the U-shaped curve is asymptotic to the vertical line through $\bar{\hat{k}}$.

The second of the two curves in the phase plane is a vertical line through $\hat{k}^*$ obtained by equating the LHS of (2.30) to zero. Along this curve, $\hat{q}$ is a constant. The intersection of the two curves represents the pair $(\hat{k}^*, \hat{q}^*)$ corresponding to optimal balanced growth.

The curves divide up the plane into four non-overlapping zones $\mathcal{P}$, $\mathcal{P}'$, $\mathcal{Q}$ and $\mathcal{Q}'$. We want to find out how the economy will behave if it starts with $\hat{k}_0 \neq \hat{k}^*$ and chooses a $\hat{q}_0$ so that the pair $(\hat{k}_0, \hat{q}_0)$ falls in any one of these regions. We shall present the arguments for $\mathcal{P}$ and leave it to the reader to carry out the arguments for the other cases. In the region $\mathcal{P}$, we have $f'(\hat{k}) > \rho + \delta + \theta\mu$. Hence, (2.30) implies $\dot{\hat{q}} < 0$, which is indicated by a downward pointing arrow. In the same region, (2.31) implies that $\dot{\hat{k}} > 0$.[23] This is indicated by a rightward pointing arrow. The directions of movements in the other three regions are indicated in Figure 2.4.

A path that starts in region $\mathcal{P}$ can either move towards the balanced growth equilibrium point (see thick arrow), or move into either of the two regions $\mathcal{P}'$ or $\mathcal{Q}'$. (Note the curved arrows, usually referred to as stream lines.) Once inside the last two regions, the path stays trapped there as the curved arrows indicate. Similarly, a path starting in $\mathcal{Q}$ may converge to the balanced growth equilibrium or get trapped in regions $\mathcal{P}'$ or $\mathcal{Q}'$. We will argue that it is either suboptimal or infeasible for a path to enter the regions $\mathcal{P}'$ or $\mathcal{Q}'$.

Suppose that the path ends up in $\mathcal{Q}'$. This means that $\hat{q} \uparrow \infty$. Hence, (2.31) and (1.9) implies that $\hat{c}$ is arbitrarily small for t large enough. Consider now an alternative feasible path along which $\hat{k} = $ constant from some t_0 onwards. Then, for $t > t_0$, $\hat{c} = $ constant also, say $\bar{\hat{c}} = \overline{C_t/A_t L_t}$. Since $A_t L_t$ is exogenously specified, the path along which $\hat{c}$ turns arbitrarily small must involve a value of $C(t)$ that is eventually smaller than the corresponding C_t in $\bar{\hat{c}}$. Consequently, such a path is suboptimal. An optimal path therefore cannot move into the zone $\mathcal{Q}'$.

Next suppose that $\{\hat{k}_t^*, \hat{c}_t^*\}$ moves into $\mathcal{P}'$. In this zone, $\hat{q}^* \downarrow 0$, Hence, (2.5) implies that $\hat{c}^*$ becomes arbitrarily large. Since the maximum possible value of $\hat{c}$ is $f(\hat{k}) + (1 - \delta)\hat{k}$, the path in question is infeasible.

Thus, the only possibility that remains is that the optimal path converges to $(\hat{k}^*, \hat{q}^*)$. The result arrived at may be stated as

PROPOSITION **2.3** *Starting from any arbitrary initial values of the capital stock and labour force, the optimal path for the Solow economy converges to the Modified Golden Rule configuration.*

---

[23]To see this, equation (2.31) is rewritten

$$\dot{\hat{k}} = f(\hat{k}(t)) - \lambda\,\hat{k}(t) - \hat{q}^{-1/\theta}.$$

When $\dot{\hat{k}} = 0$, we obtain the U-shaped relationship between $\hat{k}$ and $\hat{q}$. Each choice of $\hat{k}$ gives rise to a value of $\hat{q}$ that makes $\dot{\hat{k}} = 0$. For a higher value of $\hat{q}$, the RHS of the equation turns positive. Thus, in the entire region above the U-shaped curve, $\dot{\hat{k}} > 0$.

We have thus proved that the optimal path cannot converge to $\hat{k}^{**}$. Further, for t large enough, $f'(\hat{k}_t^*) - (\mu + n + \delta)$ is strictly positive and stays bounded away from zero. This takes us back to the transversality condition discussed in Section 2.2.1 and ensures that (2.8) holds.[24]

2.3   Growth in a Private Economy

We proceed now to the behaviour of the Private Economy. It consists of two macro agents, H and B. The first of these supplies savings and labour and the second demands capital and labour. All markets are perfectly competitive. At each t, factor markets are in equilibrium. In this section, we shall study how the economy behaves when guided by these private choices.

Agent H, whose size at t is L_t, is viewed as a dynastic household that expects to live forever. This means that H plans for all generations. An alternative assumption could be that H plans for a finite horizon and bequeaths a stock of capital to the future generations which will live beyond its planning horizon. However, this approach would require us to specify a bequest utility function in some manner or the other and thereby suggesting that H does have a preference defined over all future. The preferences of H are identically the same as the Planner's preferences, viz. (2.1), and satisfy **Assumptions u1 through u3**.

There is only one type of paper asset in the economy, a share $\mathcal{A}$ issued by B. Each unit of $\mathcal{A}$ represents the ownership right over a unit of K. The H is the owner of all capital and supplies capital services inelastically. This constitutes the supply function in the capital (services) market. Similarly, $L(t)$ is supplied inelastically in the labour market. On the other hand, factor price flexibility and the Inada conditions ensure that all savings are used up in capital formation, i.e., savings = investment.[25] The budget constraint of H at t is

$$\dot{\mathcal{A}}(t) = w(t)L(t) + r(t)\,\mathcal{A}(t) - C(t), \qquad (2.32)$$

where $\dot{\mathcal{A}}(t)$ stands for investment or disinvestment in $\mathcal{A}(t)$, $w(t)\,L(t)$ the income from inelastically supplied labour and $r(t)\,\mathcal{A}(t)$ the income

---

[24] As already noted, the result is proved more generally in Appendix 2.3 to incorporate irreversible investment.

[25] The latter reflects the non-Keynesian feature of the Solow economy.

from asset holdings. Denoting per capita asset holding by $a(t)$, equation (2.32) reduces to

$$\dot{a}(t) = w(t) + r(t)\, a(t) - c(t) - n\, a(t), \qquad (2.33)$$

where, following arguments similar to those used in the derivation of equation (1.8) in Chapter 1, $n\, a(t)$ is the per capita investment in $\mathcal{A}(t)$ necessary to keep $a(t)$ unchanged. Agent H maximizes (2.1) subject to (2.33) (or, (2.32)) being satisfied at each t.

Corresponding to any given K_0 and a path of $r(t)$ and $w(t)$, the solution to the household's problem leads to a choice of $\{C(t), \dot{\mathcal{A}}(t)\}_0^\infty$, hence $\{C(t), \dot{K}(t)\}$ at each t. Given the inherited $K(t)$ at t, the chosen $\dot{K}(t)$ and the rate of depreciation δ, the capital stock for the next instant of time is determined. Accordingly, the notion of an equilibrium of the Private Economy which Chapter 1 introduced can be elaborated as follows:

> **Definition:** (i) a path of rates of interest and wages $\{r_t^*, w_t^*\}_0^\infty$, (ii) a path of optimal choices by H, viz. $\{c_t^*, \mathcal{A}_t^*\}_0^\infty$, or equivalently, $\{c_t^*, a_t^*\}_0^\infty$, where $\mathcal{A}_t^* = K_t^*$ at each t by definition, or, $\hat{k}_t^* = a_t^*/A_t$ at each t and (iii) a path of optimal choices by B, viz. $\{K_t^*, L_t^*\}_0^\infty$, or equivalently, $\{\hat{k}_t^*, L_t^*\}_0^\infty$ satisfying (1.13) and (1.14) are said to constitute an **equilibrium** for the Private Economy.

Trivially, the path $\{r_t^*, w_t^*\}_0^\infty$ has the features of a perfect foresight equilibrium. To see this, suppose that H and B forecast the path $\{r_t^*, w_t^*\}_0^\infty$ at $t = 0$. Then, H will choose $\{c_t^*, \mathcal{A}_t^*\}_0^\infty = \{c_t^*, K_t^*\}_0^\infty$ on the basis of its dynamic optimality exercise and B will select $\{\hat{k}_t^*, L_t^*\}_0^\infty$. According to condition (iii) above, factor markets will be in equilibrium. Taking account of the CRS technology, (1.13) and $\mathcal{A}_t^* = K_t^*$, equation (2.32) reduces to (1.1). The latter implies that the commodity market is in equilibrium. Thus, all markets will be in equilibrium and $\{r_t^*, w_t^*\}_0^\infty$ will be realized if expected.

Given our derivations for the Command Economy, solving for the Private Economy will be a relatively simple exercise. Let us replace (1.9) by (2.33) and treat a rather than $\hat{k}$ as the state variable. The control variable for both problems is c. However, to distinguish between the Command and the Private economies, we shall denote the Private

Economy choice by $\bar{c}$. The necessary condition for a static optimum turns out to be

$$u'(\bar{c}) - \bar{q} = 0, \tag{2.34}$$

where $\bar{q}(t)$ is the co-state variable for the problem, i.e., the shadow price of a unit of $a(t)$ at t.

The relevant Hamiltonian for the Private Economy is

$$
\begin{aligned}
\mathcal{H}_m(c(t), a(t), \bar{q}(t)) &= u(c(t)) + \bar{q}(t)[w(t) \\
&\quad + (r(t) - n)a(t) - c(t)].
\end{aligned}
\tag{2.35}
$$

The necessary conditions for optimality are:

$$\frac{\partial \mathcal{H}_m(\bar{c}_t^*, \bar{a}_t^*, \bar{q}_t^*)}{\partial c} = 0. \tag{2.36}$$

$$\dot{\bar{q}}_t^* = \frac{d \int_t^\infty \partial \mathcal{H}_m(\bar{c}_s^*, \bar{a}_s^*, \bar{q}_s^*)/\partial a(s) \, e^{-(\rho-n)(s-t)} \, ds}{dt}. \tag{2.37}$$

Finally,

$$\frac{\partial \mathcal{H}_m(\bar{c}_t^*, \bar{a}_t^*, \bar{q}_t^*)}{\partial \bar{q}(t)} = \dot{\bar{a}}_t^*$$

$$\text{or,} \quad \dot{a}(t) = w(t) + r(t)\, a(t) - c(t) - n\, a(t). \tag{2.38}$$

2.3.1 Equilibrium Balanced Growth Rate

We have so far been discussing the optimal balanced growth rate. Is this optimal balanced growth rate an equilibrium growth rate too? In other words, we shall concentrate now on the notion of a dynamic equilibrium, somewhat in the spirit of Harrod (1939). The discussion will be restricted to the rate of growth of c alone, since the rates of growth of other variables will follow automatically. Given (2.18), equations (2.34) and (2.37) yield

$$\frac{\dot{c}}{c} = \frac{r - \rho}{\theta}. \qquad (2.39)$$

The above equation expresses the rate at which the household wishes to grow given the market rate of interest r. It is, in other words, the optimal rate of growth for the household, given the rate of interest. Consequently, we shall denote it by $g_c^d(r)$ and call it the *demand rate of balanced growth*, or simply the demand rate of growth for the Private Economy. The demand *growth rate* of c constitutes an *equilibrium* rate of growth for the Private Economy when it matches the economy's balanced growth capability.

Equation (2.39) implies that under balanced growth, the desired rate of growth will be characterized by a constant r. What is the balanced rate at which c is *capable* of growing given a constant r? First, (1.13) shows that a constant r leads to a constant $\hat{k}$ for profit maximization. From (1.9), however, whenever $\hat{k}$ is a constant, c grows at the rate μ. Thus, from supply side considerations, there is a perfectly inelastic

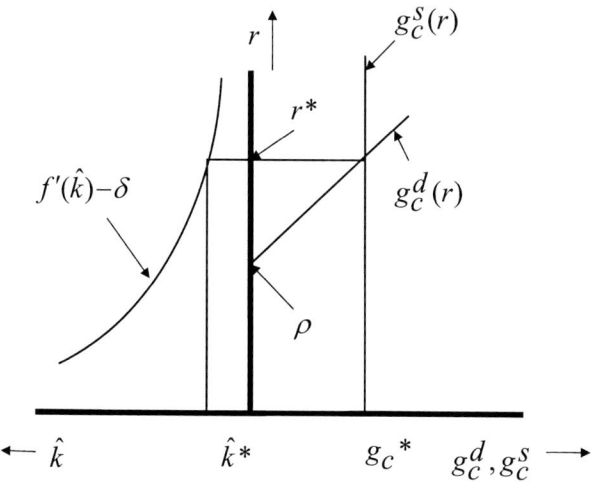

Figure 2.5: The Balanced Growth Equlibrium

relationship between r and the rate of growth of c. Refer to this as the *supply rate of balanced growth* $g_c^s(r)$, or simply the supply rate of growth.

It is the *only* balanced rate of growth of the maximum feasible value of c that the economy can afford for itself when producers maximize profit at each instant of time. 'Supply' here is not being defined in the standard economic sense an optimal choice by any agent. Rather, it is the attainable rate of growth of the best possible residual value of c, given profit maximization by producers.

> **Definition:** The per capita consumption for the Solow
> Economy displays a balanced growth **equilibrium** when
> the demand rate of balanced growth equals the supply
> rate of balanced growth.

PROPOSITION **2.4** *The equilibrium balanced growth rate of per capita consumption equals μ. The associated equilibrium rate of interest satisfies the condition $r^* = \rho + \mu\,\theta$.*

The proof of this proposition is obvious from the right hand panel of Figure 2.5.[26] Moreover, it follows from (1.9) that k and y also grow at the rate μ when c is in balanced growth equilibrium.

Even though the equilibrium rate of growth is viewed as an intersection of a demand and a supply curve, it should be obvious that it is the supply side which dominates. The equilibrium growth rate of c is $g_c^* = \mu$. Thus, a change in the parameters of demand, i.e., shifts or changes in the slope of the demand curve, will leave the equilibrium rate of growth unaffected. An increase in thriftiness, caused, say, by a tax on consumption, will fail to affect the equilibrium rate of growth of the system. In other words, the equilibrium rate of growth is uncontrollable. This diagrammatic device will find extensive use in the subsequent chapters.

The left hand panel captures the determination of $\hat{k}^*$ associated with a balanced growth equilibrium. The value of $\hat{k}^*$ follows from the equilibrium value of r^*, since (1.13) requires that the net marginal product of capital be equated to the market rate of interest.[27]

---

[26]From the definition of an equilibrium for the Private Economy, along a balanced growth equilibrium path, the *levels* of consumption demand and supply are equal too.

[27]To the extent that a balanced growth path is an equilibrium path for a Private Economy, it satisfies the property of a perfect foresight equilibrium.

2.4   Comparison of Growth Paths: Command Economy vs Private Economy

The purpose of this section is to establish that the growth path of the Private Economy is unique and identically the same as the optimal growth path for the Command Economy. The latter result is the dynamic counterpart of the First Fundamental Theorem of Welfare Economics, which states that a competitive equilibrium is Pareto Optimal.

We shall restrict attention to the function (2.18). Define a new variable p^* such that $p_t^*/A_t = \bar{q}_t^*$ at each t. Then, (2.37)) reduces to

$$\dot{p}_t^* = -f'(\bar{\hat{k}}_t^*)\, p_t^* + (\mu + \rho + \delta)\, p_t^*. \tag{2.40}$$

(2.36) yields

$$u'(\bar{c}_t^*) = \frac{p_t^*}{A_t}. \tag{2.41}$$

Also, (2.33) and (1.1) reduce to

$$\dot{\bar{c}}_t^* + A_t\, \dot{\bar{\hat{k}}}_t^* = A_t\{f(\bar{\hat{k}}_t^*) - (\mu + n + \delta)\bar{\hat{k}}_t^*\}. \tag{2.42}$$

Using our earlier methods, (1.13), (2.40), (2.41), (2.42) and the assumption of a CRS technology may now be used to show that the relevant variables for the Private Economy converge to the MGR configuration. This means that $f'(\bar{\hat{k}}_t^*) - (\mu + \delta + n)$ stays bounded away from 0 as $t \to \infty$. Let us now solve the differential equation (2.40) to obtain [28]

$$p_t^* = p_0^*\, e^{-\int_0^t (f'(\bar{\hat{k}}_s^*) - (\mu + \rho + \delta))\, ds}.$$

Multiplying both sides by $e^{-(\rho-n)\,t}$ and simplifying, we get

$$p_t^*\, e^{-(\rho-n)\,t} = p_0^*\, e^{-\int_0^t (f'(\bar{\hat{k}}_s^*) - (\mu + \delta + n))\, ds}. \tag{2.43}$$

---

[28]See Appendix A.1.2 of Barro and Sala-i-Martin (2003) for a clear exposition of the method of solution of this differential equation.

Since, $f'(\bar{\hat{k}}_t^*) - (\mu + \delta + n)$ is strictly positive from some t onwards and stays bounded away from 0 as $t \to \infty$, it follows that the RHS of the last equation converges to 0 as $t \to \infty$. Hence, p_t^* satisfies the transversality condition

$$e^{-(\rho-n)t}p_t^* \to 0 \text{ as } t \to \infty. \tag{2.44}$$

We now appeal to Appendix 2.2 to claim that (2.40), (2.41), (2.42), and (2.44) imply that the path $\{\bar{c}_t^*, \bar{\hat{k}}_t^*\}_0^\infty$ is unique and solves the Command Economy's problem. Hence, the Private Economy path is identically the same as the one followed by the Command Economy. Also, the path of $\{r_t^*, w_t^*\}_0^\infty$ determined by (1.13) is unique. Lastly, using the definition $\bar{q}^* = p_t^*/A_t$,

$$e^{-(\rho-n)t}\bar{q}_t^* \to 0 \text{ as } t \to \infty \tag{2.45}$$

also. Thus, we have proved the following proposition.

PROPOSITION **2.5** *Suppose* $\{\bar{c}_t^*, \bar{a}_t^*\}_0^\infty$ *and* $\{r_t^*, w_t^*\}_0^\infty$ *is an equilibrium path for the Private Economy. Then, there exists a path of co-state variables* $\bar{q}_t^*$ *such that (2.36), (2.37), (2.38), and (2.45) are satisfied. The equilibrium paths of the variables chosen by the Private Economy are unique. Moreover, the paths of per capita consumption and capital chosen by the Private Economy are identically the same as the ones chosen by the Planned Economy.*

Thus, the decentralized decisions of a Private Economy produce a social optimum, though, as we shall see, many of the growth models to follow violate this property. Moreover, as far as the Solow model goes, the path followed by the Private Economy, being identically the same as the one chosen by the Command Economy, will by dynamically stable in the sense of Section 2.3.2.

2.5 The Ways Ahead

Let us first take stock of where we have arrived. We may refer to the growth rate of labour as the exogenous rate and the model determined rate of growth of capital as the endogenous rate. In the absence of technical change, the Solow model predicts the impossibility of the endogenous rate staying indefinitely higher than the exogenous rate. Under the law of diminishing returns, the latter drives the former down to a level commensurate with itself. Consequently, the Solow exercise leads to the depressing conclusion that the long run growth rate of per capita magnitudes will be exactly zero, a conclusion that would appear to run counter to the very purpose of economic growth.

Fortunately, technical progress helps to get rid of this disturbing conclusion by introducing a 'wedge' between the exogenous and the endogenous rates. The force of diminishing returns still prevails, but technical progress distinguishes between the actual labour force and the effective labour force. Capital can now grow permanently faster than the *actual* labour force (the head count if one likes) in apparent violation of the law of diminishing returns! This suggests that any meaningful growth exercise must consist of finding ways of easing the economic system out of the shackles of diminishing returns.

Solow, as we have seen, succeeds in leading us to this vitally important conclusion. Unfortunately, however, he found a way out of the zero growth trap in an ad hoc manner, by supplementing the growth rate of labour by yet another exogenous growth rate, that of technical progress. Both the Private and the Command economies for the Solow world give rise to economic variables, such as c, k, y etc., that grow ultimately at the rate of growth of A. The latter though is a nebulous entity, consisting of an *exogenously* specified rate of labour augmentation arising from *unexplained* causes. The model fails to shed any light on the nature of economic forces that may affect technological progress. An implication of this observation is that the long run growth rate of the Solow economy cannot be affected by economic policy.[29] This is not a trivial issue, especially so for economies driven by private enterprise, because casual observation suggests that firms do employ resources in the shape of $R\&D$ to improve the technology. Thus, one would expect the rate of technological progress to respond to economic incentives, much as the supply of output by a firm does. But, from what we have presented so far, the supply rate of growth is completely inelastic vis-á-vis changes in known economic variables.

It is this last observation that constitutes the point of departure for Modern Growth Theory. It investigates different ways of filling up this missing link in the Solow model and adding refinements to it so as to remove the triviality associated with the rate of technological progress. Let us note the nature of difficulties that could arise in a Private Econ-

---

[29]However, a policy that affects, say, saving behaviour, will have an impact on the out of steady state path to the equilibrium. To see this, note that the variable $\dot{k}$ in equation (1.9) will change in response to changes in the instantaneous savings rate.

omy when we move in the intended direction. First, if we consider A to be the output of a conscious process of production, such as $R\&D$, then it must be paid for. Paying for A in addition to K and L brings up questions of returns to scale with respect to the three factors. The Solow model assumes F to display constant returns to scale with respect to K and AL. But this means that it will give rise to increasing returns if K, A and L are considered separately. Consequently, the assumption of competitive factor markets needs to be given up when we deal with a Private Economy. That is, explaining A might require admitting non-competitive market structures. An alternative avenue could be to view A as an unconscious by-product of the process of capital accumulation. Investment undertaken by a firm may attract high quality labour into a given area from which other existing firms benefit. Such investments lead to social improvements in productivity, which are external to the investing firm. In these situations, competitive markets can function, but the market-generated equilibria will not be socially optimal, for reasons similar to the failure of the first fundamental theorem of welfare economics in the presence of externalities.

In what follows, we shall attempt to introduce the reader to the different ways in which economic theorists have attempted to address the basic question raised by the Solow model. Invariably, however, the answers received fit into one or the other of the two approaches suggested in the preceding paragraph. As we shall see in the rest of this book, the *modus operandi* boils down to investigating if the *scarcity of natural resource*-imposed law of diminishing returns can be postponed by means of *human creativity*. Putting it somewhat philosophically, natural resources, even if growing according to some law, are ultimately scarce. On the other hand, human wants are boundlessly large. Tapping yet another potentially endless resource, viz. the unlimited variety of human ingenuity, bridges the gap between the scarce and the infinite. If human understanding of the ostensible boundaries imposed by natural phenomena can keep growing over time through a growth of wilfully acquired knowledge, then the conflict between the finite and the infinite could well be resolved. As growth economists would wish us to believe, knowledge, the most abstract of resources created by economic agents, serves as the ultimate vehicle for breaking through the barriers of diminishing returns. It constitutes, in other words, the crowning refinement in the concept of capital, the only form of capital that is not subject to the laws of natural scarcity.

The remaining four chapters of the book will present a selected set of attempts by economic theorists to carry forward the above ideas. In particular, Chapter 4 will collect, except for the model proposed by Romer

(1986), some of the attempts to view technical progress as an unconscious by product of capital accumulation. This will lead us to consider the famous Arrow (1962) exercise on Learning by Doing and its extensions. The chapter will also present models of growth which are formally similar to the Arrow type models, though motivated by different factors. A famous model it will be concerned with is due to Barro (1990) and Barro and Sala-i-Martin (2003) on the role of infrastructure in capital accumulation. Chapters 4, 5, and 6 will then be concerned with models of consciously produced technical progress. The latter will sometimes assume the form of human capital accumulation (Lucas 1998 and Rebelo 1991 in Chapter 4) and accumulation of infrastructure (Dasgupta 1999 and 2001 in Chapter 4). Other famous exercises they will be concerned with are due to Romer (1990, in Chapter 5), Grossman and Helpman (1991, in Chapters 5 and 6) and Aghion and Howitt (1992, Chapter 6). These works will be seen to link growth with profit driven $R\&D$. The models, as we shall see, will call for non-competitive market structures to allow for payment to factors responsible for technical progress. They will also open up the possibility of obsolescence of research ideas in the face of cut-throat competition.

Appendix 2.1   Optimality Conditions: General Treatment

This section has two objectives. First, it provides some of the mathematical details avoided by the intuitive discussion of the necessary first order conditions in Section 2.1.1. Secondly, it gives an integrated analysis that applies to the cases of reversible as well as irreversible investment. Note that for irreversible investment, it is not possible to rule out c hitting the upper bound. At the maximum possible value of c, all output is consumed away, but this does not exhaust the capital stock. The economy bequeaths $(1 - \delta)K$ to posterity. Hence, positive production as well as consumption is feasible at subsequent points of time. However, **Assumption u2** still rules out $c = 0$ at any t. Hence, for irreversible investment, (A1.1) reduces to

$$0 < c \leq Af(\hat{k}). \tag{A2.1.1}$$

Equation (A2.1.1) shows that the optimum for the irreversible investment case could occur at a point where $\hat{k}$ can no longer be sacrificed to yield extra c. Consequently, the marginal rate of substitution between c and $\dot{\hat{k}}$ (as measured by the slope of the level curves of the Hamiltonian) may no longer equal the rate of technical substitution between them. At points such as these, the marginal rate of substitution will be treated as the correct price ratio. The implication of this observation will be clearer below. The planner's optimisation exercise for this case is:

Optimization under Irreversible Investment

Find $\{c^*(t)\}_0^\infty$ to maximize (2.1)

subject to (1.9), (A2.1.1) and $\hat{k}(0) = \hat{k}_0$.

In what follows, we shall refer to the reversible and the irreversible investment versions of our problem as **Version 1** and **Version 2** respectively.

Necessary Conditions for Optimum

We begin our discussion with a

Definition: The function $c : R_+ \to R$ is piece-wise continuous if
(i) $c(\cdot)$ is continuous except over a finite set of points $\{a_1, \cdots, a_n\}$ and
(ii) at each a_i, $\lim c(t)$ exists for $t \uparrow a_i$ as well as for $t \downarrow a_i$, but the two limits are unequal.

In what follows, the control variable $c(t)$ will be restricted to piece-wise continuous functions satisfying (1.9). Any such $c(t)$ will be referred to as a *feasible path*.

At $t = 0$, the entire path $\{c(t)\}_0^\infty$ (leading to the associated path $\{\hat{k}(t)\}_{t>0}^\infty$) is the choice variable for the agent. To this extent, the agent is engaged in a dynamic exercise. However, we shall break up the analysis into two parts. The first part will be concerned with *static* optimality conditions, properties that must hold true for a given volume of output at t to be allocated optimally between consumption and investment. The second part will be concerned with *dynamic* conditions of optimal resource allocation across time, i.e., the way in which the optimal choice at a given point of time is linked to choices in the future.

Static Optimization, the Principle of Optimality and the Functional Equation

Strictly speaking of course, these exercises are not independent. The overall problem being dynamic in nature, even the static optimality conditions need to be derived with reference to a minimal set of dynamic considerations. In this context, we shall begin by developing Bellman's *Principle of Optimality* (Bellman 1957), a famous mathematical principle underlying multi-stage decision problems. Starting from any time point t_0, the best achievable value of welfare depends on $\hat{k}_{t_0}$. Notice that this is a deeper statement than might appear at first sight. If the planning horizon were finite, say T, then the best value of welfare would depend on $\hat{k}_{t_0}$ *as well as* t_0, since the residual time horizon shrinks with the passage of time (i.e., $T - t_0$ falls as t_0 rises). The infinite horizon problem does not involve this complication. At any value of t, the residual horizon continues to be infinitely long.

Let $V(\hat{k}_{t_0})$ stand for the optimum welfare starting from $\hat{k}_{t_0}$, as in Section 2.1.1. The function is normally referred to as the *value function*. Consider the truncated problem

$$\text{Maximize} \qquad \int_{t_o}^{\infty} u(c(t))\, e^{-(\rho-n)(t-t_0)}\, dt$$

subject to (1.9), (2.3)

(alternatively, (1.9), (A2.1.1))

$$\text{and} \qquad \hat{k}(t_0) = \hat{k}_{t_0}. \qquad\qquad (\text{A2.1.2})$$

If $\{\tilde{c}_t\}_{t_0}^{\infty}$ solves this problem, then

$$V(\hat{k}_{t_0}) = \int_{t_o}^{\infty} u(\tilde{c}_t)\, e^{-(\rho-n)(t-t_0)} dt.$$

Bellman's Principle of Optimality says:

> *An optimal path has the property that whatever be the initial conditions and control variables over some initial period, the control variables over the remaining period must be optimal for the remaining problem, with the state resulting from the early decisions considered as the initial condition.*

Let $\{c_t^*\}_0^{\infty}$ solve either **Version 1** or **Version 2** of our problem. Suppose, moreover, that it gives rise to the path $\hat{k}_t^*$. Then, according to the Principle of Optimality,

$$V(\hat{k}_{t_0}^*) = \int_{t_o}^{\infty} u(c_t^*) \, e^{-(\rho-n)(t-t_0)} dt.$$

Proof of the Principle of Optimality: Consider a small interval $0 \le t \le h$, $h > 0$. Denoting the truncated path $\{c(t)\}_0^h$ by $c_{0,h}$, it is clear that $\hat{k}_h$ is a function of $c_{0,h}$, given $\hat{k}_0$. Let $\hat{k}(h) = \phi(c_{0,h})$. Then, $V(\hat{k}(h)) = V(\phi(c_{0,h}))$. Suppose then that the agent chooses $c_{0,h}^*$ over the interval $[0,h]$, but that contrary to the Principle of Optimality, the aggregate utility from $\{c_t^*\}_h^{\infty}$ falls short of $V(\phi(c_{0,h}^*))$. If possible, let

$$
\begin{aligned}
V(\phi(c_{0,h}^*)) &= \int_h^{\infty} u(\bar{c}_t) e^{-(\rho-n)\,(t-h)} \, dt \\
&> \int_h^{\infty} u(c_t^*) e^{-(\rho-n)\,(t-h)} \, dt,
\end{aligned}
$$

where $\bar{c}_t$ is feasible from $\phi(c_{0,h}^*)$ and $\bar{c}_t \ne c_t^*$ except possibly over a set of time points which is so small that it may be ignored. Define

$$
c^{**}(t) = \begin{cases} c_t^*, & t \in [0,h] \\ \bar{c}_t & t \in (h,\infty). \end{cases}
$$

Clearly, $c^{**}(t)$ is feasible, since $c^{**}(t)$ involves possibly a single point of discontinuity at (at $t = h$) in addition to the finite number of discontinuities c_t^* or $\bar{c}_t$ might admit. Further, by construction,

$$\int_0^{\infty} u(c^{**}(t)) \, e^{-(\rho-n)t} \, dt > \int_0^{\infty} u(c_t^*) \, e^{-(\rho-n)t} \, dt$$

which contradicts the presumed optimality of $\{c_t^*\}_0^{\infty}$.

According to the Principle of Optimality then,

$$V(\hat{k}_0) = \int_o^h u(c_t^*) \, e^{-(\rho-n)t} dt + V(\phi(c_{0,h}^*))$$

$$\geq \int_{o}^{h} u(c_t) \, e^{-(\rho-n)t} dt + V(\phi(c_{0,h})),$$

$$(A2.1.3)$$

given any feasible path $\{c(t)\}_0^\infty$. Alternatively,

$$V(\hat{k}_0) = max_{c_{0,h}} \{\int_{o}^{h} u(c(t)) \, e^{-(\rho-n)t} dt + V(\phi(c_{0,h}))\}, \qquad (A2.1.4)$$

or, more generally,

$$V(\hat{k}_{t_0}) \quad = \quad max_{c_{t_0,t_0+h}} \{\int_{t_0}^{t_0+h} u(c(t)) \, e^{-(\rho-n)(t-t_0)} dt$$

$$+ V(\phi(c_{t_0,t_0+h}))\}, \qquad (A2.1.5)$$

where $max_{c_{a,b}}$ denotes maximization with respect to $c(t)$, $a \leq t \leq b$. Equation (A2.1.4) (alternatively (A2.1.5)) is referred to as a *functional equation*. This completes our discussion of Bellman's Principle of Optimality.

Necessary Conditions for Static Optimality

In what follows, we shall proceed under

Assumption V $V(\hat{k})$ is continuously differentiable.

Assumption V allows us to make some approximations concerning the *RHS* of (A2.1.5). First, for h small,

$$u(c(t)) \cong u(c(t_0)), \quad t_0 \leq t \leq t_0 + h.$$

If t_0 is a point of discontinuity, we choose c_{t_0} as the right hand limit of $c(t)$ at t_0.[30]

---

[30]Note that replacing the optimal value of $c(t_0)$ by the right hand limit does not affect the value of the utility integral.

Therefore,

$$\int_{t_o}^{t_0+h} u(c(t))\, e^{-(\rho-n)(t-t_0)} dt \cong u(c(t_0)) \int_{t_o}^{t_0+h} e^{-(\rho-n)(t-t_0)} dt$$

$$= u(c(t_0))[-\frac{e^{-(\rho-n)(t-t_0)}}{\rho-n}]_{t_0}^{t_0+h}$$

$$= u(c(t_0))[-\frac{e^{-(\rho-n)h}}{\rho-n} + \frac{1}{\rho-n}]$$

$$= u(c(t_0))[\frac{1}{\rho-n}\{1 - e^{-(\rho-n)h}\}]$$

$$\cong u(c(t_0))$$

$$\times[\frac{1}{\rho-n}\{1 - (1 - (\rho-n)h)\}]$$

by Taylor's approximation ,

$$= u(c(t_0))h.$$

Thus, (A2.1.5) can be written as

$$V(\hat{k}_{t_0}) \cong max_{c(t_0)} \{h\, u(c(t_0)) + V(\hat{k}(t_0 + h))\}, \qquad (A2.1.6)$$

where $\hat{k}(t_0+h)$ results from the choice of $c_{t_0,t_0+h} = c(t_0)$, $t_0 \le t \le t_0+h$. A necessary condition for this optimum is

$$\frac{h\, \partial u(c(t_0))}{\partial c(t_0)} + \frac{\partial V(\hat{k}(t_0 + h))}{\partial c(t_0)} \ge 0. \qquad (A2.1.7)$$

The *inequality* is explained by the fact that under irreversible investment, the optimum value of $c(t_0)$ might hit its upper bound given by (A2.1.1). This being a corner solution, the partial derivative may turn out to be strictly positive.

Next, note that

$$\frac{\partial V(\hat{k}(t_0 + h))}{\partial c(t_0)} = \frac{\partial V(\hat{k}(t_0 + h))}{\partial \hat{k}(t_0 + h)} \cdot \frac{\partial \hat{k}(t_0 + h)}{\partial c(t_0)}.$$

Linearizing again

$$\hat{k}(t_0 + h) \cong \hat{k}(t_0) + h \, \dot{\hat{k}}(t_0),$$

where, according to (1.9),

$$\dot{\hat{k}}(t_0) = f(\hat{k}(t_0)) - (\mu + n + \delta)\hat{k}(t_0) - \frac{c(t_0)}{A_{t_0}}.$$

Thus,

$$\frac{\partial \hat{k}(t_0 + h)}{\partial c(t_0)} \cong -\frac{h}{A_{t_0}}.$$

Denote $\partial V(\hat{k}_t^*)/\partial \hat{k}(t)$ by q_t^*. The variable $q(t)$ stands for the maximum possible change in the social welfare from t onwards on account of a marginal change in $\hat{k}(t)$. In other words, it is the marginal value or shadow price of $\hat{k}$ at t along the optimal path. The assumption that V is differentiable implies that at any given value of $\hat{k}(t)$, the value of $q(t)$ is uniquely defined. Using these facts, the optimality of $\{c_t^*\}_{t_0}^\infty$ and the definition of q_t^*, (A2.1.7) reduces to

$$\frac{h \, \partial u(c_{t_0}^*)}{\partial c(t_0)} - q_{t_0+h}^* \frac{h}{A_{t_0}} = \frac{h \, \partial u(c_{t_0}^*)}{\partial c(t_0)} - \frac{h \, q_{t_0}^*}{A_{t_0}} - \frac{h \, (q_{t_0+h}^* - q_{t_0}^*)}{A_{t_0}}$$

$$\geq \quad 0,$$

or,

$$\frac{\partial u(c_{t_0}^*)}{\partial c(t_0)} - \frac{q_{t_0}^*}{A_{t_0}} - \frac{(q_{t_0+h}^* - q_{t_0}^*)}{A_{t_0}} \geq 0.$$

Allowing $h \to 0$, replacing t_0 by t and using **Assumption V**, we see that for $\{c_t^*\}_0^\infty$ to be optimal,

$$\frac{\partial u(c_t^*)}{\partial c(t)} - \frac{q_t^*}{A_t} \geq 0, \text{ with equality}$$

$$\text{if } c_t^* \text{ is interior },\quad \text{(A2.1.8)}$$

$$\text{and } \left(\frac{\partial u(c_t^*)}{\partial c(t)} - \frac{q_t^*}{A_t}\right) z^*(t) = 0 \qquad \text{(A2.1.9)}$$

must hold for all t.

The Maximal Principle

Section 2.1.1 introduced the reader to the terminology *Maximal Principle* and the connection between the static optimization exercise and the auxiliary Hamiltonian function. We fill in some of the mathematical details of that discussion here and, in the process, generalize it to apply the case of irreversible investment also.

Consider first the reversible investment case. We shall argue that in this case, c_t^* maximizes $\mathcal{H}$ subject to (1.9), $\hat{k}(t) = \hat{k}_t^*$ and $q(t) = q_t^*$ for each t. Moreover, the *FOC* characterising such a solution is identically the same as the equality version of (A2.1.8). To see this, use (1.9) to get

$$\dot{\hat{k}}(t) = \{f(\hat{k}^*(t)) - (\mu + n + \delta)\hat{k}^*(t)\} - \frac{c(t)}{A_t}.$$

Substituting in (2.4), $\mathcal{H}$ reduces to

$$\begin{aligned}\mathcal{H}(c(t), \hat{k}^*(t), q^*(t)) &= u(c(t)) + q^*(t)[\{f(\hat{k}^*(t)) \\ &\quad -(\mu + n + \delta)\hat{k}^*(t)\} - \frac{c(t)}{A_t}],\end{aligned}$$

which is a function of $c(t)$ alone. Differentiating $\mathcal{H}$ with respect to $c(t)$, we obtain $\partial u(c(t))/\partial c(t) - q^*(t)/A_t$. By assumption, $\exists$ a value of c_t^* satisfying (1.9) and $\hat{k}(t) = \hat{k}_t^*$ such that

$$\frac{\partial u(c_t^*)}{\partial c(t)} - \frac{q_t^*}{A_t} = 0.$$

The shape of the level curves of $\mathcal{H}$ tell us further that c_t^* is a unique solution to the problem

$$\text{Maximize } \mathcal{H}(c(t), \hat{k}_t^*, q_t^*) \text{ subject to (1.9).} \qquad\qquad \text{(A2.1.10)}$$

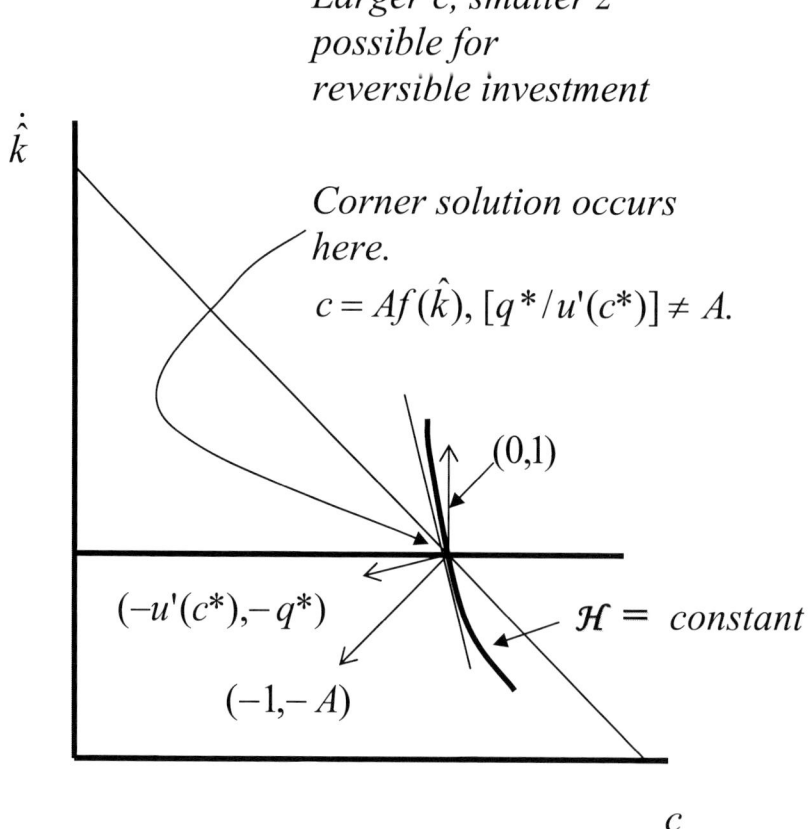

Larger c, smaller z possible for reversible investment

Corner solution occurs here.

$c = Af(\hat{k}), [q*/u'(c*)] \neq A.$

$(0,1)$

$(-u'(c*), -q*)$

$(-1, -A)$

$\mathcal{H} = constant$

Figure 2.6: Equilibrium with Irreversible Investment

Next, consider a corner solution corresponding to irreversible investment. To relate it to the Hamiltonian, let us reformulate the relevant constraints in the Kuhn-Tucker form. Rewrite (1.9) as the inequality constraint

$$A_t\{f(\hat{k}(t)) - (\mu + n + \delta)\hat{k}(t)\} - c(t) - A_t\,\dot{\hat{k}}(t) \geq 0 \qquad (A2.1.11)$$

Similarly, note that

$$(\mu + n + \delta)\hat{k}(t) + \dot{\hat{k}}(t) \geq 0 \qquad (A2.1.12)$$

must hold. The inequality (A2.1.8) may now be viewed as the *FOC* satisfying a corner solution to the problem

$$\text{Maximize} \quad \mathcal{H}(c(t), \hat{k}^*(t), q_t^*)$$

$$\text{subject to} \quad (A2.1.11) \text{ and } \quad (A2.1.12).$$

$$(A2.1.13)$$

Figure 2.6 shows that at the corner solution, both constraints are binding. The gradients to these constraints at the optimum point are $(-1, -A_t)$ and $(0, 1)$ respectively and the gradient to the objective function is $(u'(c_t^*), q_t^*)$. As per the Kuhn-Tucker conditions then, $\exists$ nonnegative Lagrange multipliers λ_1 and λ_2 such that

$$(-u'(c_t^*), -q_t^*) = \lambda_1\,(-1, -A_t) + \lambda_2\,(0, 1).$$

Moreover, it is easy to read from Figure 2.6 that (A2.1.8) must hold as a strict inequality.

Dynamic Optimality

We shall consider the following perturbation in the optimal path (See Figure 2.2):

(i) at t_0, consumption is lowered and investment increased marginally so as to raise $\hat{k}_{t_0}^*$ to $\hat{k}_{t_0}'$, where $\hat{k}_{t_0}' - \hat{k}_{t_0}^* = \Delta$;

(ii) $\hat{k}'_s = \hat{k}^*_s + \Delta \ \forall \ s > t_0$, or, as shown in Figure 2.2, $\hat{k}'_s$ is merely a parallel upward shift in $\hat{k}^*(s)$ for $s > t_0$;

(iii) $\forall \ s > t_0$, the extra *per capita* output realized by the higher $\hat{k}'_s$ *after maintaining the additional Δ for all time* is consumed away.[31]

The definition of $q(\cdot)$ implies that the price of a unit of $\hat{k}(t_0)$ in units of $c(t_0)$ is $q^*_{t_0}/u'(c^*_{t_0})$ along the optimal path. Thus, the sacrifice of $c(t_0)$ required to raise $\hat{k}^*_{t_0}$ by Δ equals $(q^*_{t_0}/u'(c^*_{t_0})) \ \Delta$. This entails a loss of *utility* equal to $u'(c^*(t_0)) \times \Delta \ (q^*_{t_0}/u'(c^*_{t_0})) = \Delta \ q^*_{t_0}$.

Let us now compute the extra utility provided by the new path $\forall \ s > t_0$. The extra per capita output brought forth by Δ at s equals $A_s f'(\hat{k}^*_s) \ \Delta$. This extra output is partly invested to maintain $\hat{k}(s)$ at the higher level. In units of z, the required investment is $(\mu + n + \delta) \ \Delta$, which equals $(q^*_s/u'(c^*_s)) \ (\mu + n + \delta) \ \Delta$ in units of c. The extra per capita consumption permitted by the extra output after subtracting the investment is $A_s f'(\hat{k}^*_s) \ \Delta - (q^*_s/u'(c^*_s)) \ (\mu + n + \delta) \ \Delta$. Multiplying out by $u'(c^*_s)$, the extra utility from the extra consumption at each s is given by $[A_s \ u'(c^*_s) \ f'(\hat{k}(s)) - q^*_s \ (\mu + n + \delta)] \ \Delta$. Thus, the total discounted gain in utility at t_0 from the perturbation equals $\Delta \int_{t_0}^{\infty} e^{-(\rho-n)(s-t_0)} \{A_s u'(c^*_s) f'(\hat{k}^*_s) - q^*_s \ (\mu + n + \delta)\} ds$.

Optimality, as noted, requires that the gain and the loss be equal. Hence,

$$\Delta \ q^*_{t_0} = \Delta \ \int_{t_0}^{\infty} e^{-(\rho-n)(s-t_0)} \{A_s u'(c^*_s) \ f'(\hat{k}^*_s) - q^*_s \ (\mu + n + \delta)\} ds,$$

or,

$$q^*_{t_0} = \int_{t_0}^{\infty} e^{-(\rho-n)(s-t_0)} \{A_s u'(c^*_s) \ f'(\hat{k}^*_s) - q^*_s \ (\mu + n + \delta)\} ds. \quad \text{(A2.1.14)}$$

Replacing t_0 by t for notational ease, consistency between (A2.1.8) and (A2.1.14) implies

$$q^*_t \geq \int_t^{\infty} e^{-(\rho-n)(s-t)} q^*_s \ \{f'(\hat{k}^*_s) - (\mu + n + \delta)\} ds. \quad \text{(A2.1.15)}$$

---

[31] The construction of the perturbed path follows Solow (2000).

For q_t^* to be well-defined, the integral on the RHS must exist for each t. We shall demonstrate in Appendix 2.2 (Proposition A2.2.1) that the optimality of $\{c_t^*, \hat{k}_t^*\}_0^\infty$ implies $f'(\hat{k}_s^*) - (\mu + n + \delta)$ is bounded strictly away from zero for s sufficiently large. Anticipating this result, the integral can exist $\forall\, t$ only if the transversality condition (2.8) is satisfied. Differentiating (A2.1.14) with respect to t to get

$$
\begin{aligned}
\dot{q}_t^* \;=\; & -\{A_t u'(c_t^*) f'(\hat{k}_t^*) - q_t^*(\mu + n + \delta)\} \\
& + (\rho - n) \int_t^\infty e^{-(\rho-n)(s-t)} \{A_s u'(c_s^*) f'(\hat{k}_s^*) \\
& - q_s^*(\mu + n + \delta)\} ds.
\end{aligned}
$$

Using (A2.1.14), the last equation reduces to

$$
\dot{q}_t^* = -\{A_t u'(c_t^*) f'(\hat{k}_t^*) - q_t^*(\mu + n + \delta)\} + (\rho - n)q_t^*. \qquad \text{(A2.1.16)}
$$

The necessary conditions for static and dynamic optimality are renumbered and stated below for easy reference as

PROPOSITION **A2.1.1** *If $\{c_t^*, \hat{k}_t^*\}_0^\infty$ is optimal, then there exists a path of co-state variables $\{q_t^*\}_0^\infty$ such that*

$$
u'(c_t^*) \;\geq\; \frac{q_t^*}{A_t}, \quad \text{with equality for an interior } c_t^*; \quad \text{(A2.1.17)}
$$

$$
\dot{\hat{k}}_t^* = f(\hat{k}_t^*) - \frac{c_t^*}{A_t} - (\mu + n + \delta)\hat{k}_t^*; \qquad \text{(A2.1.18)}
$$

$$
\begin{aligned}
\dot{q}_t^* \;=\; & -\{A_t u'(c_t^*) f'(\hat{k}_t^*) - q_t^*(\mu + n + \delta)\} \\
& + (\rho - n)q_t^* \\
\;=\; & -A_t u'(c_t^*) f'(\hat{k}_t^*) + (\mu + \rho + \delta)q_t^*; \qquad \text{(A2.1.19)}
\end{aligned}
$$

$$
\text{and} \qquad e^{-(\rho-n)t}\, q_t^* \to 0 \ \text{ as } t \to \infty. \qquad \text{(A2.1.20)}
$$

The Hamiltonian Function Again

The link between (A2.1.17) of Proposition A2.1.1 and the Hamiltonian was already indicated by (A2.1.10) and (A2.1.13). The remaining parts of this proposition can also be stated in terms of the same Hamiltonian function. Equation (A2.1.18) follows from (2.17).

Equation (2.15) established the link between (A2.1.19) and the Hamiltonian for the reversible investment case. For irreversible investment, use (1.9) and (A2.1.1) to get

$$\mathcal{H} = u(Af(\hat{k})) - q(\mu + n + \delta)\hat{k}, \text{ when } c \text{ has a corner solution}.$$

Differentiating $\mathcal{H}$ with respect to $\hat{k}$, we see that

$$\frac{\partial \mathcal{H}(c_s^*, \hat{k}_s^*, q_s^*)}{\partial \hat{k}(s)} = u'(c_s^*) \, A_s \, f'(\hat{k}_s^*) - q_s^*(\mu + n + \delta).$$

Using (A2.1.14) now, $q_t^* = \int_t^\infty (\partial \mathcal{H}/\partial \hat{k}(s)) \, e^{-(\rho-n)(s-t)} ds$. Thus,

$$
\begin{aligned}
\dot{q}_t^* &= \frac{d(\int_t^\infty (\partial \mathcal{H}(c_s^*, \hat{k}_s^*, q_s^*)/\partial \hat{k}(s)) \, e^{-(\rho-n)(s-t)} ds)}{dt} \\[2mm]
&= -\frac{\partial \mathcal{H}(c_t^*, \hat{k}_t^*, q_t^*)}{\partial \hat{k}(t)} + (\rho - n) \, q_t^* \\[2mm]
&= -A_t u'(c_t^*) f'(\hat{k}_t^*) + (\mu + \rho + \delta)q_t^*, \quad\quad\quad\text{(A2.1.21)}
\end{aligned}
$$

which is none other than equation (A2.1.19). Let us collect the necessary conditions stated in terms of the Hamiltonian function as[32]

PROPOSITION **A2.1.2** *Suppose* $\{c_t^*, \hat{k}_t^*\}_0^\infty$ *solves* **Version 1** *or* **Version 2** *of the problem. Then, there exists a path of co-state variables* q_t^* *such that* (A2.1.10) *(alternatively* (A2.1.13)*),* (2.17)*,* (A2.1.21)*, and* (A2.1.20) *are satisfied.*

---

[32]The conditions resemble standard representations of the first three necessary conditions, except for (A2.1.21). Equation (A2.1.21) is borrowed from Cass (1965 and 1966). The advantage of choosing the form (A2.1.21) is that it makes direct reference to the economic interpretation of a co-state variable. Moreover, it uses a single differential equation to describe the evolution of the co-state variable for both reversible and irreversible investment.

Appendix 2.2   Sufficient Conditions for an Optimum

We proceed now to prove that under **Assumptions u1** and **f1**, any path $\{c_t^*, \hat{k}_t^*, q_t^*\}_0^\infty$ satisfying (2.6), (2.17), (2.15), and (2.8) constitutes a unique solution to the problems stated as **Version 1** and **Version 2** above. Assume then that $\{c(t), \hat{k}(t)\}_0^\infty$ is any feasible path. Then, equation (1.7) gives

$$A(f(\hat{k}) - \hat{z}) - c = 0, \qquad (\text{A2.2.1})$$

where the time index t has been dropped for convenience. In what follows, we shall also use the fact that u1 and f1 imply

$$u(c^*) - u(c) - u'(c^*)(c^* - c) \quad > \quad 0$$

$$f(\hat{k}^*) - f(\hat{k}) - f'(\hat{k}^*)(\hat{k}^* - \hat{k}) \quad > \quad 0. \qquad (\text{A2.2.2})$$

Our claim is established if we can show that

$$D \quad = \quad \int_0^\infty \{u(c^*) - u(c)\}\, e^{-(\rho - n)t} dt$$

$$> \quad 0.$$

By adding and subtracting terms, we may use (A2.2.1) and the identity $\hat{z} = \dot{\hat{k}} + (\mu + n + \delta)\hat{k}$ to write

$$D \quad = \quad \int_0^\infty [\{u(c^*) - u(c)\} + u'(c^*)\{(A(f(\hat{k}^*) - \hat{z}^*) - c^*)$$

$$- (A(f(\hat{k}) - \hat{z}) - c)\} + q^*\{(\hat{z}^* - \lambda \hat{k}^* - \dot{\hat{k}}^*)$$

$$- (\hat{z} - \lambda \hat{k} - \dot{\hat{k}})\}]\, e^{-(\rho - n)t}\, dt,$$

where $\lambda = \mu + n + \delta$. Collecting terms,

$$D \; = \; \int_0^\infty [\{u(c^*) - u(c) - u'(c^*)(c^* - c)\} + \{q^*(\hat{z}^* - \hat{z})$$

$$-Au'(c^*)(\hat{z}^* - \hat{z})\} - q^*\{\lambda(\hat{k}^* - \hat{k}) + (\dot{\hat{k}}^* - \dot{\hat{k}})\}$$

$$+Au'(c^*)\{f(\hat{k}^*) - f(\hat{k})\}] \; e^{-(\rho-n)t}dt, \qquad\qquad \text{(A2.2.3)}$$

Equation (A2.2.3) may be reduced further by integrating $\int_0^\infty q^*(\dot{\hat{k}}^* - \dot{\hat{k}})e^{-(\rho-n)t}dt$ by parts. Thus,

$$\int_0^\infty q^*(\dot{\hat{k}}^* - \dot{\hat{k}})e^{-(\rho-n)t}dt \; = \; e^{-(\rho-n)t}q^*(\hat{k}^* - \hat{k}) \; |_0^\infty$$

$$- \int_0^\infty (\hat{k}^* - \hat{k})\{\dot{q}^*e^{-(\rho-n)t}$$

$$-(\rho - n)q^*e^{-(\rho-n)t}\}dt.$$

Proposition 1 has demonstrated that any feasible path $\{\hat{k}\}$ is bounded above. Using (2.8), the last equation reduces to

$$\int_0^\infty q^*(\dot{\hat{k}}^* - \dot{\hat{k}})e^{-(\rho-n)t}dt \; = \; - \int_0^\infty (\hat{k}^* - \hat{k})\{\dot{q}^*e^{-(\rho-n)t}$$

$$-(\rho - n)q^*e^{-(\rho-n)t}\}dt.$$

$$\text{(A2.2.4)}$$

Plugging (A2.2.4) into (A2.2.3), we get

$$D \; = \; \int_0^\infty [\{u(c^*) - u(c) - u'(c^*)(c^* - c)\} + \{q^* - Au'(c^*)\}$$

$$\times(\hat{z}^* - \hat{z}) - q^*\lambda(\hat{k}^* - \hat{k}) + (\dot{q}^* - (\rho - n)q^*)(\hat{k}^* - \hat{k})$$

$$+Au'(c^*)\{f(\hat{k}^*) - f(\hat{k})\}] \; e^{-(\rho-n)t}dt$$

$$= \int_0^\infty [\{u(c^*) - u(c) - u'(c^*)(c^* - c)\} + \{q^* - Au'(c^*)\}$$

$$(\hat{z}^* - \hat{z}) + (\hat{k}^* - \hat{k})\{\dot{q}^* - (\rho + \lambda - n)q^* + Au'(c^*)f'(\hat{k}^*)\}$$

$$+ Au'(c^*)\{f(\hat{k}^*) - f(\hat{k}) - f'(\hat{k}^*)(\hat{k}^* - \hat{k})\}] \; e^{-(\rho-n)t} \; dt,$$

$$(A2.2.5)$$

adding and subtracting $Au'(c^*)f'(\hat{k}^*)(\hat{k}^*-\hat{k})$. Note that $(q^*-Au'(c^*))\hat{z}^* = 0$ according to (A2.1.9). Further, $(q^* - Au'(c^*))\hat{z} = 0$ for reversible investment. In case of irreversible investment, $q^* - Au'(c^*) \leq 0$ and $\hat{z} \geq 0$. Hence, $(q^* - Au'(c^*))(\hat{z}^* - \hat{z}) \geq 0$ in all cases. Appealing to this fact along with (A2.2.2), the definition of λ and (A2.1.19), equation (A2.2.5) implies

$$D > \int_0^\infty [(\hat{k}^* - \hat{k})\{\dot{q}^* - (\rho + \lambda - n)q^*$$

$$+ Au'(c^*)f'(\hat{k}^*)\}] \; e^{-(\rho-n)t} \; dt$$

$$= \int_0^\infty [(\hat{k}^* - \hat{k})\{\dot{q}^* - (\rho + \delta + \mu)q^*$$

$$+ Au'(c^*)f'(\hat{k}^*)\}] \; e^{-(\rho-n)t} \; dt$$

$$= \int_0^\infty (\hat{k}^* - \hat{k})\{\dot{q}^* - \dot{q}^*\} \; dt$$

$$= 0.$$

This establishes that $\{c_t^*, \hat{k}_t^*\}_0^\infty$ is a unique optimum path. We may note in passing that the last inequality will be weak if both u and f are weakly concave. Thus, we have proved the following result[33]:

PROPOSITION **A2.2** *The conditions enumerated in Proposition 2.1, along with the strict concavity of u and f, are sufficient for the existence of a unique solution to the planner's problem.*

---

[33]Mangasarian (1966) proved the corresponding result for the finite horizon problem.

Appendix 2.3   Suboptimality of Golden Rule

We are now ready to prove the following

PROPOSITION **A2.3** *For any optimal path* $\{c_t^*, \hat{k}_t^*\}_0^\infty$, $\exists$ *a* t_0 *such that* $f'(\hat{k}_t^*) - (\mu + n + \delta)$ *is bounded strictly away from zero* $\forall\, t > t_0$. *In other words, the optimal path of capital accumulation stays away from the GR in the long run.*

Proof: Although the arguments will be posed in terms of a Command Economy, they will hold *mutatis mutandis* for a Private Economy also. The proof holds for both reversible and irreversible investment. The result will be derived in two steps. The first will demonstrate that the GR per capita consumption path $\{A_t \hat{c}^{**}\}$ associated with indefinite maintenance of $\hat{k}^{**}$ is a suboptimal policy. The second step will then show that a path for which $f'(\hat{k}_t^*) \rightarrow (\mu + n + \delta)$ is suboptimal.

Step 1.

In what follows, we shall abbreviate by writing $\lambda = \mu + n + \delta$. Equation (2.23) implies that along the GR path

$$\hat{c}^{**} + \lambda \hat{k}^{**} = f(\hat{k}^{**}), \qquad\qquad (A2.3.1)$$

As an alternative to the path $\{A_t \hat{c}^{**}, \hat{k}^{**}\}$, consider a path which raises per capita consumption at $t = 0$ above $A_0\, \hat{c}^{**}$ by reducing $\hat{k}^{**}$ to $\hat{k}' = \hat{k}^{**} - \Delta$. It is possible to achieve this by reducing $\hat{z}$ below $\lambda\, \hat{k}^{**}$.[34] Thus, we have

$$
\begin{aligned}
f(\hat{k}^{**}) &= \hat{c}^{**} + \lambda \hat{k}' + \lambda(\hat{k}^{**} - \hat{k}') \\
&= \hat{c}^{**} + \lambda \Delta + \lambda \hat{k}'.
\end{aligned}
$$

Thus, the change in $\hat{c}^{**}$ is $\lambda \Delta$ and the rise in per capita consumption at $t = 0$ is $A_0\, \lambda\, \Delta$.

---

[34]One may consume part of the capital also in the reversible case, but we do not follow up this possibility. The proof we construct instead works for both reversible as well as irreversible investment.

The alternative path is constructed to maintain $\hat{k}$ at this constant value $\hat{k}'$ $\forall$ $t > 0$. Per capita consumption for all $t > 0$ is $A_t \hat{c}'$ along the alternative path, where $(\hat{c}', \hat{k}')$ solves (A2.3.1). Linearizing around $A_0 \hat{c}^{**}$, the gain in utility at $t = 0$ from the change is

$$
\begin{aligned}
\mathcal{G}(0) &= u(A_0 \hat{c}^{**} + A_0 \, \lambda \, \Delta) - u(A_0 \hat{c}^{**}) \\
&\cong u(A_0 \hat{c}^{**}) + A_0 \, \lambda \, \Delta \, u'(A_0 \hat{c}^{**}) - u(A_0 \hat{c}^{**}) \\
&= A_0 \, \lambda \, \Delta \, u'(A_0 \hat{c}^{**}).
\end{aligned}
\tag{A2.3.2}
$$

Denote $u'(A_0 \hat{c}^{**})$ by u'^{**}.

We proceed now to compare the initial gain $A_0 \, \lambda \, \Delta \, u'^{**}$ with subsequent losses. The loss in utility from the change at each $t > 0$ is

$$
\begin{aligned}
\mathcal{L}(t) &= u(A_t \hat{c}^{**}) - u(A_t \hat{c}') \\
&= u(A_t \hat{c}^{**}) - u(A_t(f(\hat{k}') - \lambda \hat{k}')).
\end{aligned}
$$

Linearizing around $\hat{k}^{**}$,

$$
\begin{aligned}
\mathcal{L}(t) \;\cong\; & u(A_t \hat{c}^{**}) - u[A_t(f(\hat{k}^{**}) - \Delta f'(\hat{k}^{**}) + \frac{\Delta^2}{2} f''(\hat{k}^{**}) \\
& - \lambda \hat{k}^{**} + \lambda \Delta)] \\[1em]
= \; & u(A_t \hat{c}^{**}) - u[A_t((f(\hat{k}^{**}) - \lambda \hat{k}^{**}) - \Delta(f'(\hat{k}^{**}) \\
& - \lambda) + \frac{\Delta^2}{2} f''(\hat{k}^{**}))] \\[1em]
= \; & u(A_t \hat{c}^{**}) - u(A_t(\hat{c}^{**} + \frac{\Delta^2}{2} f''(\hat{k}^{**}))), \text{ using (2.24)}, \\[1em]
\cong \; & u(A_t \hat{c}^{**}) - (u(A_t \hat{c}^{**}) + \frac{\Delta^2}{2} A_t \, f''(\hat{k}^{**}) u'(A_t \hat{c}^{**})),
\end{aligned}
$$

(linearizing around $A_t \hat{c}^{**}$),

$$= -\frac{\Delta^2}{2} A_t f''^{**} u'(A_t \hat{c}^{**}), \qquad \text{(A2.3.3)}$$

where $f''^{**} = f''(\hat{k}^{**})$. The discounted stream of losses incurred during $(0, \infty)$ is

$$\int_0^\infty \mathcal{L}(t)\, e^{-(\rho-n)t} dt \;=\; \frac{\Delta^2}{2} \int_0^\infty (-f''^{**} A_t\, u'(A_t\, \hat{c}^{**}))\, e^{-(\rho-n)t} dt$$

$$> \;\; 0, \qquad \text{(A2.3.4)}$$

since $f'' < 0$ by **Assumption f1** The net change in welfare to the household from the perturbation is

$$\omega \;=\; \mathcal{G}(0) - \int_0^\infty \mathcal{L}(t)\, e^{-(\rho-n)t} dt$$

$$= \;\; A_0\, \lambda\, \Delta\, u'^{**} - (\Delta^2/2) \int_0^\infty (-f''^{**} A_t\, u'(A_t\, \hat{c}^{**})) e^{-(\rho-n)t} dt.$$

Let

$$\xi^* = \int_0^\infty (-f''^{**} A_t u'(A_t\, \hat{c}^{**})) e^{-(\rho-n)t} dt,$$

so that

$$\omega \;=\; A_0\, \lambda\, \Delta u'^{**} - (\Delta^2/2)\, \xi^*$$

$$= \;\; \Delta\, \xi^* (A_0\, \lambda\, u'^{**}/\xi^* - \Delta/2).$$

Since A_0, λ, u'^{**} and ξ^* are fixed, $\exists$ an ϵ such that $\Delta < \epsilon \Rightarrow \omega > 0$. So long as the reduction in $\hat{k}$ falls short of ϵ, the perturbation from the path $\{A_t\, \hat{c}^{**}, \hat{k}^{**}\}$ constructed above is welfare improving.

Step 2.

Suppose now that the proposition is false. Then, $\exists$ an optimal path $\{\hat{c}_t^*, \hat{k}_t^*\}$ such that $|\hat{c}_t^* - \hat{c}^{**}|$ and $|\hat{k}_t^* - \hat{k}^{**}|$ are arbitrarily small for t large enough. Consider the following perturbation. At a large enough t_0, disinvest down to $\hat{k}'$ (defined in Step 1) and maintain $\{\hat{c}', \hat{k}'\}$ then onwards. The extra consumption generated is Δ_{t_0}, where $|\Delta_{t_0} - A_{t_0} \lambda \Delta|$ is arbitrarily small for t_0 large enough (given the definition of Δ in Step 1).

The per capita consumption at t_0 changes to $A_{t_0}\hat{c}_{t_0}^* + \Delta_{t_0}$ and the gain in utility from the increased consumption is $u(A_{t_0}\hat{c}_{t_0}^* + \Delta_{t_0}) - u(A_{t_0}\hat{c}_{t_0}^*) = \nu$ (say). For large enough t_0, the value of $\nu \cong u(A_{t_0}\hat{c}^{**} + A_{t_0} \lambda \Delta) - u(A_{t_0}\hat{c}^{**})$. Thus, using Step 1 again, we may assume $\nu \cong A_{t_0}\lambda \Delta u'(A_{t_0} \hat{c}^{**})$.

Since $\hat{k}_t^* \to \hat{k}^{**}$, it is possible to assume *wlog* that $u(c_t^*) - u(A_t\hat{c}') > 0 \ \forall \ t > t_0$. Thus, utility falls by $u(c_t^*) - u(A_t\hat{c}')$ at each $t > t_0$. The discounted present value of the stream of losses is $\int_{t_0}^{\infty}(u(c_t^*) - u(A_t\hat{c}'))e^{-(\rho-n)(t-t_0)}dt$. We have, by definition GR,

$$\int_{t_0}^{\infty}(u(A_t\hat{c}^{**}) - u(A_t\hat{c}')) \ e^{-(\rho-n)(t-t_0)}dt$$
$$> \int_{t_0}^{\infty}(u(c_t^*) - u(A_t\hat{c}'))e^{-(\rho-n)(t-t_0)}dt,$$

or,

$$-\int_{t_0}^{\infty}(u(A_t\hat{c}^{**}) - u(A_t\hat{c}')) \ e^{-(\rho-n)(t-t_0)}dt$$
$$< -\int_{t_0}^{\infty}(u(c_t^*) - u(A_t\hat{c}'))e^{-(\rho-n)(t-t_0)}dt,$$

or,

$$-(\Delta^2/2) \ \xi_{t_0}^* < -\int_{t_0}^{\infty}(u(c_t^*) - u(A_t\hat{c}')) \ e^{-(\rho-n)(t-t_0)}dt,$$

where $\xi_{t_0}^*$ corresponds to ξ^* of Step 1 with due alteration of details. Thus, the net gain is approximately equal to

$$A_{t_0} \lambda \Delta \ u'(A_{t_0}\hat{c}^{**}) - \int_{t_0}^{\infty}(u(c_t^*) - u(A_t\hat{c}')) \ e^{-(\rho-n)(t-t_0)}dt$$

$$> A_{t_0} \lambda \Delta \ u'(A_{t_0}\hat{c}^{**}) - (\Delta^2/2) \ \xi_{t_0}^* > 0$$

for an appropriately small value of Δ.

This completes the proof.

Appendix 2.4   Halkin's Counter-example

Section 2.2.1 ended with an example of an optimum path that does not satisfy the transversality condition. This section discusses one more case, a famous example due to Halkin (1974), for which the transversality condition is not a necessary characterization of optimality.

Before stating the details of the example, let us go back to (5.46) and analyse the reason why it leads to (2.8). The inequality (5.46) is a relationship between the shadow price of investment q_t^* and all subsequent shadow prices over infinite time. Note that, given the objective function and the technology, (2.8) holds because optimality imposes nontrivial restrictions on the behaviour of the capital accumulation path for all $t > t_0$. (See Proposition A2.3 above.) Halkin, on the other hand, constructs an objective function that leaves the path of accumulation unrestricted.

To get a feel for Halkin's example, consider an agent engaged in wealth accumulation. Her lifetime utility depends on the difference between the terminal (i.e., limiting) value of her wealth and the initial wealth she owns. Suppose that the maximum possible value of the terminal wealth is $\bar{K}$ and that her initial wealth is K_0. Then, the optimum value of her welfare is $\bar{K} - K_0$. The important characteristic of this objective function is that the agent's welfare is independent of the path followed for approaching $\bar{K}$. The marginal social product of a rise in K_0 is thus $q(0) = \partial(\bar{K} - K_0)/\partial K_0 = -1$, which is independent of the marginal social productivities of K along the way to the optimum $\bar{K}$. Consequently, the value of the shadow price at $t = 0$ does not put any restriction on future values of the shadow price. The same argument holds for the shadow price at any later point in time. In other words, $q(t) = \partial(\bar{K} - K(s))/\partial K(s) = -1 \ \ \forall s > t$. Hence, for this problem, the co-state variable does not converge to zero.

Let us now state and work out the example algebraically. The problem is stated as follows:

$$\text{Maximize } \int_0^\infty (1 - y)\, u\; dt$$

subject to

$$\dot{y} = (1 - y)\, u, \; y(0) = 0, \; u \in [0, 1].$$

Obviously, u and y are respectively the control and state variables for this problem.

Solution: Substituting the state equation in the objective function,

$$\int_0^\infty \dot{y}\; dt \;=\; y\big|_0^\infty$$

$$=\; \lim{}_{t \to \infty}\, y(t).$$

The problem thus reduces to maximizing $\lim_{t \to \infty} y(t)$. To find the upper bound of y, we solve the equation

$$\dot{y} + (y - 1)\, u = 0.$$

Substituting $z = y - 1$, the equation reduces to

$$\dot{z} + zu = 0.$$

The solution to this equation is

$$z(t) = b e^{-\int_0^t u(v)dv}, \; b = \text{constant},$$

or,

$$y(t) = 1 + b\, e^{-\int_0^t u(v)\; dv}.$$

At $t = 0$, $y(0) = 0 = 1 + b$, or, $b = -1$. Hence, the general solution is $y(t) = 1 - e^{-\int_0^t u(v)dv}$. Writing $\int_0^t u(v)dv = h(t) \geq 0$, the solution is $y(t) = 1 - e^{-h(t)}$, whence $y(t) \in [0, 1)$. Thus, the upper bound of $y(t)$ is unity and any path leading to it is a solution to the problem. There is no unique optimum path. Indeed, any constant $u \in (0, 1)$ is a solution to the problem. Suppose such a constant u^* is selected.

The Hamiltonian for the problem is

$$\mathcal{H} = (1 - y)\, u + \lambda\, (1 - y)\, u$$
$$= ((1 - y)(1 + \lambda))\, u.$$

The FOC's are:

$$\dot{y} = u\, (1 - y),$$
$$\dot{\lambda} = (1 + \lambda)\, u,$$
$$(1 - y)(1 + \lambda) = 0.$$

Choose $\lambda^* = -1 \ \forall \ t$. Then $(u, \lambda) = (u^*, -1)$ satisfies all the optimality conditions, but $\lim_{t \to \infty} \lambda(t) \neq 0$. Note that the value of the co-state variable tallies with the one we obtained above from purely economic arguments. This completes the counter-example.

Summary

1. The optimal rate of saving, hence investment under Solow assumptions, is chosen by maximizing the discounted sum of population weighted utilities from per capita consumption at each point of time over an infinite time horizon. The optimal choice satisfies three conditions. First, the marginal rate of substition between present and future utilities is equal to the slope of the transformation locus between c and $\dot{k}$. Second, the loss in utility from a marginal reduction in present consumption equals the discounted present value of the stream of gains in future utilities. Third, optimal paths view capital stocks far out in the future to be increasingly useless. The conditions are necessary and sufficient for optimality.

2. The optimality conditions may be derived with the aid of a reduced form welfare function called the Hamiltonian. The Hamiltonian function expresses at each point of time the utility derived by a planner or a private agent from an arbitrary but feasible consumption-investment pair, under the assumption that future decisions will be arrived at optimally.

3. Balanced growth occurs when output, capital, and consumption grow at constant rates over time.

4. Optimal balanced growth paths can be derived under the assumption that the instantaneous utility function satisfies the condition of constant elasticity of marginal utility. General utility functions cannot handle optimal balanced growth paths in the presence of technical progress.

5. The Golden Rule of accumulation refers to a sustainable level of capital-effective labour ratio which maximizes per capita consumption at each point of time. The Golden Rule requires the marginal product of capital to equal the sum of population growth rate, rate of technical progress and the discount parameter. When utility is discounted, the optimal path converges to a value of per capita consumption in the long run that falls short of the Golden Rule value. On account of discounting, the smaller utility from the less than Golden Rule consumption in the long run is more than compensated by larger utility in the present from a larger than Golden Rule consumption made possible through capital consumption.

6. Under the assumptions of the model, a market-driven competitive economy behaves the same way as a social utility maximizing planned economy.

7. A balanced growth *equilibrium* path for a welfare maximizing Private Economy can be represented as the point of intersection of a curve representing the balanced rate at which society wishes to grow as a function of the rate of interest and a curve that represents the society's capability of growing at a balanced rate.

8. In the long run, the rate of growth of per capita consumption adjusts to the rate of growth of technical progress. However, the rate of technical progress is an unexplained concept in the Solow model. Consequently, this model needs to be sharpened to incorporate factors determining technical progress. Subsequent literature has done this in two different ways. First, a part of the literature views technical progress as an externality caused by interaction between firms' workers who learn from each other through interactions outside their work houses. In this case, the equilibrium growth path can be sustained by market-driven competitive firms. However, on account of the externality, the competitive path may not be socially optimal. Second, technological progress can be the product of expenditure on *R&D*. When agents need to be paid for causing technical change, the assumption of constant returns to scale is not tenable. As a result, competitive market structures fail to sustain the optimal growth path of an economy.

9. Necessary and sufficient conditions for optimality of growth paths must allow for corner solutions under irreversible investment.

Problems

1. Derive equation (2.33).

2. Show that under the assumption of a CRS technology, equation (1.13) and the fact that $A_t^* = K_t^* \; \forall \; t$, equation (2.32) reduces to (1.1).

3. Read up Cass (1965) and derive (2.33) of problem 1 once again under the assumption that investment is irreversible.

4. Assume that the production function has the form $Y = K^\alpha (AL)^{1-\alpha}$, $0 < \alpha < 1$, where $A(t) = A_0 \, e^{\mu \, t}$ represents Harrod-neutral technical progress and $L(t) = L_0 \, e^{nt}$. Study the path of the Solow economy starting from any arbitrarily given initial triplet (K_0, L_0, A_0) under the assumption that a dynastic household representing the Private Economy maximizes the welfare function $U = \int_0^\infty [c(t)^{1-\theta} - 1/1 - \theta] \, e^{-(\rho - (\mu + n))t} \, dt$ subject to an appropriate budget constraint at each instant of time. State the form of the budget constraint.

5. Use (2.36) and (2.37) to derive

$$\frac{\dot{c}}{c} = \frac{r - \rho}{\theta}.$$

6. Derive equation (2.40).

7. Derive equation (2.41).

8. Carry out the analysis of Section 2.3.2 in terms of a phase diagram which is different from Figure 2.4. In the new phase diagram, measure $\hat{c}$ along the vertical axis and $\hat{k}$ along the horizontal axis. [Hint: Read Barro and Sala-i-Martin (2003), Chapter 2.]

9. In the Solow model, the optimal path converges to a long rund balanced growth equilibrium. Present this convergence result with the help of the transformation frontier between c and $\hat{k}$ and the level curves corresponding to the Hamiltonian.

10. How would the results derived in this chapter change if, instead of a single dynastic household, there were finitely many equal sized

households in the economy which differed from each other in terms of asset holdings and labour productivities? [Hint: This problem was discussed in Barro and Sala-i-Martin (2003) with reference to Caselli and Ventura (2000).]

11. Suppose that the instantaneous utility function changes to

$$u(c) = \frac{(c - \bar{c})^{1-\theta} - 1}{1 - \theta},$$

where $\bar{c}$ represents the subsistence level of per capita consumption.

(i) Compare the properties of this utility function with the utility function of Section 2.2.

(ii) What are the likely changes in the optimal path that will occur if the utility function of Section 2.3 were to be replaced by this new function?

Part II: Selected Models of New Growth Theory

Chapter 3

Technical progress as a Spillover

3.1 Introduction

Chapter 2 concluded with the suggestion that there are two possible avenues for modelling technical progress. First, one might view it as the conscious result of $R\&D$, attempts to acquire knowledge based skill and so on, requiring expenditure on factors responsible for the activities in question. We noted that the latter might in turn call for the introduction of market structures that are radically different from the Solow type conventional perfectly competitive markets. The second approach suggested was to view technical progress as an unplanned by-product of the process of privately conducted economic activities, a possible example of which was suggested in Section 2.5. Typically, when technical progress is brought forth unconsciously by the private actions of one economic agent or the other, it assumes the form of a non-internalizable externality generated by the relevant agent. In that event, the Private Economy can continue to be supported by standard competitive markets. Consequently, one can breathe life into the notion of technical progress with minimal changes in the one sector competitive Solow model.

We shall accordingly present a series of models in this chapter which avoid the complexities of alternative market structures. Except for the model of Romer (1986) (See Section 3.2.8), the models we shall describe will have technical similarities, though they will not necessarily be attempts to model the same economic idea. To start with, we will be concerned with the notion of technical progress as a spillover or externality. These models will try to capture two types of externalities. The first of them (Section 3.2) will be induced by the process of private investment activities, a class of models initiated by Arrow (1962) and Frankel (1962) and carried forward by Romer (1986), d'Autume and Michel (1993) and others. The nature of technical progress introduced by these models is referred to as Learning by Doing, a terminology that goes back to Arrow's seminal paper. Under the Learning by Doing hypothesis, technical progress is viewed as an improvement in workers' skills caused by exposure to capital brought into existence by continuing investment activity.

This will be followed by models involving fixed coefficients of production. These models are often confused with the fixed coefficients type behaviour of the models of d'Autume and Michel (1993) as well as models due to Barro and Sala-i-Martin (2003) to be introduced in Chapter 5. Our discussion will clarify the distinctions between these models. We shall also briefly discuss the models of Harrod (1939) and Domar (1946) in this context, since these models too are often mis-identified with the fixed coefficient model we shall present. Finally, we will round up the discussion of the chapter by bringing up the simplest type of endogenous growth model, viz. the AK model and show how it is linked to the fixed coefficients model.

3.2   Learning by Doing

In Section 1.2 and Appendix 1.2, we introduced the notion of Harrod-neutrality in the context of labour augmenting technical change. However, we noted later that the parameter A reflecting technological growth is itself an unexplained phenomenon. While the original exercise did not search deeper into the nature of A, in a subsequent paper Solow (1969) did try to repair this shortcoming by linking technical progress to the process of capital accumulation itself. Higher productivity was *embodied* only in new equipment. The exact numerical value of the rate of increase in productivity, however, was *exogenously* specified and, in the face of diminishing returns, the equilibrium growth rate adjusted once again to exogenous factors alone. Thus, from the point of view of a theory of technical progress, Solow's new approach, though rich in insights, did not qualify as an improvement over Solow (1956).[1]

---

[1]Other similar attempts at explaining technical progress may be found in Phelps (1962) and Drandakis and Phelps (1966).

Arrow (1962) took a significant step towards offering a theory of labour augmentation, thereby endogenizing the equilibrium rate of technical progress for the economy. He attributed productivity increases over time to learning, i.e., the accumulation of experience, on the part of the labour force. Experience is gathered in workshops while producing output with the help of machinery and equipment. Hence, technical progress amounts to 'Learning by doing'. Every new piece of equipment has to be 'broken in' so to speak, thus creating room for learning.[2] Since it is experience in machinery handling that leads to learning, Arrow constructs an index for experience. The index consists of the value of cumulative *gross* investment (CGI) at any point of time.[3] As he viewed it, an increase in investment today raises the size of CGI from tomorrow onwards above what it would have been had the investment not taken place. More specifically, suppose the economy's capital stock is growing along the path $K(t)$. Imagine now that at $t = t_0$, an entrepreneur changes his investment decision and raises it by Δ, but that the investment decisions of all future entrepreneurs remain unchanged. Then, the path of gross capital stock t_0 onwards gets altered to $K(t) + \Delta$. The CGI for the economy is thus increased by Δ units for all $t > t_0$. Consequently, the labour force at all time points subsequent to t_0 will have the opportunity of being exposed to a larger CGI than what would have been the case had the extra investment not occurred at t_0. In this sense, the altered investment plan by the entrepreneur at t_0 has the effect of bequeathing a more experienced and productive labour force to the future, compared to the experience they would otherwise have possessed. The extra investor will of course himself gain from the act of his investment (in the form of improved labour skills in his own organization), but he would be causing gains for future entrepreneurs also. The latter would gain on account of the larger stock of aggregate capital in the economy, a gain that cannot be internalised by the investor at t_0. This form of technical change generates an *intertemporal externality*, causing later machines to be more productive than earlier ones.

---

[2]In Arrow's words: 'Each new machine put to use changes the production environment, thereby inducing the workers to learn.'

[3]Thus, in the presence of physical depreciation of capital, experience is measured by the aggregate capital stock that *would be* in existence in its absence. Arrow also offers reasons as to why cumulative gross output is not a satisfactory index of learning.

3.2.1   Description of the Economy

In what follows, however, a *disembodied*[4] version of the Arrow exercise
(suggested by Sheshinski (1967)) will be considered and, as mentioned
in Section 1.2, the value of δ will henceforth be assumed to be zero.
Technical change is still an externality, but it is atemporal. An investment activity, irrespective of the firm in which it is located, adds to the
CGI for the entire economy, and the benefit of increased labour productivity in the initiating firm *spills over* to *all* coexisting firms, increasing
the effective size of the labour force in each firm. It is this last fact that
makes technical change disembodied; it raises the output generated by
all machines in existence, *irrespective* of their vintages, even if the firms
in which they are located have not raised their investments. The exact
manner in which this happens may be understood by visualising workers
from different organisations interacting beyond office hours and learning
from one another as an outcome of the social intercourse. [5]

Formally speaking, this introduces a change in the specification of
$A(t)$ in the Solow (1956) model. It is now a function of *CGI* at t. In
the absence of physical depreciation, the latter is equal to the aggregate
capital stock $K(t)$. The exact functional form assumed by Arrow and
Sheshinski is

$$A(t) = K(t)^{\alpha}, \quad \alpha > 0. \tag{3.1}$$

Capital accumulation has diminishing, constant or increasing productivity in the *learning activity* depending on whether $\alpha < 1, = 1$, or, > 1.

The technology is given by

$$Y = F(K, K^{\alpha}L), \tag{3.2}$$

where (3.2) satisfies Assumptions **F1** and **F2** of Chapter 1. The function
$F(.,.)$ can be expressed as in (1.5), with $\hat{y} = Y/K^{\alpha}L$ and $\hat{k} = K/K^{\alpha}L$.
The properties of $f(\hat{k})$ remain unaltered too vis-á-vis $A = K^{\alpha}L$. As
with the case of intertemporal externality (Arrow 1962), equation (3.2)
introduces a distinction between the private and the social marginal productivity of capital. A private producer, in computing the profitability
of an additional dose of capital, will be ignoring the gain it generates
for other producers. Intuitively speaking, the productive sector may be
imagined to be made up of M identical firms, each producing according

---

[4]See footnote 13, Chapter 1 for a definition of embodied and disembodied technical
progress.

[5]In concrete terms, it might help to think of labourers from different organisations
exchanging information during community gatherings.

to $F(K/M, K^\alpha(L/M))$. Given constant returns in K and $K^\alpha L$, this means that aggregate production is still represented by (3.2). An increase in K/M in all firms brings about a corresponding rise in K, but each firm is negligibly small (M being a large number) and is aware only of the change in its own capital stock. Hence, it does not take into account the effect of the social marginal productivity of the change in the private capital stock. In other words, $[\partial F/\partial K|_{K^\alpha=constant}] = F_1 = f'(\hat{k})$ measures the private marginal product of capital.

As opposed to the private return, however, the *social* marginal productivity of capital is $\partial F/\partial K$, which is stricly greater than the private marginal product, since capital accumulation has a spillover effect on the level attained by AL (as captured by $\alpha > 0$).[6] The spillovers may or may not give rise to nondecreasing *social* returns to capital. But the returns are external to individual firms. Consequently, the equilibrium for the system is sustainable by a perfectly competitive Private Economy. In other words, the private marginal productivity of capital will still be equated to the market rate of interest by private producers. To appreciate the nature of social returns to capital on the other hand, consider its average product

$$\frac{Y}{K} = F(1, K^{\alpha-1}L), \qquad (3.3)$$

which, given L, decreases, remains constant or increases with K according as α falls short of, equals or exceeds unity.

The learning by doing hypothesis is expected to change the Solow conclusion on the equilibrium rate of balanced growth. The crucial factor underlying Solow's result was that under the law of diminishing returns, sustained growth would require K to grow at the exogenously specified combined rate of growth of A and L. In the learning by doing scenario, the law of diminishing returns continues to hold. What changes, however, is the status accorded to the rate of growth of A. It is no longer an exogenous parameter for the model and depends instead on the rate of growth of K itself. Consequently, while diminishing returns still predicts a constant value of K/AL in the long run, the rate of growth of K has a feedback effect on the rate of growth of A, instead of the causality being unidirectional as in the Solow case.

We will divide up the discussion into three parts depending on the value of α.

---

[6]For later use, note that $\partial F/\partial K$ is neatly expressed as $\alpha f(\hat{k})/\hat{k} + (1-\alpha)f'(\hat{k})$. That is, the social marginal product of capital is a convex combination of the average product of capital and its private marginal product.

3.2.2   Case 1 ($\alpha < 1$): The Private Economy

This was the case considered by Arrow as well as Sheshinski. As already indicated, the rate of growth of efficient labour is a blend as it were of an endogenous factor, viz. the rate of growth of learning, which is a function of the rate of capital accumulation, and the exogenous population growth rate. Thus, while the supply rate of capital growth is determined by the rate of growth of efficient labour, the latter is itself influenced by the former. As a result, the rates of growth of capital and efficient labour are solutions to a pair of simultaneous equations and hence, endogenously determined. In other words and as distinct from Solow, the rate of technical progress is *solved for* by the model. As such, Arrow's view of technical change is less arbitrary than Solow's. Nevertheless, as will be seen, the rates of change of relevant variables continue to be impervious to policy changes in balanced growth equilibrium.

Thus, similar to Solow's Private Economy, the position of the supply rate of balanced growth curve is determined by a constant value of μ in Arrow's work also. Nonetheless, as already noted, Arrow's progress lies in the fact that the value of μ is determined internally and specified in terms of other parameters of the model. This is the content of the next result.

PROPOSITION **3.1** *The equilibrium balanced growth rate of per capita consumption equals μ.*

$$\mu = \frac{n\alpha}{1 - \alpha}.$$

The associated equilibrium rate of interest satisfies the condition

$$r^* = f'(\hat{k})$$

$$= \rho + \frac{n\alpha\theta}{1 - \alpha}. \tag{3.4}$$

Proof: Following Proposition 2.4, it is clear that the equilbrium rate of growth is μ. It is enough to prove therefore that $\mu = n\alpha/1 - \alpha$. Profit maximisation at constant r implies $K/AL = constant$, i.e.,

$$\frac{\dot{K}}{K} = \mu + n.$$

On the other hand, (3.1) yields

$$\mu = \alpha \frac{\dot{K}}{K}.$$

Solving these simultaneous equations in $\dot{K}/K$ and μ,

$$\frac{\dot{K}}{K} = \frac{n}{1 - \alpha} \tag{3.5}$$

$$\text{and} \qquad \mu = \frac{n\alpha}{1 - \alpha}. \tag{3.6}$$

Following (2.22) and substituting for the value of μ, the value of r^* follows.

Since μ is completely determined by demographic and technological factors, Arrow's conclusions were somewhat disappointing insofar as they failed to suggest how policy prescriptions (say the response of the demand rate of growth to a tax on interest income) might influence the *equilibrium* balanced growth rate. Moreover, as Romer (1986) observed, Arrow's work predicts that an economy with a low rate of growth of labour would have technology growing at a small rate. This conclusion does not conform to the behaviour of technologically advanced economies. An interesting feature of the Arrow model, however, arises from the fact that although demand parameters do not affect the rate of growth, they do have an influence of the equilibrium value of $\hat{k}$ or r. This is evident from (3.4) and has a policy implication. The fact will be clarified from our discussion of the Command Economy.

3.2.3 Case 1 ($\alpha < 1$): The Command Economy

We have already noted that the social marginal productivity of capital is higher in Arrow's economy than its private marginal productivity. There is no way the private sector can internalise this externality. However, an all perceiving social planner, were she/he to exist, would be in a position to do so. Keeping this in mind, we may write the planner's optimization exercise as:

Maximise (2.1) subject to (1.9), (2.18) and, (3.1).

In the planner's problem, there is no free market equating the marginal product of capital to the rate of interest. Secondly, the planner internalises all externalities and replaces the private marginal product of capital by its social marginal product.

To appreciate the manner in which the planner internalises the externality, let us go back to equation (1.9). The planner is aware of the exact manner in which μ is affected by the process of capital accumulation. In particular, he is aware that $A = K^\alpha = (\hat{k}L)^{\alpha/1-\alpha}$, so that

$$
\begin{aligned}
\mu &= \dot{A}/A \\[2mm]
&= \frac{\alpha}{1-\alpha}\left(\frac{\dot{\hat{k}}}{\hat{k}} + n\right).
\end{aligned}
\tag{3.7}
$$

Substituting for this in (1.9) and solving for $\dot{\hat{k}}$, we get

$$
\dot{\hat{k}} = (1-\alpha)\, f(\hat{k}) - n\,\hat{k} - (1-\alpha)\,\frac{c}{(\hat{k}L)^{\alpha/1-\alpha}}.
\tag{3.8}
$$

The Hamiltonian for the planner's problem is accordingly

$$
\begin{aligned}
\mathcal{H} &= \frac{c^{1-\theta}-1}{1-\theta} \\[2mm]
&\quad + q\left((1-\alpha)f(\hat{k}) - n\,\hat{k} - (1-\alpha)\,\frac{c}{(\hat{k}L)^{\alpha/1-\alpha}}\right).
\end{aligned}
\tag{3.9}
$$

The static condition for optimality, i.e.,

$$
\frac{\partial \mathcal{H}}{\partial c} = 0
$$

yields

$$
\begin{aligned}
c^{-\theta} &= (1-\alpha)\,\frac{q}{(\hat{k}L)^{\alpha/1-\alpha}} \\[2mm]
&= (1-\alpha)\,\frac{q}{A}.
\end{aligned}
\tag{3.10}
$$

The condition for dynamic optimality implies

$$
\begin{aligned}
\dot{q} &= -\frac{\partial \mathcal{H}}{\partial \hat{k}} + (\rho - n)\,q \\[2mm]
&= -\left((1-\alpha)\,f'(\hat{k}) - n + \alpha\,\frac{c}{A\,\hat{k}}\right) q + (\rho - n)\,q.
\end{aligned}
\tag{3.11}
$$

Denote the Command Economy's optimal balanced growth rate of c by G^*. Differentiating (3.10) with respect to t and substituting from (3.11) we obtain

$$G^* = \frac{\alpha \, f(\hat{k}^{**})/\hat{k}^{**} + (1-\alpha)f'(\hat{k}^{**}) - \rho}{\theta}, \qquad (3.12)$$

where $\hat{k}^{**}$ stands for the optimal level of $\hat{k}$ corresponding to G^*. Following the arguments of Section 2.3.1, we conclude that $G^* = \mu = n\alpha/1-\alpha$. Thus, the balanced growth rate for the Private Economy is identical with the rate achieved by the Command Economy in equilibrium. There will nonetheless be a difference between the solutions for the two systems. To see this, substitute $G^* = \mu = n\alpha/1-\alpha$ in (3.12) to get

$$\left(\alpha \frac{f(\hat{k}^{**})}{\hat{k}^{**}} + (1-\alpha)f'(\hat{k}^{**}) \right) = \rho + \frac{n\alpha\theta}{1-\alpha} \qquad (3.13)$$

3.2.4 Comparison of Command and Private Economies

The planner's balanced growth equilibrium is the best possible balanced growth path for the economy since it corresponds to the internalisation of all externalities. Since the social marginal product of capital, viz. $\alpha f(\hat{k})/\hat{k} + (1-\alpha)f'(\hat{k})$, is larger than its private marginal product, viz. $f'(\hat{k})$, it is evident from (3.4) and (3.13) that in balanced growth equilibrium, $\hat{k}^{**} > \hat{k}^*$. In other words, the Private Economy underinvests and is unable to achieve the (higher) socially optimal value of $\hat{k}$. The result amounts to a failure of the First Fundamental Theorem of Welfare Economics. The market failure creates room for policy intervention in Arrow's model. The rise in social marginal productivity, brought about by labour augmentation as of any given value of capital, is not recognised by the market. Hence, the market pays capital less than its true marginal product, while it awards to labour the marginal product of efficient labour, which in turn is created by the investment generated learning process. The market solution can be improved by a tax-subsidy scheme. The private producers will raise their investments to increase $\hat{k}^*$ to the level $\hat{k}^{**}$, if the private return at $\hat{k}^{**}$, viz. $f'(\hat{k}^{**})$, were to be supplemented by a subsidy to raise the effective return to $\alpha(f(\hat{k}^{**})/\hat{k}^{**}) + (1-\alpha)f'(\hat{k}^{**})$. The subsidy can be provided by taxing labour income appropriately.

PROPOSITION **3.2** *The Private Economy's equilibrium balanced growth* *path is not socially optimal in the Arrow model. A Private Economy equilibrium supported by wage taxation and capital subsidization can restore the social optimum.*

Apart from the equilibrium rate of growth turning out to be inert to policy manipulations,[7] a second major shortcoming of the Arrow theory is that technical progress, though endogenously generated, is viewed as an inevitable (or, unavoidable) *byproduct* of the process of capital accumulation. It is not linked to the *rational* actions of economic agents who are known in real life to innovate in search of higher profits from production.

Figure 3.1 summarizes the conclusions for the Arrow exercise.

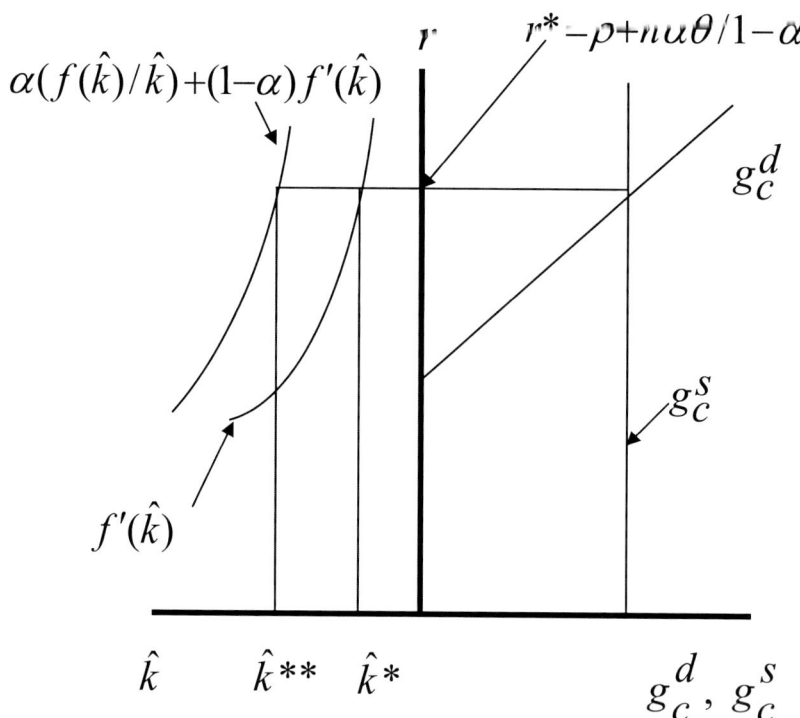

Figure 3.1: Arrow: Private vs Command Solutions

---

[7]Notice, however, that as with the Solow model, policy has a role to play in out of steady state dynamics in Arrow's model.

As indicated in Chapter 2, a part of the difficulty lies in the structure of markets. We may end this section by drawing the readers' attention to a difficulty that will arise in the context of appropriate designing of markets. Arrow's technical change is a non-marketable commodity in that it is both nonrival as well as nonexcludable, i.e., it is a pure public good. It is non-rival since all firms enjoy it simultaneously; and it is non-excludable, since it has the form of an external effect. This suggests that the classic public good problem will need to be handled appropriately if technical progress has to be properly dealt with. We shall return to this question in Section 3.2.8 and Chapter 6 where we discuss Romer (1986 and 1990).

3.2.5 Case 2 ($\alpha = 1$): The Private Economy

Arrow's model shares most features of the Solow world and it is possible to carry out an out of balanced growth analysis to prove that both the Private and the Command Economies eventually grow at the rate $\mu = n\,\alpha/(1 - \alpha)$. We have already noted, however, that Romer (1986) criticized this aspect of Arrow's conclusion, since, given α, it implies that the per capita consumption c in economies characterised by a low value of n will grow at negligible rates in the long run. The prediction is clearly not borne out by facts, because the richest economies in the world have a low population growth rate, though they are known to experience significant growth rates of c.

The problem arises on account of the restriction $\alpha < 1$ imposed by Arrow. This gives rise to diminishing social productivity of capital and a weak spillover effect of capital accumulation. (See equation (3.3)). Romer's criticism does not apply when $\alpha \geq 1$, in which case the average productivity is non-diminishing and hence stronger than the Arrow case. In this connection, we begin with the work of d'Autume and Michel (1993), who assume $\alpha = 1$. In the interest of continuity, the neoclassical framework will be maintained, although the original results were presented in Arrow's embodied form.

By definition, $\mu = \dot{K}/K = constant$ along a balanced growth path. However, with $\alpha = 1$, the assumption of balanced growth does not yield the value of the supply rate of growth as in the earlier model. Of course, the supply rate of growth continues to be equal to μ, but the value of μ remains unknown until $\dot{K}/K$ is determined. More precisely, the requirement that $\dot{K}/K = \dot{A}/A + \dot{L}/L$ leads to

$$
\begin{aligned}
\frac{\dot{K}}{K} &= \mu + n \\
&= \frac{\dot{K}}{K} + n, \text{ since } \alpha = 1
\end{aligned}
\tag{3.14}
$$

and this can happen only if $n = 0$. On the other hand, (3.14) cannot solve for $\dot{K}/K$ with $n = 0$.

A necessary condition for positive balanced growth being a *stationary* level of population, $L = \bar{L} = constant$. As a result, and as opposed to the case $\alpha < 1$, $\hat{k}^* = K/(K\bar{L}) = 1/\bar{L}$. This represents, once again, a departure from the models studied so far, where the equilibrium value of $\hat{k}$ depended on demand as well as supply parameters. Further, (1.13) admits a unique profit maximising value of r, viz,, $r^* = f'(1/\bar{L})$, quite independently of the value assumed by μ. (Compare with Figure 2.5.) Alternatively, r^* can sustain *any* rate of balanced growth of k. Note, moreover, that with $n = \delta = 0$, (1.9) implies

$$
\frac{\dot{\hat{c}}}{\hat{k}} = \frac{f(\hat{k})}{\hat{k}} - \mu,
\tag{3.15}
$$

where $\mu = \dot{K}/K = constant$, along a balanced growth path. Given a fixed value of μ (which remains to be determined) and a fixed value of $\hat{k} = \hat{k}^* = 1/\bar{L}$, the above equation implies that the value of $\hat{c}/\hat{k}$ is a constant. A fixed value of $\hat{c}/\hat{k}$, while assuring us that c and k grow at an equal rate in balanced growth equilibrium does not throw any light on the exact magnitude of that growth rate (i.e., μ). This implies that g_c^s is a perfectly elastic function at r^*. Hence, g_c^s is a horizontal curve passing through r^*.

The g_c^d curve is identically the same as in the earlier models. Consequently, the equilibrium rate of balanced growth, $g_c^* = (r^* - \rho)/\theta$, is determined once again by the intersection of demand and supply. However, as opposed to the earlier cases, and this is the second crucial departure from earlier models, it is demand now that has the driver's seat in the determination of the equilibrium growth rate.[8] Indeed, a change in ρ and θ would now have an effect on the growth rate. So

---

[8]The reader cannot fail to note the diametrically opposite roles played by g_c^d and g_c^s for the two cases $\alpha < 1$ and $\alpha = 1$. In the former, they interact to fix the equilibrium value of $\hat{k}$, leaving the rate of growth of the economy to be determined by exogenous supply side parameters. In the latter, the opposite is the case.

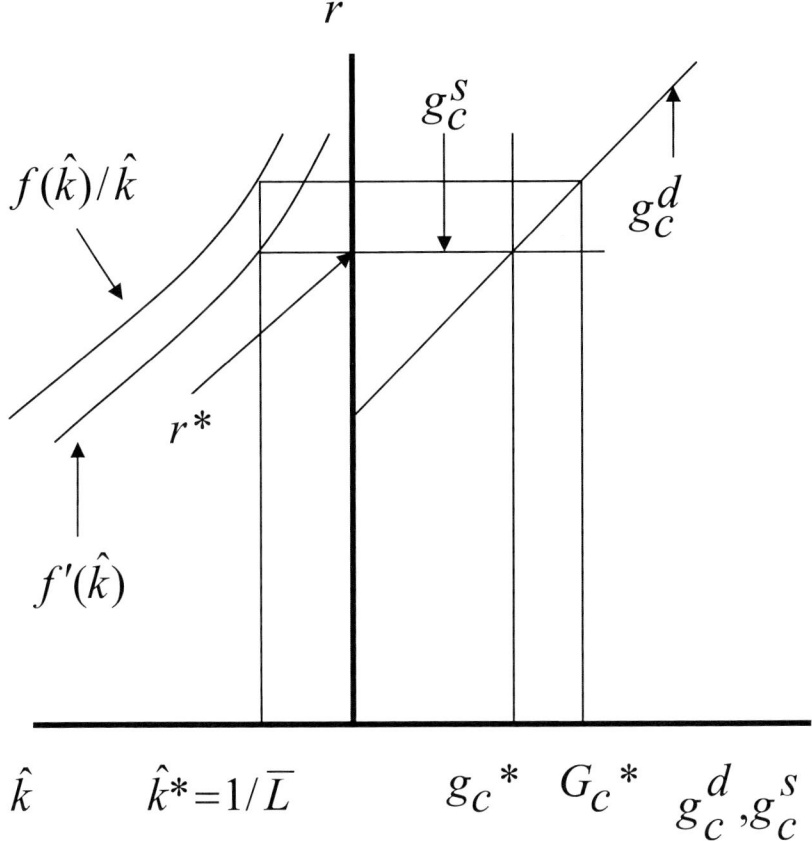

Figure 3.2: d'Autume and Michel: Private vs Command Solutions

would policy, such as a proportional tax on interest income. As opposed to Arrow's case, the growth rate is *controllable*. The equilibrium is depicted in Figure 3.2.

It follows now that, despite the fact that the rate of population growth is zero, the equilibrium rate of growth is non-zero. Hence, the criticism raised by Romer (1986) against Arrow's exercise (with which this section started) does not apply to the d'Autume and Michel model.[9] Note, however, that while the equilibrium solution is no longer tied to the *rate* of population growth, it does still depend on the *size* of the

---

[9]Moreover, as will be evident from Section 3.2.7, the model does not permit out of balanced growth dynamics in any case.

labour force, since the latter determines the equilibrium rate of interest and hence the equilibrium growth rate. In this connection, recall the restriction (2.27) discussed in Chapter 2, which reduces now to

$$g_c^* (1 - \theta) < \rho. \tag{3.16}$$

The rate g_c^* being endogenously determined, there is no guarantee that the above restriction will be satisfied. Of course, a low enough value of r^* will ensure that the restriction will not be violated. A low r^* follows from a high value of $1/\bar{L}$, which amounts to a low value of $\bar{L}$. Consequently, one way of ensuring that the model gives rise to meaningful results is to impose an upper bound on $\bar{L}$. Another possibility to explore is to impose bounds on ρ and θ.

The link between g_c^* and $\bar{L}$ imply a comparative static result. A higher $\bar{L}$ leads, *ceteris paribus*, to a higher value of g_c^* via a larger value of r^*. One may interpret this to mean that the effect of Learning by doing is higher when the labour force is larger, i.e., the aggregate of skills acquired is higher. This phenomenon will show up in a major way again when we discuss Romer (1990) in Chapter 5. As Romer argues, a rise in the stock of *human capital* or skilled work force has a growth rate enhancing effect.

The conclusions are summarized below.

PROPOSITION **3.3** *When $\alpha = 1$, balanced growth equilibrium implies zero growth of population. Further, the rate of equilibrium growth of c, k and y is determined by demand as well as technological parameters. A change in preference parameters affects the growth rate, while a change in the size of the labour force affects both the growth rate as well as the equilibrium value of the effective capital-labour ratio.*

3.2.6   Command Economy and Private Economy

Once again, the Command Economy takes into account the externality factor in its optimality calculation and this shows up in the form of a higher value accorded to the social marginal product of capital as compared to the market economy. Since the production function can be rewritten as $Y = K\bar{L}f(1/\bar{L})$, the social marginal product is a constant $\bar{L}f(1/\bar{L})$ and equals the social average productivity $f(\hat{k})/\hat{k}$.[10]   As a

---

[10]A model that may be considered to be a close parallel of the d'Autume and Michel model is one due to Frankel (1962). The only difference between the two lies in the value of the coefficient of labour augmentation. Frankel takes it to be per capita capital K/L, rather than K.

result, the optimal balanced growth rate for the Command Economy is

$$G_c^* = \frac{\bar{L}f(1/\bar{L}) - \rho}{\theta}. \tag{3.17}$$

Since the average product is larger than the marginal product, the following proposition emerges:

PROPOSITION **3.4** *The equilibrium rate of growth in a Private Economy is strictly less than the equilibrium growth rate in a Command Economy.*

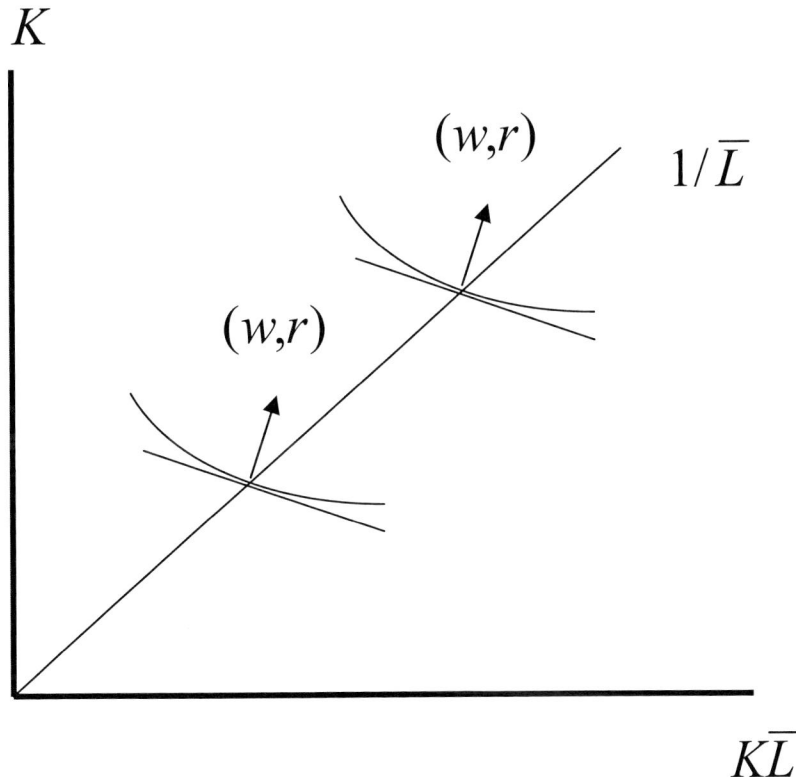

Figure 3.3: d'Autume and Michel: Alternative Representation

As opposed to the case $\alpha < 1$, it is now the *rate of growth* that is higher in the Command Economy rather than the equilibrium value of $\hat{k}$. The

Private Economy and Command Economy equilibria are compared in Figure 3.2. Figure 3.3 is an alternative depiction of the model. This diagram shows that the ratio $K/K\bar{L} = 1/\bar{L}$ is a ray through the origin in the isoquant plane along which the economy moves. The wage-rental ratio is tangential to the isoquants at their points of intersection with the ray $1/\bar{L}$. There is full employment of both factors along the balanced growth path. The rate at which the economy moves along the ray is determined by the rate of interest corresponding to the wage-rental ratio quoted above. The Command Economy too moves along the same ray, but the rate of change is determined by the social marginal productivity of capital $\bar{L}f(1/\bar{L})$ which is larger than the rate of interest in the Private Economy.

3.2.7   Lessons from Case 2

An important feature of the model is that it adjusts to the equilibrium rate of growth $g_c^* = (f'(\hat{k}^*) - \rho)/\theta$ instantaneously at time point $t = 0$. This follows because $\hat{k} = 1/\bar{L}$. Given g_c^*, (3.15) yields $c_0 = k_0\,(f(\hat{k})/\hat{k} - \mu)$.[11] The entire paths of k_t^* and c_t^* are solved for then onwards. The Private Economy jumps on to the balanced growth path independent of the value of K_0 and continues on that path forever. There is no scope for out of balanced growth behaviour.

Exactly the same observation holds, *mutatis mutandis*, for the Command solution. The only difference lies in the values chosen of the variable G^* and the paths of $K(t)$ and $C(t)$, beginning from a given K_0.

Two features of the model stand out vis-á-vis the Solow and the Arrow models. First, demand parameters now affect the growth of technology in a straightforward manner and this in turn influences the growth rate of important macro variables like the GDP, capital stock, consumption etc. In this sense, this is the first example of an endogenous growth model that we have come across in this book. Secondly, and as already noted, the model links up the endogenously determined growth rate to the exogenously given *level* of the work force. In particular, the higher the latter, the higher is the growth rate that the economy enjoys (subject to (3.16) being satisfied). This second feature has the important implication that scarce resources (labour in this case) impose an upper bound on the achievable growth rate of technology, GDP and so on. The bound can be relaxed therefore through an expansion of the

---

[11]Writing $\Lambda = f(\hat{k})/\hat{k} - \mu$, $\hat{c} = \Lambda\,\hat{k}$ may be looked upon as the consumption function for the economy under balanced growth.

resource base.[12] Apart from this, there is no technological constraint
on an economy's rate of growth. In subsequent chapters, we shall have
occasions to refer back to these two basic characteristics of the model.
As we shall observe in connection with our discussion of more sophisticated models, not all of them are capable of incorporating the two
features equally well. It should be obvious that even if a model succeeds
in determining the growth rate endogenously, its predictions would be
somewhat pessimistic if it ends up by imposing a *technological* bound
on the rate of growth of *technology* itself.

3.2.8 Case 3 ($\alpha > 1$): Private and Command Economies

This case takes us back to Romer (1986) and constitutes the most tech-
nically demanding of the three alternatives under consideration. Since
the mathematical derivations involved are nontrivial, we shall strip the
model down to its bear essentials, ignoring details that do not play major roles in the model. To compare the model with the previous two, we
shall capture externalities[13] with the aid of an Arrow type production
function $Y = F(K, K^\alpha L)$, though the original Romer model is far more
general.[14]

As opposed to the first two models of Learning by Doing, Romer
distinguishes between physical and knowledge capital. It is the latter
that is responsible for the Harrodian labour augmentation.[15] Thus, K
denotes the total stock of knowledge in a society and K is accumulable.
Romer's explanation of labour augmentation can be viewed as the effect
of an educated environment on labour skills. The externality lies in the
fact that such an environment leads to improvements in the skills of
those who lack formal education (say). Given that $\alpha > 1$, the effect is
strong. The term $K^\alpha L$, $\alpha > 1$ increases the size of the effective labour
force at an increasing rate as K or knowledge grows.

The improvement in knowledge comes about through a knowledge
producing technology. Unlike Arrow, for whom technical progress is an
unplanned by-product of physical capital accumulation, it is the accu-

---

[12]See, however, footnote 9 in Chapter 5 for criticisms of the second feature of the
model.

[13]The externality discussed so far is the strongest in the present case.

[14]First, the function is posed at the micro firm level. Secondly, in his most general
treatment, Romer does not assume any specific form for the learning by doing effect.

[15]His model admits both kinds of capital. However, this simplified exposition ig-
nores physical capital to stick to the essence of the exercise.

mulation of *knowledge* through an explicit *R and D* activity that con-
tributes to an increase in labour productivity in Romer's economy. In
the changed scenario, $I = Y - C$ still stands for investment in the sense
of foregone consumption. However, unlike the previous models, I is used
up completely in the creation of more knowledge (through research for
example).[16] Thus, savings (S) translates one-to-one into investment (I)
as in Solow, Arrow and others, but I is not identically the same as $\dot{K}$.
It is a costly input that is used to produce $\dot{K}$.

Explicitly, new knowledge or $\dot{K}$ is assumed to be a linear homogeneous function of I and the *entire* stock of knowledge capital (i.e., K)
in existence and concave in each argument. The *R and D* production
function is written $G(I, K)$. In other words,

$$\dot{K} = G(I, K) = Kg\left(\frac{I}{K}\right),$$ (3.18)

where $g(I/K) = G(I/K, 1)$.

Given these specifications,

$$\frac{\dot{\hat{k}}}{\hat{k}} = \frac{\dot{K}}{K} - \alpha\frac{\dot{K}}{K} - n < 0,$$ (3.19)

whenever $\dot{K}/K > 0$. Thus, $\hat{k}$ must fall continuously, thereby making it
necessary for the demand rate of growth to change over time.[17] Thus,
this system can never hope to be in balanced growth equilibrium. However, paths of c, k and y satisfying the definition of a perfect foresight
equilibrium will exist as we shall indicate below.

Let us assume, without loss of generality, that $n = 0$, though it is
not logically necessary to do so as in d'Autume and Michel, since, in
any case, the Romer model rules out balanced growth. In particular,
normalise $\bar{L} = 1$. Thus, (3.2) reduces to

$$Y = F(K, K^\alpha), \quad \alpha > 1,$$ (3.20)

---

[16]At this stage of Romer's work, the precise form of knowledge capital is left
somewhat vague.

[17]To the extent that $f'(\hat{k})$ rises as $\hat{k}$ falls, one expects the growth rate of the
economy to rise over time. For models represented so far, this could make the marginal
product of K rise unboundedly (via Inada conditions), causing the demand rate
of growth to explode also. The utility integral will correspondingly diverge and no
optimal path would exist. Romer avoids this problem by assuming that $g(I/K) = G(I/K, 1)$ in (3.18) is bounded above.

where Y is viewed as being produced by means of costly knowledge capital and efficient labour. Further,

$$I = Y - C$$

$$= F(K, K^\alpha) - C$$

$$= F(K, K^\alpha) - c. \tag{3.21}$$

New knowledge capital (i.e., $\dot{K}$) is developed through research via the technology specified in (3.18). The fact that the whole of K is present simultaneously in both F and G indicates that it is being viewed as a nonrival good. The household sells the services of K and $\bar{L}$ to firms producing Y. The income so derived is spent wholly on C and I. The latter is used in producing $\dot{K}$, with the help of the nonrival K, which implies that K is a free input as far as the production of $\dot{K}$ is concerned. Since K has to be paid for in producing Y but not $\dot{K}$, knowledge capital is a *partially excludable* commodity in the model.[18] Following Arrow's basic idea, however, the labour augmenting effect of capital accumulation (viz. K^α) is external to the firm. Consequently, the market structure may still be assumed to be perfectly competitive as in Solow (1956).

At the cost of repetition, let us emphasize that technical progress in this model is not a pure externality as was the case for the two previous models. It does assume the form of an Arrow-type externality in the production of Y. However, the externality is generated by knowledge capital and the latter is accumulated through conscious effort involving expenditure on a costly economic resource, viz. I.[19]

As indicated above, the algebra of the Romer model is complicated. We work out below some of its salient features, though these had best be treated as initial steps designed to help students interested in details. Concretely speaking, the Private Economy problem will be solved in the same way as the planner would solve the Command Economy exercise, subject to the restriction that producers are unable to internalise the external effect of learning. This amounts to doing away with the household-firm separation and solving a grand optimisation exercise similar to the one studied in Section 2.1.[20] Let

$$\mathcal{H} = \frac{c^{1-\theta} - 1}{1 - \theta} + \bar{q}\, K\, g\left(\frac{I}{K}\right)$$

---

[18] The conceptual implication of a nonrival and partially excludable K is brought out in great detail in Romer (1990). See Chapter 5.

[19] One could identify I as wages paid to research workers.

[20] The procedure will be repeated later on in the book also. See Chapter 4, Section 4.2.

$$= \frac{c^{1-\theta} - 1}{1 - \theta} + \bar{q} \, K \, g\left(\frac{F(K, K^{\alpha}) - c}{K}\right), \qquad (3.22)$$

using (3.21). The conditions of static and dynamic optimality are captured by the following pair of equations:

$$\frac{\partial \mathcal{H}}{\partial c} = 0,$$

$$\text{and} \qquad \dot{\bar{q}} = -\frac{\partial \mathcal{H}}{\partial K} + \rho \, \bar{q} \qquad (3.23)$$

respectively. Using these two, the system reduces to a differential equation

$$\frac{\dot{c}}{c} = \Phi(K, c). \qquad (3.24)$$

On the other hand, (3.18) is similarly rewritten

$$\frac{\dot{K}}{K} = g\left(\frac{I}{K}\right),$$

$$= \Psi(K, c). \qquad (3.25)$$

The two equations (3.24) and (3.25) represent the fundamental equations of motion for the system. These are difficult to solve analytically. Hence, Romer illustrates their behaviour through a series of examples using specific functional forms for F and g and values of θ. The resulting paths, as already noted, do not display balanced growth equilibrium. To the extent that they are solved for by the model, the rates of growth of c, K and A at each t are endogenously determined.[21] Moreover, unlike Arrow's case, despite the absence of population growth, the economy does not converge to a zero-growth equilibrium in the long run.[22]

The Command Economy solves exactly the same problem as above, but for the internalisation of the externality. As a result, Romer is able to argue that the rate of research will be higher for the Command Economy and the level of consumption lower. Summarising, we have

---

[21] Note that the out of steady state path in Case 1 had the same characteristic.

[22] In general, K and c are seen to diverge for all of Romer's examples. The examples differ, however, in terms of whether they impose asymptotic bounds on the rates of growth, though the possibility of increasing growth rates is not ruled out.

PROPOSITION **3.5** *When $\alpha > 1$, the economy is not in balanced growth equilibrium at any finite t. The out of balanced growth equilibrium paths of both the Private and Command Economies are endogenously determined and are different from one another. The economy does not converge to zero growth equilibrium even though the population growth rate is zero.*

As far as balanced growth is concerned, there was a *logical* need in d'Autume and Michel for assuming the rate of population growth to be zero. Although there is no such necessity in the remaining models, it is convenient to make the assumption in any case. Apart from simplifying the algebra, it helps to establish the fact that an exogenous specification of the population growth rate has no role to play in determining the growth rate of an economy. Also, it isolates clearly the role of technology in generating economic growth.

3.3 Fixed Coefficients and Related Models

We end up this chapter with a discussion of the so-called Leontief fixed coefficients model of growth popularized by Dorfman, Samuelson and Solow (1958).[23] The model will serve several purposes. First, it will study the stability properties of growth paths in the absence of smooth substitution possibilities for a Command Economy. The discussion will lead us naturally to two of the earliest models of growth due to Harrod (1939) and Domar (1946). These models will be brought up very briefly to clarify a long standing misconception in growth theory that they are no different from the Leontief fixed coefficient model. Finally, we shall introduce, using a special case of the fixed coefficient model, the most elementary of the endogenous growth models. This is the AK-Model of growth. Though apparently similar, the AK-Model too will be seen to be quite different in spirit from the Leontief fixed coefficient model.[24]

Denoting labor by L, capital by K and output by Y, assume that isoquants are right angled corners and that the production function is given by

$$Y = min\ \{AK, BL\},\ A > 0,\ B > 0, \tag{3.26}$$

where A and B are constants. Figure 3.4 captures this production function and associated properties. First, the right angled corners fall on a ray OF through the origin with slope B/A. If the ratio of the economy's

---

[23]Dorfman *et al* (1958), Chapters 9 and 10.

[24]This section is based on Dasgupta (2008).

capital and labor supply happens to fall on this ray, then both factors
will be fully employed. Second, if the economy's capital and labor fall
above the ray, there will be underemployment of capital, while if it falls
below the ray, there will be underemployment of labor.

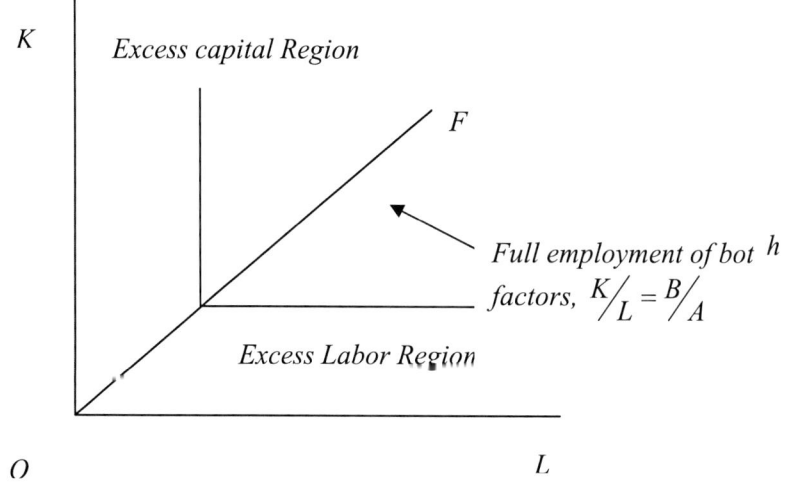

Figure 3.4: Fixed Coefficient Technology

Thus, as opposed to Solow's model of perpetual full employment, we
shall be dealing in general with unemployment of either labor or capital
in this model.

3.3.1   Growth Paths of Capital and Labour

We will treat the following growth model in a non-market environment
and return back to markets towards the very end. What follows therefore is a Command Economy exercise unless explicitly stated. Labour
grows according to **Assumption L** of Chapter 1 and the basic growth
equation is given by $\dot{K} = s\,Y$, where s is the constant marginal and
average propensity to save out of income. The value of s, as opposed to
our exercises so far, is specified as an ad hoc constant. As before there
is zero depreciation of capital. The output will be $BL(t)$ and $AK(t)$
respectively above and below the ray OF.

Initial Point in Excess Supply of Labor Zone

By assumption, $K_0^1/L_0^1 < B/A$, where $K(0) = K_0^1$ and $L(0) = L_0^1$ as in Figure 3.5. In this region, $Y = AK$. Thus, $\dot{K}/K = s A$. Since n, s and A are exogenous, two sub-cases arise.

Case: $sA > n$.

Here, starting from (K_0^1, L_0^1), both K and L rise, but K rises faster than L, since $sA > n$. Thus, $\dot{K}/K - n = \dot{k}/k = s A - n$. Hence, $k(t) = k_0 e^{(sA-n)t}$. Thus, $\exists\, \bar{t} > 0$ such that $k(\bar{t}) = B/A$ and the economy is on OF with $\dot{K}/K = sA = sBL/K > n$, since $AK = BL$. So, K keeps on rising faster than L, with K/L rising above B/A and the economy moves to the capital surplus region, the production function changing to $Y = BL$.

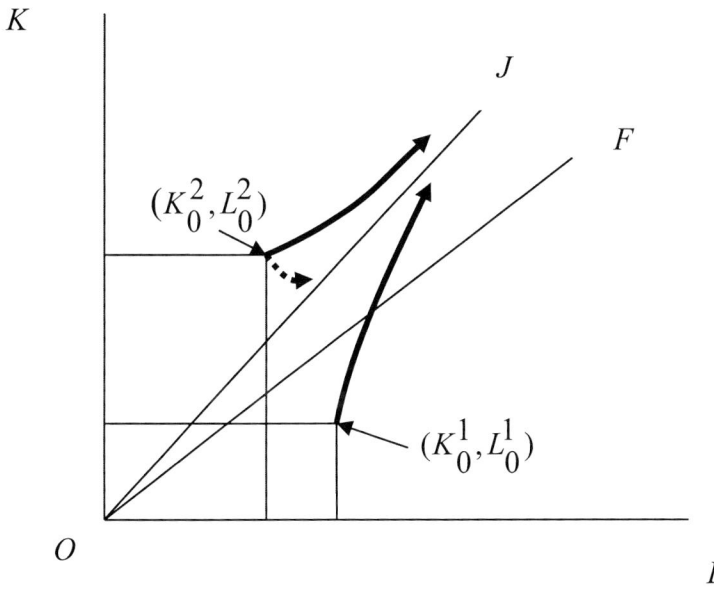

Figure 3.5: Growth Paths when $sA > n$

The behaviour of $\dot{K}$ changes now to $\dot{K}/K = sBL/K > n$. Since $\dot{K}/K > n$, , it follows that L/K falls so long as $sBL/K > n$. The growth rate of capital is greater than n, but it declines over time, asymptotically approaching n. Thus, although both K and L increase, the rate of increase of K falls towards n and K/L converges to a number higher than B/A. In the limit, $\dot{K}/K = sBL/K = n$ and $K/L \to sB/n$. The unbroken curve starting from (K_0^1, L_0^1) in Figure 3.5 demonstrates this.

Note that along the ray OJ, both capital and labor are growing at the same rate n. Thus, in the long run, the model behaves the same way as the Solow model, as far as the rate of growth is concerned. Capital, labor and final output rise at the rate n. However, unlike Solow, we do not have full employment of both factors. In particular, all capital is not employed. Actual employment of capital falls on the ray OF. The vertical distance between OJ and OF measures the extent of unemployed capital in long run equilibrium.

Denoting the actual employment of capital by $\tilde{K}(t)$, we see that both $\tilde{K}(t)$ and $K(t)$ grow at the rate n. Thus, the ratio

$$\frac{K(t) - \tilde{K}(t)}{K(t)} - 1 - \frac{\tilde{K}(t)}{K(t)}$$

approaches a positive constant, which is less than unity. The excess supply of capital as a proportion of the growing capital stock converges to a steady positive value.

Case: $sA < n$.

We have $\dot{K}/K = sA < n$. Thus, $\dot{K}/K - n = \dot{k}/k = sA - n < 0$ and $k(t) = k_0 \, e^{(sA-n)\,t} \to 0$. Note, however, that $\dot{K}/K = sA > 0$, so that both K and L rise. In other words, the broken line starting from (K_0^1, L_0^1) cannot represent the behaviour of the economy. The correct behavior is captured by the unbroken arrow starting from (K_0^1, L_0^1) in Figure 3.6. At any point on this curve, the slope is less than unity, since capital grows at a slower rate than labor. The ratio K/L moves through flatter and flatter rays such as OQ and eventually approaches zero. Since the economy continues to remain below the ray OF, there is full employment of capital.

The actual employment of labor, $\tilde{L}$ solves $K/\tilde{L} = B/A$. In other words, K and $\tilde{L}$ continue to grow at the same rate, but K/L approaches zero. This means $\tilde{L}/L$ also approaches zero. The quantity of employed labor as a fraction of the labor force becomes infinitesimally small with time.

Finally, note that output growth is given by $\dot{Y}/Y = \dot{K}/K = sA$. Thus, output grows with full employment of capital at the rate sA. The

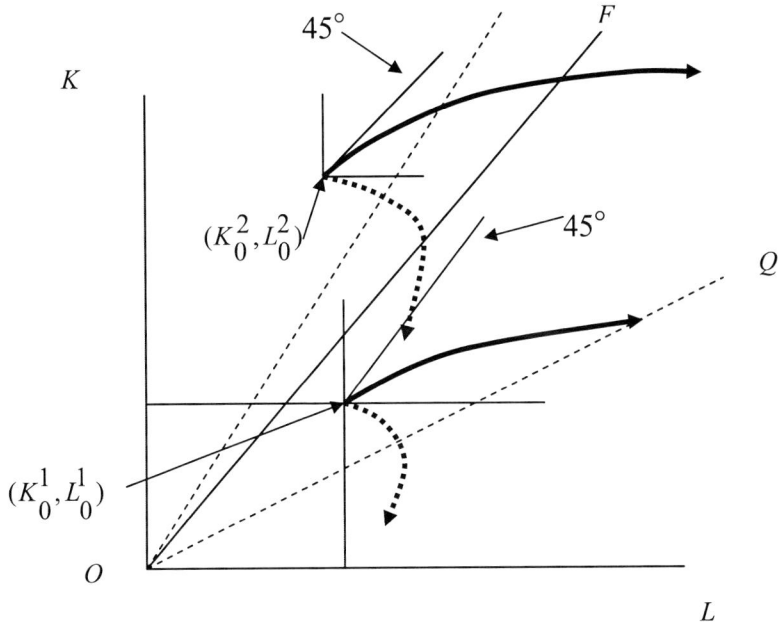

Figure 3.6: Growth Paths when $sA < n$

rate of growth of labor force is n, which is different from the rate of growth of output. The long run behavior differs from Solow's economy.

Initial Point in Excess Supply of Capital Zone

There are two cases again.

Case: $sA > n$.

The economy behaves the same way as in the excess-supply-of-labor case if (K_0^1, L_0^1) is trapped inside OJ and OF. Initial excess-supply-of-capital leads to the same behavior as initial excess-supply-of-labor.

Since $sBL/K = n$ on OJ, we must have $sBL/K < n$ above OJ. Thus, starting from (K_0^2, L_0^2) in Figure 3.5, we get $\dot{K}/K = sBL/K < n$ and $\dot{K}/K - n = sBL/K - n < 0$. Therefore, L rises faster than K and K/L asymptotes to OJ from above, as shown by the unbroken arrow starting from (K_0^2, L_0^2). The economy ends up in the long run with properties similar to the excess-supply-of-labor case. Note that both K and L must grow. Hence, the broken line starting from (K_0^2, L_0^2)

cannot represent the way the system behaves.

Case: $sA < n$.

When $k_0 = K_0/L_0 > B/A$, we have $\dot{K}/K = sBL/K < sA < n$. Thus, $\dot{K}/K - n = \dot{k}/k = sBL/K - n < 0$. So, K keeps on rising slower than L and $k(t)$ falls below B/A. Once this happens, the behavior of $\dot{K}$ changes to $\dot{K}/K - n = sA - n < 0$. This implies K/L falls indefinitely, though K and L both keep rising. Once again, the limiting behavior of the economy is the same as in the excess-supply-of-labor case. In particular, Y and K both grow at the rate sA. The economy moves along the unbroken arrow from (K_0^2, L_0^2) and not along the broken arrow.

In all the cases shown, either capital or labor remains unemployed despite the fact that capital employment, labor employment and output grow in the long run at positive rates. Full employment occurs if K_0/L_0 falls on OJ. In this case, through a proper choice of s, the economy grows at the rate n from the beginning, without any unemployment.

3.3.2   Comparisons with Other Models

We now try to distinguish these results from other models with which the model of Section 3.3.1 has often been compared and sometimes even (incorrectly) identified.

The Harrod Model

There are two principal features of the Harrod model, the warranted rate of growth and the natural rate of growth. The former is derived as follows. First, as in the above model, $S = sY$, where S is aggregate savings. Aggregate investment I is supposed to be a function of expected change in output, $\dot{Y}$, with $I = \dot{Y}/A$, where A is constant. Thus,

$$S = I \Leftrightarrow \frac{\dot{Y}}{Y} = sA. \tag{3.27}$$

Here, $\dot{Y}/Y$ stands for the expected rate of growth of output. According to (3.27), when the expected rate of growth of output equals sA, investment will equal saving at each t. That is, sA is the rate of growth of output which, if expected, will lead investors to equate investment and saving at each point of time, thus leading to expectations realization. Harrod called sA the warranted rate of growth of the economy.

As opposed to the warranted rate of growth, the natural rate of growth of the economy, n, is that rate of growth that keeps all resources fully employed at each t. If $n = sA$, then the expectations fulfilling growth rate is consistent with full employment.

Suppose, however that $n > sA$. Since $n = \dot{Y}/Y$, it follows that $\dot{Y}/Y > sA$ or,

$$I = \frac{1}{A}\dot{Y} > sY = S. \tag{3.28}$$

Thus, aggregate investment will exceed aggregate saving, leading to excess demand for output. So, trying to grow faster than the warranted rate will make entrepreneurs conclude they are growing too slowly. This will make them want to grow even faster, giving rise to unabated inflation.

Supppose that $n < sA$. Then,

$$I = \frac{1}{A}\dot{Y} < sY = S. \tag{3.29}$$

Now there will be a cut back on output and a continual downward revision of the rate of investment. The entrepreneurs will feel they are growing too faast and invest even less.

In the fixed coefficients model, the system could end up with unemployment, but it will be growing at a constant rate. Harrod's rate of growth will contract under (3.29). The only similarity between the two systems lies in the full employment cases, which can occur under very special circumstances.

The Domar Model

Domar looked at two implications of investment. The first was income generation. The second was novel, the increase in productive capacity. Domar pointed out that capacity may grow at a higher rate than output unless investment grew at a well specified rate.

Denote the ratio of productive capacity to investment by the constant κ. The potential output of investment projects would thus be $I\kappa$. However, the productive capacity of the whole economy may rise by less than κ, since new projects may involve transfer of resources from existing projects. Denoting aggregate social productivity by P, Domar assumed the potential social productivity of investment to be another constant

$$\sigma = \frac{dP/dt}{I}. \qquad (3.30)$$

The change in output demanded, however, must satisfy the condition

$$\frac{dY}{dt} = \frac{dI}{dt}\frac{1}{s}. \qquad (3.31)$$

If at time $t = 0$, we have $P_0 = Y_0$ and we require output and capacity to grow at the same rate, then equations (3.30) and (3.31) imply $I = I_0\, e^{s\sigma t}$. However, there is no guarantee that private investors would invest at the rate $s\sigma$. Assume then that they invest at the constant rate r. If $\sigma = \kappa$, then using the fact that aggregate capital stock at $t = T$ is $K(T) = \int_0^T I(t)\, e^{rt} dt$, it can be shown that $lim_{t\to\infty} Y/P = r/s\, \sigma$. If $r < s\sigma$, then unused capacity and unemployment will emerge. Note that the problem of capacity unemployment is distinct from that of capital unemployment in the fixed coefficient case.

If $\sigma < \kappa$, we end up again with $lim_{t\to\infty} Y/P = r/s\, \sigma$. For developing economies, it has an undesirable implication that forced obsolescence of older installed capacity may result.

The AK Model of Endogenous Growth

In Section 3.3.1, the case $sA < n$ implied a long run rate of growth of the system equal to sA. The corresponding production function was

$$Y = AK. \qquad (3.32)$$

When the production function assumes this form, it is common to refer to it as an AK production function and it leads to a growth rate equal to sA. By varying s, the rate of growth of the model can be controlled and to that extent, this is an example of an endogenous growth model. A pure AK model incorporates only a single factor of production K. It leads to a rate of growth equal to sA and can be sustained by a perfectly competitive market that pays K its marginal product A. As with the d'Autume-Michel (1993) model (and the Barro-Sala-i-Martin (2003) model to be developed in Chapter 5), the AK model too does not permit out of balanced growth dymamics, a fact that the reader can easily check.

Referring back to our treatment of the fixed coefficients model, one can reinterpret the AK model as a two factor model by linking it to the situation that arises *eventually* in the $sA < n$ case. We noted there that while capital and labour were being employed in fixed proportion to produce Y, there was excess supply of labour in the face of full employment of capital. In this case, labour employed ($\tilde{L}$) equals $(A/B)\,K$. Assuming a subsistence wage rate for labour ($\underline{w}$) and the return to capital to be $\tilde{r}$, the total factor payment will be

$$(\tilde{r} + \underline{w}\,A/B)K$$

and total profit amounts to

$$AK - (r + \underline{w}\,A/B)K.$$

With this interpretation, profit maximization leads to $(\tilde{r} + \underline{w}\,A/B) = A$ rather than $r = A$. In other words, A represents here a payment to the composite factor of production. Given $\underline{w}$, it is possible to solve for $\tilde{r} = A - \underline{w}\,A/B$. The existence of a perfectly competitive capital market in the face of fixed coefficients of production, allows for the determination of the joint return to the two factors as the marginal product of capital alone. The actual return to capital depends on the level of subsistence wages.

Summary

1. Arrow (1962) and Frankel (1962) offered theories of technological progress which amounted to learning by doing. A society's exposure to capital improved the efficiency of labour working across the economy. The reason underlying a rise in labour efficiency was thus explained. This viewpoint allowed for the determination of the rate of technological progress, and hence the rate of per capita growth, endogenously. However, it was still the supply side that dominated and manipulation of demand parameters through profit taxation or a change in preference

did not have any impact on the rate of growth. The rate of growth did not respond to policy changes.

2. In this class of models, the social rate of return to capital diminishes with rising capital. But it exceeds the private rate of return. There is therefore a positive spill-over element across firms, but it is external to the firms thereby allowing perfectly competitive markets to sustain the Private Economy. In the Command Economy, however, the planner internalizes the externality. As a result, the equilibrium capital-effective labour ratio in the long run is higher for the Command Economy. However, the Command Economy grows at the same rate as the Private Economy. By taxing labour and subsidising capital, it is possible to sustain the socially optimum capital accumulation path as a market driven equilibrium.

3. d'Autume and Michel (1993) demonstrated that the endogenous rate of growth turns susceptible to policy changes in the learning by doing model if the social rate of return to capital accumulation is a constant. In this case, the endogenously determined rate of growth can be affected by policy. Also, the Command Economy's socially optimal growth rate exceeds the Private Economy's growth rate. A tax-subsidy scheme will now be able to move the Private Economy's rate of growth towards the Command Equilibrium. The model does not allow for out of balanced growth behaviour.

4. Romer (1986) allowed for increasing social returns from capital formation through the learning channel. However, he distinguished physical from knowledge capital and held knowledge capital to be responsible for labour augmentation. Knowledge is accumulated through a research technology that employs the investible surplus generated in final good production. The total stock of knowledge enters the production of the final consumption good technology as a costly input, though it is a free input in the production of knowledge itself. Thus, Romer's model is driven by two important factors. First, a strong Arrow type learning effect and second a knowledge accumulation technology. Knowledge itself is a partially excludable public good. On account of the powerful learning effect, the economy cannot grow at a balanced rate. While capital and effective labour grow for ever, the capital to effective labour ratio approaches a zero value asymptotically.

5. Leontief's fixed coefficients technology allows for interesting out of balanced growth dynamics in a Planned Economy. In the long run, depending on parameter specifications, the economy can grow at a balanced rate with either excess capital or excess labour. The excess labour case led us to consider a special class, the AK models of endogenous

growth. Such models do not allow for out of balanced growth dynamics and can be interpreted to involve two factors of production used in fixed proportion, with excess supply of one factor. Perfectly competitive capital markets can operate in this case, but the returns to the factors need to be carefully interpreted. Except for the single factor interpretation, the return to capital is not the same as the marginal product of capital.

6. The growth models Harrod (1939) and Domar (1946) are often interpreted as examples of the fixed coefficient technology model. This interpretation is not correct. Harrod was concerned with a razor's edge balanced growth path that was highly unstable and Domar studied the possibility of the growth of excess capacity and obsolescence with capital accumulation.

Problems

1. Derive equation (3.12).

2. Derive equation (3.17).

3. With reference to equation (3.16), discuss if the parameters of the Arrow model described in Sections 3.2.2 and 3.2.3 need to be restricted to ensure meaningful solutions.

4. Consider the Frankel (1962) model which assumes $A = K/L$. Work out the Private and Command Economy balanced growth rates for this case. Discuss the relationship between the two rates.

5. Use the pair of equations (3.23) to derive (3.24). You do not need to specify the exact functional form of Φ.

6. Consider the following extension of the production function (3.2) (based on Dasgupta and Marjit (2004)):

$$Y = F(K, K^\alpha C^{1-\alpha} \bar{L}).$$

This function attempts to capture an externality additional to Arrow's K^α. Development economists have often argued that the quality of life itself has a labour efficiency improving role in production. In the function above, the level of C is used as an index of the quality of life. Assume that the model satisfies all other Solow assumptions, except that L is assumed to be a constant.

(i) Calculate the Private Economy equilibrium rate of balanced growth for this model.

(ii) Calculate the Command Economy equilibrium rate of balanced growth for this model.

(iii) How does the Command Economy equilibrium differ from the Private Economy equilibrium?

(iv) How does a rise in the discount rate ρ for this model affect the growth rates? Interpret your answer.

7. Read Barro and Sala-i-Martin, Economic Growth, Second Edition, Section 1.4 and compare with our treatment of the fixed coefficient model in this book.

8. (Based on Barro and Sala-i-Martin, Economic Growth, Second Edition, Chapter 4.) Assume that the production function for the firm i is

$$Y_i = AK_i^\alpha L_i^{1-\alpha} K^\lambda,$$

where $0 < \alpha < 1, 0 < \lambda < 1$.

(i) What is the balanced growth rate of Y, K and C in this model if $\lambda < 1 - \alpha$ and L is a constant.

(ii) If $\lambda < 1 - \alpha$ and L grows at the rate $n > 0$, what is the balanced growth rate of Y, K and C?

Chapter 4

Technical progress as a Conscious Economic Activity-I: Human Capital Formation

4.1 Resource Allocation for Technological Advancement

By now, we are reasonably familiar with economic models of growth for which the balanced growth rates are determined by endogenous forces. Chapter 2 taught us why the only sustainable rate of growth of per capita GDP would be identically the same as the rate of technical progress in the long run. The conclusion was unsatisfactory inasmuch as the Solow model had little to offer by way of explaining the nature of technical progress itself. This did not reduce the importance of the Solow exercise, since it contained a valuable insight on the role of diminishing returns in connecting up the rate of capital accumulation with the rate of growth of the effective labour force. Chapter 3 was a preliminary attempt to build up a theory of technical progress by appealing to Arrow's learning by doing hypothesis. As we saw, capital accumulation was by itself expected to have a labour enriching effect. Between two societies, one that had a larger stock of physical capital was likely to be characterised by a more efficient labour force. While this gave rise to a theory of Harrod-neutral technical progress, it suffered from the drawback that it assigned to physical capital accumulation a primary status, of which technical progress turned out to be a passive by-product. Casual empiricism suggests, on the other hand, that causality runs in the reverse direction. Usually, conscious and costly efforts devoted to the discovery of novel methods of production lead to the construction of a piece of physical machinery or equipment in which the new technology is embedded.

In plain terms, changes in the variable A measuring technical progress might appear to be the end point of a consciously driven discovery process, which in turn dictates the choice of the physical capital accumulation path. Since any *discovery* involves a deliberate effort (i.e., the shouldering of economic costs) on the part of a potential *discoverer*, technological progress should strictly speaking be thought of as a productive activity geared towards the harnessing of scarce economic resources needed to *produce* $\dot{A}$. The present chapter and Chapter 6 will be concerned with adding flesh to this bare skeleton of an idea. We shall spin alternative stories to guide the theoretical construction of models that recognise technical progress as a conscious economic activity.

There are two major differences between the two chapters. The first relates to the concrete form we shall imagine the discovery process to assume. The present chapter will mostly interpret it to mean labour skills acquired through the use of resources diverted away from the production of consumption or physical capital goods. Acquisition of novel skills by individuals (by spending time, a vital economic resource, in educating themselves) constitutes an awakening of dormant abilities and should count as self-discovery, a transformation of unskilled manpower to a skilled work force or *human capital*. Chapter 6 will view technical progress as a process of knowledge creation (or discovery once again) through R & D. This will introduce a distinction between physical and knowledge (as opposed to human) capital.[1]

The second difference arises from the fact that all the models described in these two chapters will be concerned with the specification of *technologies for technological progress*. A fundamental question that comes up in this context is whether there are technological limits to technical progress itself. In other words, is the rate of technical change producible by rational economic agents constrained by technological fac-

---

[1]The last chapter presented the Romer (1986) model, which was a preliminary attempt at conceptualising knowledge capital. Chapter 6 will carry this idea forward by viewing knowledge capital as a vitally important ingredient for the creation of an array of specialised inputs that improves the technology. An alternative paradigm will imagine knowledge as adding variety to the menu of commodities consumed by the household, thereby adding directly to utility.

tors? Models in this chapter will recognize finite bounds on the rate of technical progress. Chapter 6 will present a more optimistic view of the matter and argue that bounds on technical progress arise, not due to technological reasons, but on account of scarcity of specialised resources which may conceivably be removed over time.[2]

We shall formalise human capital in this chapter in different ways. One way, to be introduced in Section 4.3, will be to broaden the definition of physical capital and interpret it as a composite of physical and human capital. An alternative approach shall be to look at the value of AL at any point of time t as the prevailing stock of human capital and changes in it considered investment in this form of capital. (Sections 4.2 and 4.4.) A common feature shared by all the models of this chapter is that they incorporate two production sectors as opposed to the single commodity framework adopted in the last three chapters (with the sole exception of the Romer (1986) model). The broadened scope of technology in the present chapter will occasionally bring with it two state variables corresponding to two accumulable factors of production. It will also add to the number of control variables. (Note that Romer (1986) was a two sector economy, but there was a single state variable (K) and a single control variable (c).) The appearance of several control and state variables calls for extensions of the scope of optimisation techniques developed in Chapter 2. Consequently, the necessary tools for the purpose will need to be forged in this chapter. (See Sections 4.2.2, 4.2.3 and 4.2.4.)

4.2 A Two Sector Model of Growth: Rebelo-I

We shall begin with Rebelo's (1991) contributions to the area. To motivate his work, let us go back to the Solow model which demonstrated that there were two essential barriers to endogenising the growth rate: (a) diminishing returns to factors of production and (b) an exogenously specified growth rate of the composite factor AL. Rebelo shows that it is the *simultaneous* presence of both conditions that rules out endogeneity. That is, the growth rate can be endogenously determined provided any one of the two conditions is dispensed with. We shall illustrate this by means of two models. The first satisfies (a) but not (b)

---

[2]Recall from Chapter 3 that the d'Autume-Michel model had the latter characteristic. A rise in the stock of the labour force led to improvements in the equilibrium growth rate.

and the second retains (b) at the cost of a partial removal of (a). The two exercises will establish a trade off between the two Solow conditions from the point of view of endogenous growth theory and illustrate in a transparent manner the barest structural needs of an endogenous growth model.

As already indicated, we will move out of the single sector scenario of the previous chapters for both exercises. Rebelo's first model requires us to take this step since one must now specify an additional technology for 'producing the factor whose growth was left to exogenous factors in the Solow model. As far as the second model goes, one of the sectors considered has an AK structure of the type discussed in the last chapter, while the other involves a Solow technology as well as an exogenously given factor supply. Despite the latter, the AK forces dominate, thereby de-linking the growth rate from exogenous factors. Thus, the two sectors in the second Rebelo model are required to emphasise the power of the AK assumptions. The present section describes Rebelo's first model.[3]

4.2.1   Description of the Economy

There are two producible commodities, of which the first is similar to the Solow commodity that may be either consumed by the household or invested for physical capital formation. (Notice that Romer (1986) had a similar sector, but did not permit one to one transformation of the investment good into physical capital.) The second represents an additional investment good, used to build up stocks of other forms of capital. Let us denote physical capital by K as before. The second capital good, T, may be identified as human capital or the stock of skills embodied in the available labour force. [4]

The technology for the first sector is given by:

$$Y = C + \dot{K} = A(\nu\ K)^{\gamma}(u\ T)^{1-\gamma}, \qquad (4.1)$$

where ν and u stand for the shares of K and T employed in the Y-sector. Given that human capital is embodied in labourers, the factor T should have a form similar to Solow's AL, where A may be interpreted as education per worker. The technology for producing Y resembles the Solow production function, since $T = AL$. In what follows, however, we shall

---

[3]For a general treatment of two sector endogenous growth, see Bond et al (1996).

[4]Chapter 5 will deal with a similar model, but instead of interpreting the second good as human capital, it will look upon it as infrastructure.

continue to abstract from growth in L (in line with some of the exercises in Chapter 3) and concentrate attention entirely on the growth of education. This serves to trace back the source of growth to endogenous factors determining the dynamics of T. The second sector, to be referred to as the T-sector, will be viewed as producing a commodity that may be used only to add to the existing stock of T. Since T is human capital, the product of the T sector may be interpreted as new education and/or research output that helps to augment T. Accordingly, the output of the T sector will be denoted by $\dot{T}$ and the technology given by

$$\dot{T} = B((1-\nu)K)^{\beta}((1-u)T)^{1-\beta}, \tag{4.2}$$

where $1-\nu$ and $1-u$ are the shares of K and T employed in this sector. The important characteristic of the T-sector lies in the recognition it accords to the fact that human capital is an indispensable resource in the production of human capital. (The shares in the two sectors for each factor input add up to unity, i.e., either the market or a planner ensures that all resources are fully employed at each instant of time.)

The fact that we are ignoring the separation of T into A and L, forces us to define all relevant rates of growth in absolute rather than per capita terms. Thus, in what follows, $g_K = \dot{K}/K$, $g_T = \dot{T}/T$ and $g_C = \dot{C}/C$.[5]

4.2.2 Balanced growth in Two-Sector Economies

We shall mostly restrict our analysis to balanced growth paths alone. However, the study of balanced growth paths in the presence of two state variables requires an extension of the definition employed in earlier chapters. Since T replaces AL, the first natural requirement to impose for balanced growth is that

$$\frac{\dot{K}}{K} = \frac{\dot{T}}{T}$$

$$\text{i.e.,} \quad \frac{K}{T} = constant. \tag{4.3}$$

Both sectors employ K and T, however. Hence, we shall impose the above requirement on each sector in isolation also. That is, a second requirement for balanced growth in the current two-sector framework will be

---

[5]Strictly speaking, we are concerned here with the growth of C/L. However, L being a constant, it is enough to concentrate on the growth of C alone.

$$\frac{\nu\ K}{u\ T} = constant$$

$$\text{and} \quad \frac{(1-\nu)\ K}{(1-u)\ T} = constant. \tag{4.4}$$

4.2.3   Private and Command Economies

Private accumulation of T is best viewed as an activity carried out by the household as part of its optimisation exercise. In other words, we shall imagine that agent H decides on the allocation of the stock of human capital it owns for its own augmentation. The decision cannot be separated from the simultaneous choice of the share of T to be employed in the Y-sector. The logical implication is that production decisions in the Y-sector must also be thought of as a part of the household's optimisation exercise. So conceived, the Private Economy will not distinguish between H and B and turn into a representative household firm.[6] In our previous exercises, the planner was viewed as solving an overall optimisation exercise and we did not distinguish between supply and demand rates of growth. In the present problem, the household's behaviour is identical with that of the planner. Hence, we have to separate out different parts of the planner's exercise to isolate demand from supply.[7]

The household solves the problem

$$\text{Maximise} \int_0^\infty \frac{C^{1-\theta} - 1}{1 - \theta} e^{-\rho\ t} dt$$

subject to 4.1 and 4.2.

Since this way of viewing the Private Economy amounts to removing the distinction between the Private and Command Economies, the two economies will end up with the same optimal paths *by definition*.

Unless essential, we shall drop the time argument attached to variables for notational simplicity. Denoting the prices of K and T, measured in utils, by ξ and η respectively, profit maximisation requires that the values of marginal products of each type of capital be equalised across sectors:

---

[6]Note that the Romer (1986) model was treated similarly in the last chapter. As opposed to that exercise however, there are no externalities in Rebelo's model.

[7]See Barro (1990) for another example of the household firm structure.

$$\xi \, \gamma \, A \, (\nu \, K)^{\gamma-1} \, (u \, T)^{1-\gamma} \;=\; \eta \, \beta \, B \, ((1-\nu) \, K)^{\beta-1}$$
$$\times ((1-u) \, T)^{1-\beta}, \tag{4.5}$$

$$\xi \, (1-\gamma) \, A \, (\nu \, K)^{\gamma} \, (u \, T)^{-\gamma} \;=\; \eta \, (1-\beta) \, B \, ((1-\nu) \, K)^{\beta}$$
$$\times ((1-u) \, T)^{-\beta}. \tag{4.6}$$

Dividing (4.5) by (4.6),

$$\frac{\gamma}{1-\gamma} \, \frac{u \, T}{\nu \, K} = \frac{\beta}{1-\beta} \, \frac{(1-u) \, T}{(1-\nu) \, K}. \tag{4.7}$$

We do not know as yet the equilibrium values of $uT/\nu K$ or $(1-u)T/(1-\nu)K$. Consequently, the market rate of interest is unknown. However, under the assumption of balanced growth, viz. (4.3) and (4.4), the rate of interest is a constant, since it depends on factor ratios under constant returns to scale. Since $\dot{T}/T$ and $(1-\nu)K/(1-u)T$ are constants,

$$\frac{\dot{T}}{T} = g_T^s = B \, \left(\frac{(1-\nu)K}{(1-u)T}\right)^{\beta} (1-u) \tag{4.8}$$

implies u is a constant. Hence, according to (4.7), ν is a constant also. Consider now the macro identity

$$\frac{C}{K} + \frac{\dot{K}}{K} = A \, \nu \, \left(\frac{uT}{\nu K}\right)^{1-\gamma}.$$

Under balanced growth, ν as well as the factor intensity on the RHS and $g_K^s = \dot{K}/K$ on the LHS are constants. Hence, $g_C^s = \dot{C}/C = g_K^s = $ constant.

   To solve for the demand rate of growth, let $V(K(t), T(t))$ stand for the optimal level of aggregate utility obtainable during (t, ∞) starting from $(K(t), T(t))$. Along an optimal accumulation path, $\partial V/\partial K$ and $\partial V/\partial T$ must equal the prices of $K(t)$ and $T(t)$, viz., $\xi(t)$ and $\eta(t)$. Equation (A2.1.6) continues to hold with essential changes in details. We reproduce this below:

$$V(K(t), T(t)) \;\cong\; max_{C(t)} \, \{h \, u(C(t))$$
$$+ V(K(t+h), T(t+h))\}. \tag{4.9}$$

For an optimum *wrt* C (assuming reversible investment),

$$\frac{h \ \partial u(C(t))}{\partial C(t)} + \frac{\partial V(K(t+h), T(t+h))}{\partial C(t)} = 0, \tag{4.10}$$

where

$$\begin{aligned}
\frac{\partial V(K(t+h), T(t+h))}{\partial C(t)} &= \frac{\partial V(K(t+h), T(t+h))}{\partial K(t+h)} \\
&\quad \times \frac{\partial K(t+h)}{\partial C(t)} \\
&\quad + \frac{\partial V(K(t+h), T(t+h))}{\partial T(t+h)} \\
&\quad \times \frac{\partial T(t+h)}{\partial C(t)}.
\end{aligned} \tag{4.11}$$

Linearising,

$$K(t+h) \ \cong \ K(t) + h \ \dot{K}(t),$$

$$T(t+h) \ \cong \ T(t) + h \ \dot{T}(t).$$

Using the facts that $\dot{K}(t) = A(\nu \ K(t))^{\gamma}(u \ T(t))^{1-\gamma} - C(t)$ and $T(t)$ is independent of $C(t)$, (4.11) reduces to

$$\begin{aligned}
\frac{\partial V(K(t+h), T(t+h))}{\partial C(t)} &= -h \ \xi(t+h) \\
\\
&= -\xi(t) \left(h + h^2 \ \frac{\dot{\xi}(t)}{\xi(t)} \right) \\
\\
&\cong -h \ \xi(t) \text{ (for small } h\text{).}
\end{aligned}$$

Equations (4.10) now implies that

$$C^{-\theta} = \xi \tag{4.12}$$

at each point of time. Equation (4.12) corresponds to static optimality.

    We move over now to dynamic optimality conditions. The social cost of a unit of investment in K at t is $\xi(t)$. The social return to the investment at any $s > t$, given the optimal values of ν and u, is

$\xi(s)\partial Y(s)/\partial K(s) + \eta(s)\partial \dot{T}(s)/\partial K(s).^{8}$ In order for the investment to break even, the discounted present value of the stream of returns will equal $\xi(t)$. Thus,

$$\xi(t) = \int_{t}^{\infty} \left\{ \xi(s)\frac{\partial Y(s)}{\partial K(s)} + \eta(s)\frac{\partial \dot{T}(s)}{\partial K(s)} \right\} e^{-\rho(s-t)}ds, \qquad (4.13)$$

or, taking account of the explicit forms of the production functions,

$$\begin{aligned} \xi(t) \;=\; & \int_{t}^{\infty} \{\gamma\nu A(\nu K)^{\gamma-1}(uT)^{1-\gamma}\xi(s) \\ & + \beta(1-\nu)B((1-\nu)K)^{\beta-1}((1-u)T)^{1-\beta}\eta(s)\} \, e^{-\rho(s-t)}ds. \end{aligned}$$

$$(4.14)$$

The time derivative of (4.14) yields, using (4.5),

$$\begin{aligned} \dot{\xi}(t) \;=\; & -\gamma\nu A(\nu K)^{\gamma-1}(uT)^{1-\gamma}\xi(t) \\ & -\beta(1-\nu)B((1-\nu)K)^{\beta-1}((1-u)T)^{1-\beta}\eta(t) + \rho\xi(t) \\ \;=\; & -\gamma A(\nu K)^{\gamma-1}(uT)^{1-\gamma}\xi(t) + \rho\,\xi(t). \qquad (4.15) \end{aligned}$$

The demand rate of growth, viz. equation (2.39) is obtained easily by manipulating equations (4.12) and (4.15).

To determine the equilibrium growth rate, we must find the equilibrium value of $r = r^{*}$. The solution involves several steps. Let us first use (4.6) and the parallels of (4.14) and (4.15) for η to get

$$\begin{aligned} \dot{\eta}(t) \;=\; & -(1-\gamma)uA(\nu K)^{\gamma}(uT)^{-\gamma}\xi(t) - (1-\beta)(1-u)B \\ & \times ((1-\nu)K)^{\beta}((1-u)T)^{-\beta}\eta(t) + \rho \\ \;=\; & -(1-\beta)B((1-\nu)K)^{\beta}((1-u)T)^{-\beta}\eta(t) + \rho\,\eta(t). \end{aligned}$$

$$(4.16)$$

Equations (4.15) and (4.16) constitute a two sector counterpart of (2.9) of Chapter 2. Substituting (4.5) in (4.14), we get

$$\xi(t) = \int_{t}^{\infty} \gamma A(\nu K)^{\gamma-1}(uT)^{1-\gamma}\xi(s) \, e^{-\rho(s-t)}ds. \qquad (4.17)$$

---

[8]Note that we agreed in Chapter 1 to drop the depreciation parameter Chapter 3 onwards.

Under balanced growth, $\gamma A (\nu K)^{\gamma - 1} (uT)^{1-\gamma} = constant$. Thus, for $\xi(t)$ to be well-defined

$$e^{-\rho t} \ \xi(t) \to 0 \text{ as } t \to \infty. \tag{4.18}$$

A parallel argument shows that

$$e^{-\rho t} \ \eta(t) \to 0 \text{ as } t \to \infty. \tag{4.19}$$

Finally, differentiating (4.5) and recalling that factor intensities are constant along a balanced growth path, it follows that $\dot{\xi}/\xi = \dot{\eta}/\eta$. Using this in conjunction with (4.15) and (4.16), we see that

$$\gamma \ A \ \left(\frac{u \ T}{\nu \ K} \right)^{1-\gamma} = (1 - \beta) \ B \ \left(\frac{(1 - u) \ T}{(1 - \nu) \ K} \right)^{-\beta}. \tag{4.20}$$

is satisfied. Equations (4.7) and (4.20) may be solved for the factor intensity levels $u \ T/\nu \ K$ and $(1 - u) \ T/(1 - \nu) \ K$ in balanced growth equilibrium. This determines the constant equilibrium value of r^*. Thus, g_C^s is perfectly horizontal at $r = r^*$. Substituting for r^* in (2.39), we obtain the equilibrium rate of growth g^* for the Private Economy.[9]

We may now utilise (4.8) to solve for u. Next, ν is found using the equilibrium value of $uT/\nu K$ and $(1 - u)T/(1 - \nu)K$. Plugging in the equilibrium values of u, ν and $g_T^s = g^*$ in (4.8), an equilibrium value of T/K follows. There is no guarantee of course that the arbitrarily given initial value of T_0/K_0 would equal the balanced growth equilibrium value of T/K. This gives rise to a stability problem somewhat similar to the one faced by the original Solow model. As will be recalled, in that model, balanced growth fixed the value of K/AL. However, the initial value $K_0/A_0 L_0$ being specified in an ad hoc manner, it was necessary to argue that any equilibrium path starting from $K_0/A_0 L_0$ would converge to the balanced growth value of K/AL.[10] The stability analysis for the Rebelo I model will be more complicated than the one developed for the Solow model, since the economy is now characterised by two sectors of production rather than one. This book will not concern itself with stability problems in general, though it is a serious issue and cannot be ignored altogether. Consequently, Chapter 5 will present a stability analysis for a two-sector model of growth sharing some of the features of the Rebelo-I model. Readers interested in the stability properties of the original Rebelo exercise will find a clear analysis in Chapter 5 of Barro & Sala-i-Martin (2003).

---

[9]By definition of balanced growth, $g_C^s = g_K^s = g_T^s$. Therefore, (4.8) implies that g_C^s takes values in the set $(0, B((1-\nu)K/(1-u)T)^\beta)$. This puts some obvious restrictions on the parameters of the model.

[10]Chapter 3 presented examples of models that avoided this problem altogether.

PROPOSITION **4.1** *The two-sector Rebelo model of growth with physical and human capital allows for the endogenous determination of the balanced rate of growth of the economy. The balanced growth equilibrium has associated with it a fixed value of the ratio of physical and human capital stocks. Consequently, the model calls for out of balanced growth dynamics.*

4.2.4 The Hamiltonian Approach

We may represent the above results in compact form by referring to the Hamiltonian function

$$\mathcal{H}(C, \nu, u, \xi.\eta, K, T) = u(C) + \xi \dot{K} + \eta \dot{T}.$$

For a path $\{C, \nu, u, \xi, \eta, K, T\}_0^\infty$ to be optimal, it is necessary that

$$\frac{\partial \mathcal{H}(C, \nu, u, \xi, \eta, K, T)}{\partial C} = 0,$$

$$\frac{\partial \mathcal{H}(C, \nu, u, \xi, \eta, K, T)}{\partial \nu} = 0,$$

$$\frac{\partial \mathcal{H}(C, \nu, u, \xi, \eta, K, T)}{\partial u} = 0,$$

$$\frac{\partial \mathcal{H}(C, \nu, u, \xi, \eta, K, T)}{\partial \xi} = \dot{K},$$

$$\frac{\partial \mathcal{H}(C, \nu, u, \xi, \eta, K, T)}{\partial \eta} = \dot{T}. \tag{4.21}$$

Equations (4.15) and (4.16) are rewritten

$$\dot{\xi} = -\frac{\partial \mathcal{H}}{\partial K} + \rho \xi \quad \text{and}$$

$$\dot{\eta} = -\frac{\partial \mathcal{H}}{\partial T} + \rho \eta. \tag{4.22}$$

Finally, the two transversality conditions (4.18) and (4.19) are satisfied.

4.3 A Two Sector Model of Growth: Rebelo-II

4.3.1 Description of the Economy

The earliest version of a neoclassical two-sector growth model which Rebelo's second model resembles goes back to Uzawa (1961b and 1963). It draws a physical distinction between the consumption good C and investment good $\dot{K}$.[11] Rebelo retains this contrast but replaces Uzawa's technology for producing the investment good by an AK production function.

The factors of production are divided up into technologically reproducible and non-reproducible groups, say, K and L. The former is a composite of physical and human capital, while the latter will be referred to as unskilled labour, or simply labour. The non-reproducibility of L ($=\bar{L}$, say) implies the existence of diminishing returns to the variable factor K. As already noted, Rebelo establishes the possibility of endogenous growth despite this fact. The two sectors produce respectively an investment good (I) (which is qualitatively the same as the composite of physical and human capital) and a consumption good (C). Since labour is explicitly brought back, we may once again speak of per capita consumption c. However, $L = \bar{L}$ implies c is (effectively) identical with C. The investment good is produced by the non-sector specific composite capital good (K) using an AK technology

$$I = b(1 - \nu)K, \tag{4.23}$$

where b is a technological constant and $1 - \nu$ the endogenously determined share of capital used for producing I. The linearity of the production function for I, hence the absence of diminishing returns, may be explained as follows. Diminishing returns is caused by a disproportionate use of one or more factors relative to others. Thus, in the Solow model, diminishing returns to capital in producing Y could arise when increasing quantities of capital were combined with a fixed amount of labour. In the Rebelo model on the other hand, K has already been

---

[11]Retracing our steps back to the Solow model, the one for one transformation of saving into investment might appear to be too narrow a representation of the production of capital goods. In Uzawa's framework, the traditional macro separation of GDP between consumption and saving is replaced by a division of resources allocated for consumption and investment goods production. The most general multisector model of economic growth goes back to von Neumann (1945-6). The reader should try and compare this approach with Romer (1986).

interpreted as a combined factor of production. Thus, (4.23) represents the production of a *vector* of human and physical capital (symbolised by I) by means of yet another *vector* of human and physical capital (symbolised by K), where the ratio of human to physical capital is a constant and identically the same for I and K.[12] Diminishing returns will not arise under the circumstances, since the two factors are being employed in the same proportion. The consumption good is produced by a Cobb-Douglas technology using K and $\bar{L}$:

$$C = B(\nu K)^\gamma \bar{L}^{1-\gamma}, \tag{4.24}$$

where B is a constant. As before, we shall be concerned with determining the balanced growth rate of the economy. Since there is a single capital good, but two sectors which use it, the definition of balanced growth reduces to the requirement that

$$\frac{\dot{K}}{K} = constant \tag{4.25}$$

$$\frac{(\nu \dot{K})}{\nu K} = constant. \tag{4.26}$$

4.3.2 The Private Economy

In the absence of (4.24), i.e., if the model had a single sector with (4.23) as the technology, the supply curve would be infinitely elastic at the level b.[13] On the other hand, if (4.24) represented an *aggregate* production function as in Solow, the supply curve would be perfectly inelastic, passing through a point determined by the exogenously given rate of growth of natural resources (zero, in Rebelo's case, since $L = \bar{L}$). The simultaneous existence of the two sectors in Rebelo, however, leads to a supply curve that lies in between the two extremes.

Under competition, profit maximising firms will ensure that capital is allocated across sectors to equate the (value of) its marginal productivity for every t. In other words,

$$p\,b = \gamma B(\nu K)^{\gamma-1} \bar{L}^{1-\gamma}, \tag{4.27}$$

---

[12]Of course, the last section has already demonstrated that it is possible to analytically separate out physical and human capital.

[13]This is typical for the AK technology and follows from the fact that the marginal productivity of K, which equals the rate of interest, is a constant b irrespective of the level of K. We saw an instance of this phenomenon in Section 3.3.2.

where p represents the price of K relative to C. Dividing both sides of (4.27) by p, we see that although the marginal productivity of K falls in the C-sector, its value measured in units of K remains a constant. For this to happen, $1/p$ rises (i.e., p declines) in the same proportion as the fall in the marginal product of K in the C- sector, which helps avoid the depressing effects of diminishing returns. Differentiation of (4.27) (given a constant ν) yields

$$g_p = \frac{\dot{p}}{p} = (\gamma - 1)g_K^s, \tag{4.28}$$

where g_K^s is the supply rate of growth of K, since the derivation of this rate of growth of K does not involve any demand side arguments. The RHS of (4.28) represents the rate of fall of marginal productivity in the C-sector. This is a constant under balanced growth, i.e., when g_K^s is a constant. Thus, g_p is a constant under balanced growth. Equation (4.24) implies that g_C^s satisfies

$$g_C^s = \gamma g_K^s,$$

which, using (4.28), implies

$$g_C^s = \frac{\gamma}{\gamma - 1} \, g_p.$$

It is possible to reduce g_C^s to a function of the rate of interest. To do so, we must invoke a second no arbitrage condition signifying equilibrium asset holding by the household. Notice that this means appealing to household equilibrium conditions to derive the supply rate of growth. This amounts to mixing up supply and demand factors. However, as shown below, the no arbitrage condition requires knowledge of market parameters alone and, to that extent, can be internalised by the firms.

Going over to the said condition now, the household should be indifferent between holding capital assets in the two sectors. Denote the rate of return at s from holding a unit of capital employed in the C-sector by $r_C(s)$. (Note that the ultimate objective being to derive the balanced growth path, we assume ν to be a constant.) On the other hand, the own rate of return in the I-sector is b. In order to be indifferent between assets in the two sectors, the Household should satisfy a condition parallel to (2.11). Hence, using the arguments used to derive (2.11),[14] we have

$$\dot{p}(t) = -b \, p(t) + r_C(t) \, p(t). \tag{4.29}$$

---

[14]A unit of investment in either sector at time t costs $p(t)$. A unit of investment in the I-sector at t leads to a stream of returns $p(s)b \, \forall \, s > t$. For the investment to break even, the discounted present value of the stream must equal $p(t)$ and the discount

Dividing out by $p(t)$, we obtain

$$r_C(t) = b + g_p(t). \tag{4.30}$$

Substituting this in the expression for g_C^s, we end up with

$$g_C^s = g_C^s(r_C) = \frac{\gamma(b - r_C)}{1 - \gamma}. \tag{4.31}$$

This downward falling function of r_C is the Rebelo supply rate curve for C.

As far as the demand rate of growth is concerned, the household maximises

$$\int_0^\infty u(C(t))\, e^{-\rho\, t} dt$$

subject to

$$C + pI = r_C K + w\bar{L}.$$

We may solve this problem using the Hamiltonian function

$$\mathcal{H} = u(C) + \xi\, \frac{r_C K + w\bar{L} - C}{p}.$$

The necessary conditions of optimum are

$$C^{-\theta} = \frac{\xi}{p}$$

and

$$\dot{\xi} = -\frac{\partial \mathcal{H}}{\partial K} + \rho\xi$$

$$= -\frac{\xi r_C}{p} + \rho\xi.$$

---

rate used for the purpose stands for the *rate* of return to a unit of investment in the *I*- sector. The latter rate must be equal to $r_C(s)$ for the household to be indifferent between investing in the two sectors. Thus, the second no arbitrage condition boils down to

$$p(t) = \int_t^\infty p(s)\, b\, e^{-\int_t^s r_C(x)dx} ds,$$

which, differentiated with respect to t, yields (4.29).

The last two equations along with (4.27) and (4.30) imply (2.39). The equilibrium value of g_C, say g_C^*, is determined as before by the intersection of the demand and the supply rate curves. Thus,

$$g_C^* = \frac{\gamma(b - \rho)}{1 - \gamma(1 - \theta)}. \tag{4.32}$$

Also, using $g_C^s = \gamma\, g_K^s$,

$$g_K^* = \frac{(b - \rho)}{1 - \gamma(1 - \theta)}. \tag{4.33}$$

The determination of equilibrium is shown in Figure 4.1 below. It is easy to see from the diagram that the condition for a positive rate of equilibrium growth is $b > \rho$. Writing $Y = C + pI$, the equilibrium rate of growth of Y is $g_Y^* = g_C^* = \gamma g_K^*$.

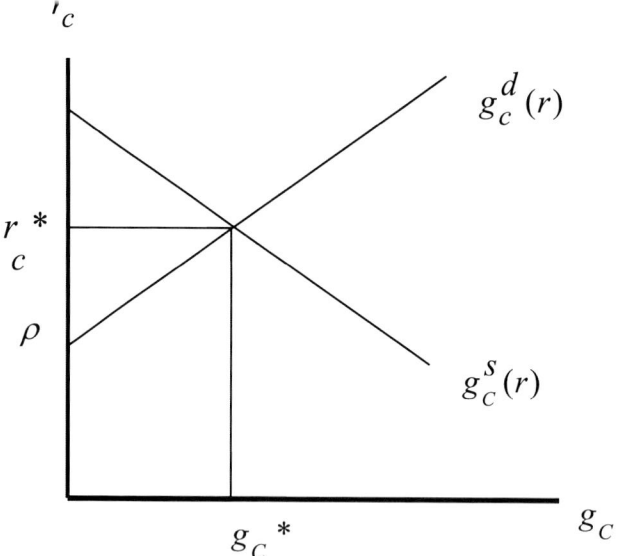

Figure 4.1: Equilibrium in the Rebelo-II Economy

The variable ν showing the allocation of K between the two sectors was left indeterminate. This is found from (4.23) which shows that the supply rate of growth of capital satisfies

$$g_K^s = \frac{\dot{K}}{K} = b\,(1 - \nu).$$

Unlike Rebelo I, the present model does not admit any out of balanced growth dynamics. To see this, observe that substitution of the equilibrium value of ν and K_0 in (4.24) yields the initial value of C_0 uniquely. Starting from this value and with K growing at the rate g_K^*, consumption grows at the equilibrium balanced rate g_C^* forever.

Rebelo's results may be summarised as follow:

PROPOSITION **4.2** *Even in the presence of strong diminishing returns in parts of the economy, balanced growth capital accumulation is possible at an endogenously chosen rate so long as there is a subsector of the economy which produces capital goods by using capital goods alone and there are perfectly functioning asset markets. All other sectors into which the capital good enters as an input and where production is carried out under diminishing returns, adjust to this rate of growth through a continuous fall in the relative price of capital goods. The model does not admit out of balanced growth dynamics.*

The astute reader will not fail to note that the equilibrium rates of growth in (4.32) and (4.33) do not depend on the level of the fixed factor $\bar{L}$. This is a shortcoming of the Rebelo II exercise, for one would intuitively expect $\bar{L}$ to act as a shift variable, whose increase boosts the rate of growth of the system. The idea of a shift variable affecting the rate of growth plays a major role in the growth models of Chapters 6 and 7. Recent research has looked deeply into this aspect of growth models and Dinopoulos and Sener (2003) offers a lucid summary.

4.3.3 The Command Economy

Denote the shadow price $\partial V/\partial K$ of K by ξ. There is a single control variable ν for the problem. As before,

$$V(K(t)) \cong max_{(\nu_{t,t+h})} \{h\, u(C(t)) + V(K(t+h))\}, \qquad (4.34)$$

where $(\nu_{t,t+h})$ denotes the truncated path $\{\nu(s)\}_t^{t+h}$.[15] An optimum *wrt* ν requires

$$\frac{h\, \partial u(C(t))}{\partial \nu(t)} + \frac{\partial V(K(t+h))}{\partial \nu(t)} = 0, \qquad (4.35)$$

---

[15] The notation was introduced in Appendix 2.1 in the Proof of the Principle of Optimality.

where

$$\frac{\partial V(K(t+h))}{\partial \nu(t)} = \frac{\partial V(K(t+h))}{\partial K(t+h)} \cdot \frac{\partial K(t+h)}{\partial \nu(t)} \tag{4.36}$$

Linearising,

$$K(t+h) \cong K(t) + h \; \dot{K}(t).$$

Using (4.23), (4.36) reduces to

$$\frac{\partial V(K(t+h))}{\partial \nu(t)} = - \; \xi(t) \; h \; b \; K.$$

Also, (4.24) shows that $h \; \partial u(C)/\partial \nu = h \; u'(C) \; B \; \gamma \; (\nu \; K)^{\gamma-1} \; K \; \bar{L}^{1-\gamma}$. Thus, (4.35) gives

$$u'(C) \; B \; \gamma \; (\nu \; K)^{\gamma-1} \; \bar{L}^{1-\gamma} = \xi \; b. \tag{4.37}$$

As far as the dynamic restriction on ξ goes, the social cost at t of a unit of investment at t is ξ. The discounted present value of the stream of returns is

$$\int_t^\infty \{\nu \; u'(C) \; B \; \gamma \; (\nu \; K)^{\gamma-1} \; \bar{L}^{1-\gamma}$$

$$+ (1-\nu)\xi b\} \; e^{-\rho(s-t)}ds \;\; = \;\; \int_t^\infty \xi b e^{-\rho(s-t)}ds,$$

given (4.37). Equating cost and benefit and differentiating, we get

$$\dot{\xi} = -\xi \; b + \xi \; \rho.$$

Thus,

$$\frac{\dot{\xi}}{\xi} = - \; b + \rho. \tag{4.38}$$

Differentiating (4.37) *wrt* to t and using (4.38),

$$-\theta \; \frac{\dot{C}}{C} + (\gamma - 1) \; \left(\frac{\dot{\nu}}{\nu} + \frac{\dot{K}}{K} \right) = - \; b + \rho.$$

Under balanced growth, ν is a constant. Equation (4.24) implies $\dot{K}/K = (1/\gamma) \; \dot{C}/C$ as before. Substituting this into the last equation, we obtain the rate of growth of C to be identically the same as (4.32). This establishes that in balanced growth equilibrium, the Private Economy succeeds in attaining the Command Economy growth path. Hence, the socially optimal growth path is decentralisable, as was the case in Proposition 4.1. The derivation of the results of this section with reference to the Hamiltonian function is left as an exercise.

A drawback of this model arises from the AK specification of (4.23). It is easy to see that the rate of growth of K for the system is bounded above by b, a technological parameter. The model to be considered in the next section suffers from a similar restriction. Chapter 6 will present attempts to solve this problem, though we have come across simple structures in the previous chapter also which link the ultimate limitation on the growth rate to scarce resources alone.[16]

4.4 Human Capital Formation: The Uzawa-Lucas Approach

4.4.1 Description of the Economy

To the extent that Rebelo I and Rebelo II typify two alternative approaches to modelling human capital accumulation (or, more generally, consciously generated technical progress), one expects to come across models that occupy an intermediate position between them. Two such exercises go back to Uzawa (1965) and Lucas (1988). To appreciate these contributions, let us return to Rebelo I but retain the AK aspect of Rebelo II by replacing (4.2) of Rebelo I by (4.23):

$$\dot{T} = b(1 - \phi)T, \tag{4.39}$$

where $1 - \phi$ stands for the share of human capital engaged in producing additions to its own stock. (Instead of justifying the AK structure of (4.39) by appealing to a composite factor as in Rebelo II, we are merely *assuming* a linear technology.) However, human capital has other uses, as in Rebelo I. Hence, a fraction ϕ of T is employed in producing the final good Y. The other input into that process is physical capital K, which, unlike Rebelo I, has no role to play in producing $\dot{T}$. The production function for Y is given by

$$Y = B(K)^{\gamma}(\phi T)^{1-\gamma}. \tag{4.40}$$

---

[16]It will be a worthwhile effort on the part of the reader to try and discover the factors explaining bounds on the growth rate for the remaining models of the present chapter.

Under balanced growth, the model will satisfy (4.26). With these specifications, we may proceed now to analyse the balanced growth equilibria
of the relevant Private and Command Economies.

4.4.2   Uzawa: The Private Economy

To begin with we shall present the basic outlines of the Uzawa approach.[17] The household's optimisation problem is assumed to be similar to that of Section 4.2.3. From (4.39), the own rate of return for T
is b. On the other hand, the real rate of interest r (on K) is

$$r = \gamma B(K)^{\gamma-1}(\phi T)^{1-\gamma}. \tag{4.41}$$

Let p stand for the price of T relative to Y. Then, an equation similar
to (4.27) must be satisfied. This is given by

$$b = \frac{(1-\gamma)BK^{\gamma}(\phi T)^{-\gamma}}{p}. \tag{4.42}$$

By virtue of the equality between g_K^s and g_T^s and the constancy of ϕ
under balanced growth, it follows that $g_p = 0$. Hence, the no arbitrage
condition relating to household's asset holdings turns out to be

$$r = b \tag{4.43}$$

and the supply curve is horizontal at the level $r = b$. Intersection with
the demand curve now determines the equilibrium rate of growth for the
Uzawa model. Since there are no externalities, the Private Economy's
behaviour does not differ from that of the Command Economy.

4.4.3   Lucas: The Private Economy

The above idea may be pushed further to elucidate Lucas (1988). The
latter introduces an Arrovian touch of externality to the Uzawa model
by recognising the fact that the production of human capital would
normally generate a positive spillover for society as a whole, but in
particular on simultaneously operated production processes, such as the
technology for producing Y. For example, interactions with educated
members of the population outside the workplace could lead to better
utilisation of all resources. Thus, the production function for Y is written

$$Y = BK^{\gamma}(\phi T)^{1-\gamma}T^{\alpha}, \tag{4.44}$$

---

[17]This is a simplified version of the Uzawa paper and differs from it in details.

where T^α stands for the external effect. The accumulation of human capital continues to be governed by (4.39). Defining r to be the real rate of interest as above, it follows that

$$r = \gamma B(K)^{\gamma-1}(\phi T)^{1-\gamma}T^\alpha. \qquad (4.45)$$

Under balanced growth, differentiation of (4.45) gives

$$g_T^s = \frac{1-\gamma}{1+\alpha-\gamma}g_K^s. \qquad (4.46)$$

The basic macro identity requires

$$\frac{C}{K} + \frac{\dot{K}}{K} = B(K)^{\gamma-1}(\phi T)^{1-\gamma}T^\alpha.$$

The constancy of the RHS under balanced growth implies as before that C and K grow at the same rate. In other words,

$$g_C^s = g_K^s. \qquad (4.47)$$

In a *private* economy, entrepreneurs would ignore the externality caused by T^α in computing the marginal product of T in the Y-sector. Thus, for such an economy, the equality of the values of marginal products of T leads to

$$p\,b = (1-\gamma)BK^\gamma\phi^{-\gamma}T^{\alpha-\gamma}, \qquad (4.48)$$

which, on differentiation and substitution from (4.46) and (4.47) yields

$$g_p = \frac{\alpha}{1-\gamma+\alpha}\,g_C^s. \qquad (4.49)$$

As in Rebelo II, r and b must be related according to

$$r = b + g_p.$$

Substituting this in (4.49), the equation for the supply rate of growth follows. Thus,

$$g_C^s(r) = \frac{(1-\gamma+\alpha)}{\alpha}(r-b).$$

Combining with the demand rate of growth,[18] the equilibrium rate of growth of C turns out to be

$$g_C^* = \frac{(1+\alpha-\gamma)(b-\rho)}{\theta(1+\alpha-\gamma)-\alpha}. \qquad (4.50)$$

---

[18]It will be useful for the reader to derive the expression for the demand rate for this model.

Finally, using (4.46), it follows that

$$g_T^* = \frac{(1-\gamma)(b-\rho)}{\theta(1+\alpha-\gamma)-\alpha}. \tag{4.51}$$

To the extent that $1 \geq \phi \geq 0$, equation (4.39) implies, like Rebelo II, that the maximum rate of growth of human capital possible in the Lucas model is given by b. This in turn puts an upper bound on g_C also, viz. $b\,(1+\alpha-\gamma)/(1-\gamma)$, since $g_C = ((1+\alpha-\gamma)/(1-\gamma))g_T$.

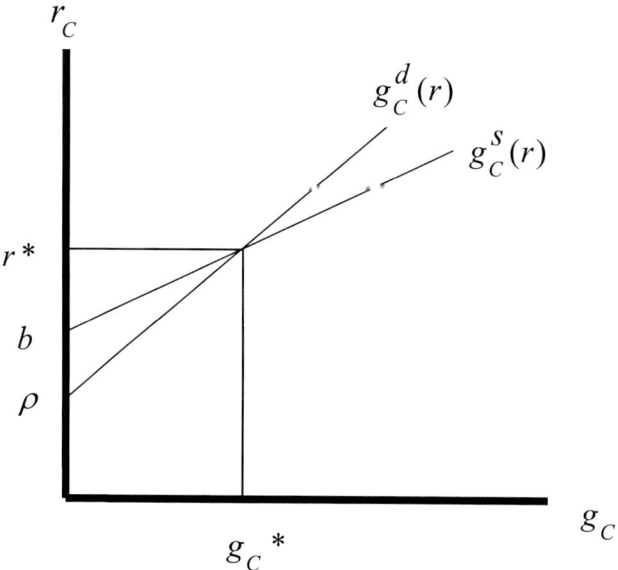

Figure 4.2: Lucas: Private Economy

The demand and supply curves as well as the equilibrium rates of interest and growth are depicted in Figure 4.2. The supply curve is drawn under the assumption of a positive externality. In case the latter is negative, the curve *could* be downward sloping.[19] A possible set of sufficient conditions for positive solutions to exist is

(i) The curve $g_C^s(r)$ in Figure 4.2 is flatter than the curve $g_C^d(r)$, i.e., $\alpha/(1+\alpha-\gamma) < \theta$;
and

---

[19]Balanced growth equilibrium, as in the case of Rebelo I, fixes the value of K/T, thus bringing up the question of stability of the equilibrium path. The issue has been analysed by Arnold (1997) and Xie (1994).

(ii) the intercept of $g_C^s(r)$ on the r axis in Figure 4.2 > intercept of $g_C^d(r)$, i.e., $b > \rho$.

4.4.4   Lucas: The Command Economy

Our discussion of the Rebelo I model treated the Private Economy problem from the Command Economy perspective. We reverse that procedure now and present the planner's exercise as one solved by a Private Economy that is aware of all externalities. Since the planner will internalise the effect of T^α in (4.44), the production function for Y is given by

$$Y = BK^\gamma(\phi T^{(1+\alpha-\gamma)/(1-\gamma)})^{1-\gamma}.$$

or alternatively, as

$$Y = BK^\gamma(\phi T')^{1-\gamma}, \tag{4.52}$$

where $T' \equiv T^{(1+\alpha-\gamma)/(1-\gamma)}$. The substitution of T by T' in the production function, thus reducing it to one free of external effects, merely expresses the fact that the planner takes account of the social productivity of T rather than its private productivity as in (4.44). Given this change, the planner's technology for producing Y is formally equivalent to that of a private producer faced with (4.52) rather than (4.44).

To complete the model, one needs to specify the technology for producing $\dot{T}'$. This is done by differentiating T' with respect to t and using (4.39) to get

$$\dot{T}' = \frac{1+\alpha-\gamma}{1-\gamma} b (1-\phi)T'. \tag{4.53}$$

Equations (4.52) and (4.53) accord to the Command Economy exactly the same structure as the Uzawa economy described by (4.39) and (4.40) above. The conclusions that applied to that economy, must hold here also. The planner will compute the real rate of interest r as

$$r^{**} = \frac{1+\alpha-\gamma}{1-\gamma} b, \tag{4.54}$$

which is the exact counterpart of (4.43). Thus, in the Command Economy, the supply curve is horizontal[20] at the level $r = [(1+\alpha-\gamma)/(1-\gamma)]b$. The equilibrium is depicted in Figure 4.3.

---

[20]There is now no change in the relative price. The Command Economy is aware of the true social productivity of T'. As a result, the marginal product of T' is unchanging along the balanced growth path.

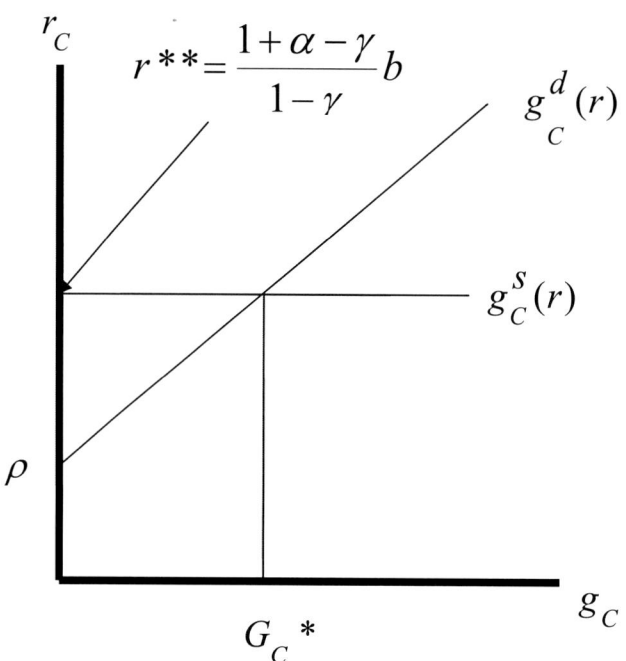

Figure 4.3: Lucas: Command Economy

It is easy to see that (4.46) and (4.47) are satisfied by the Command Economy also. Using this fact, the equilibrium growth rates of C and T work out to

$$G_C^* = \theta^{-1} \left(\frac{b(1 + \alpha - \gamma)}{1 - \gamma} - \rho \right) \tag{4.55}$$

and[21]

$$G_T^* = \theta^{-1}(b - \frac{\rho(1 - \gamma)}{1 + \alpha - \gamma}). \tag{4.56}$$

A sufficient condition for a positive solution to G_C^* to exist now is that

$$r^{**} = b \left(\frac{1 + \alpha - \gamma}{1 - \gamma} \right) > \rho.$$

In order to compare the two rates

$$g_T^* = \frac{(1 - \gamma)(b - \rho)}{\theta(1 + \alpha - \gamma) - \alpha}$$

---

[21]The derivation of G_T^* uses (4.46)

and

$$G_T^* = \frac{(1-\gamma)(b-\rho) + b\alpha}{\theta(1+\alpha-\gamma)},$$

note first that meaningful solution to the two problems require that both rates be bounded above by b. Imposing this restriction on g_T^* and G_T^* by turn, we can easily see that in each case the following common inequality is satisfied:

$$\theta \geq 1 - \frac{(1-\gamma)\,\rho}{(1+\alpha-\gamma)\,b}.$$

This inequality may also be written as

$$\theta\,b\,(1+\alpha-\gamma) - (1-\gamma)(b-\rho) \geq \alpha\,b. \qquad (4.57)$$

Noting now that

$$G_T^* - g_T^* = \frac{\alpha\{\theta\,b\,(1+\alpha-\gamma) - (1-\gamma)(b-\rho)\} - \alpha^2\,b}{\theta(1+\alpha-\gamma)\{\theta(1+\alpha-\gamma) - \alpha\}},$$

it follows that human capital accumulation will be faster for the Command Economy than in the Private Economy whenever (4.57) is satisfied as a strict inequality.[22] Using this conclusion along with (4.46) and (4.47), it follows that

$$G_C^* \;>\; g_C^*,$$

$$G_K^* \;>\; g_K^*.$$

Thus, as with previous models, the existence of positive externalities implies further that the rates of growth of C and K for the Command Economy are higher than those of the Private Economy

Lucas' results are summarised as[23]

PROPOSITION **4.3** *In a model of endogenous human capital formation along with accumulation of physical capital, the growth rate of the system is endogenously determined by the parameters of the preference function and technology. In the presence of a positive spillover effect generated by human capital formation, the equilibrium rates of growth of consumption, physical capital as well as human capital for the Command Economy dominate those for the Private Economy.*

---

[22]For meaningful solutions, the strict inequality alone must hold, or else the Y-sector produces nothing.

[23]The Lucas model too raises questions relating to the stability of out of balanced growth paths. Barro and Sala-i-Martin (2003), Chapter 5 deals with this issue in detail.

We end by noting that the present chapter has recognized a form of savings that is fundamentally different from the Solow notion in that it takes the form of allocating resources away from the production of final goods for the sake of human capital development. It is this form of savings that plays a vital role in determining the rate of growth of the economy. We shall come across this idea of savings repeatedly in the rest of the book.

Summary

1. We came across technical change as a conscious economic activity in Chapter 3 in connection with the Romer (1986) exercise. In this connection we also encountered the notion of human capital as opposed to physical capital. This chapter pursues the idea further.

2. As with Romer (1986), we were concerned once again with technical change as a conscious economic activity.

3. The chapter introduces the reader to two sector models of endogenous growth involving two state variable. In particular, the Rebelo-I model is used, in the same way the Solow model was used in Chapter 2, to derive the necessary conditions of dynamic optimization for two sector models.

4. Rebelo (1991) identifies two sources of endogenous growth rate. First, one may give up the assumption of an exogenously growing factor, retaining the CRS production function. Second, Rebelo-II shows that despite the presence of strong diminishing returns, the growth rate of the model will be endogenously determined, so far as one of the sectors of the economy has an AK structure.

5. Two other well-known models of endogenous growth, due to Uzawa (1965) and Lucas (1988), are shown to be simple applications of the Rebelo logic. Further, the Command Economy exercise due to Lucas turns out to be equivalent to Uzawa's model.

Problems

1. (Based on Aghion and Howitt (1998)). Replace the Solow production function by

$$Y = K^\alpha T^{1-\alpha},$$

where T stands for accumulable human capital (as in Rebelo-I and Lucas). A proportion of income s_k is invested on physical capital and s_T in human capital. The depreciation rates for the two forms of capital are δ_k and δ_T.

(i) Use an appropriate no arbitrage condition (See Rebelo) to find the equilibrium ration of K and T. (ii) Show that the production function can be written in the AK form and find the growth rate.

2. (Based on Barro and Sala-i-Martin (2003)). Augment the model in problem 1 by assuming that the rates s_k and s_T are chosen endogenously. The instantaneous utility function is (2.18) and the aggregate welfare is represented by (2.1). Show as in problem 1 once again that the production function can be written in the AK form and find the growth rate.

3. Solve problem 1 by replacing the production function by the CES production function

$$Y = \{a(bK)^{\psi} + (1-a)((1-b)T)^{\psi}\}^{1/\psi}$$

where where $0 < a < 1$, $0 < b < 1$, and $\psi < 1$.

4. Can you solve problem 2 using the production function of problem 3?

5. Read Uzawa (1961——– and S. Marjit (2004) 'Consumption, Quality of Life and Growth', Discussion Paper No. ERU 2002–12, Kolkata Indian Statistical Institute, (Revised).

—— (2004) 'Public Infrastructure and Sustainable Growth in a Small Open Economy with and without Foreign Direct Investment', *Arthabeekshan*, Vol. 14: 11–26. b) and (1965).

6. Read Rebelo (1991).

7. Read Lucas (1988) and (1990).

Chapter 5

Growth and Infrastructure

5.1 Introduction

The last two chapters have identified several different factors that may affect the (endogenous) growth rate of a macro-economy. The two most important amongst these consisted of viewing technolgical improvement (a) as a learning by doing process (Arrow (1962) and Frankel (1962)) and (b) as human capital accumulation (Lucas (1988), Rebelo (1991) and Uzawa (1965)). Both learning by doing as well as human capital creation are addressed in one way or the other to the problem of dissemination of technological knowledge. The scarcity of such knowledge constitutes a serious constraint on economic growth and we have seen how a relaxation of the constraint causes economic growth. Along with these, yet another serious constraint on the growth potential of developing economies assumes the form of inadequate infrastructure. This chapter utilizes the techniques developed in Chapters 3 and 4 to address this issue.

Infrastructure could assume a variety of forms, starting from clean environment to road networks, power supply and so on. The predominant characteristic of infrastructure consists of the fact that a single piece of infrastructure, such as an airport or a railway station, can cater to the needs of many producing organizations at the same time. Put dramatically, it is an input that can be simultaneously used by parallely running productive activities. This is particulary evident in the case of environment viewed as infrastructure. It has properties common to pure public goods, non-rivalry and non-excludability. Such infrastructure is comparable to free television programmes for which there is no restriction on the number of individuals who watch it. In the Indian case, Doordarshan TV is the obvious example. However, more often than not, infrastructure is not a pure public good. This is obviously the case for road networks, power plants and so on. There is a limit on the number of trucks that can carry commodities between producing firms and the markets. The power supply too has capacity restriction. Thus, most infrastructure is both rival as well as excludable. As a result, it is characterized by scarcity.

On the other hand, to make a growing economy take advantage of any given infrastructure, the latter must itself grow in order to handle the growing demand from firms, the latter growing in number as well as size. Most policy makers in developing economies are aware of the need to develop infrastructure in the interest of growth. Infrastructure growth, therefore, is a *sine qua non* for economic development. Accordingly, this chapter is devoted to studying the links between growth and infrastructure. In what follows, we shall introduce infrastructure in two different forms, a flow (such a clean environment) and a stock (such as public highways). The first of these will be based on the works of Barro (1990) and Barro and Sala-i-Martin (2003). The second will present stock models of infrastructure based on Dasgupta (1999, 2004) and Dasgupta and Shimomura (2006). From the point of view of modelling, the structure of the flow infrastructure model will share features of the one sector models of Chapter 3. The stock model on the other hand will try to extend the Rebelo-I model of Chapter 4.

5.2 Flow Infrastructure: Growth with a Public Input

We proceed now to Barro and Sala-i-Martin (2003), who studied the role of public inputs in growth.[1] We visualise identical household producers indexed by i, each endowed with the production function

$$Y_i = A \, L_i^{1-\alpha} \, K_i^\alpha \, \Gamma^{1-\alpha}, \tag{5.1}$$

where A is a constant, Y_i, L_i and K_i have standard meanings and Γ stands for the aggregate *flow* of a public input supplied free of user cost by the government. As is obvious from (5.1), Γ has the classic features

---

[1]While the treatment of this section is influenced strongly by Barro and Sala-i-Martin (2003), they are closely related to Barro (1990), where public inputs are accorded the status of private rather than public goods.

of a public good, non-rivalry and non-excludability. For concreteness, we may refer to Γ as infrastructure.

5.2.1   The Private Economy

As with the preceding models of the chapter, L_i will be assumed to be a constant and normalised to unity. However, the reader should note that the size of L_i will have a positive comparative statics effect on the rate of growth of the system as in those same models. The public input is provided out of tax revenue generated by a proportional tax $\tau \in [0, 1]$ imposed on aggregate output $Y = \sum Y_i = N\, Y_i$, assuming that there are N identical firms in the economy. Under these conditions, the aggregate output is

$$Y = NAK_i^\alpha \Gamma^{1-\alpha}. \tag{5.2}$$

Thus,

$$\Gamma = \tau\, Y,$$

$$= (\tau\, N\, A)^{1/\alpha}\, K_i, \tag{5.3}$$

using (5.2) to cancel out the term $\Gamma^{1-\alpha}$. Equations (5.2) and (5.3) show that Y/Γ and Γ/K_i have fixed and known values given a fixed τ. Consequently, Y/K_i is also fixed and known. Firms maximize $(1-\tau)\,Y_i - r\,K_i - w$, so that the market rate of interest equals

$$r = (1-\tau)\,\alpha\, A\, K_i^{\alpha-1}\, \Gamma^{1-\alpha}$$

$$= (1-\tau)\,\alpha\, A\, \left(\frac{\Gamma}{K_i}\right)^{1-\alpha}. \tag{5.4}$$

It follows from (5.3) and (5.4) that τ determines r independent of the rate at which the economy grows. Thus, appealing to arguments similar to those used in Section 3.2.5, the $g_c^s(r)$ function is perfectly elastic at a level determined by τ.[2] Solving for r as a function of τ from (5.4), the equilibrium rate of growth for the system is found then by substituting the value of r in the expression for g_c^d. The latter is calculated by maximising the aggregate utility[3] of any representative household subject to a budget constraint for each instant of time.

---

[2]Students should note the similarity with the d'Autume-Michel model.
[3]For the utility integral to be well-defined, the familiar condition $\rho + (\theta - 1)g > 0$ needs to be imposed. See problem 1 below.

Proceeding as before, $g_c^d(r)$ is given by (2.39). Equating with $g_c^s(r)$, the equilibrium growth rate is

$$g = \frac{r - \rho}{\theta}$$

$$= \frac{(1 - \tau) \, A \, \alpha \, (\Gamma/K_i)^{1-\alpha} - \rho}{\theta}. \tag{5.5}$$

Substituting (5.3), the last equation reduces to

$$g = \frac{\alpha \, A^{1/\alpha} \, N^{1-\alpha/\alpha} \, (1 - \tau) \, \tau^{1-\alpha/\alpha} - \rho}{\theta} \tag{5.6}$$

The equilibrium rate of growth g is responsive now to policy specifications, viz. the choice of the tax rate τ, which is equivalent to choosing the size of the government Γ/Y. Hence, it is important to specify the value of τ optimally. Two alternative policy objectives suggest themselves, maximisation of the growth rate and maximisation of welfare. We take these up in turn.

Growth Rate vs. Welfare Maximisation in a Private Economy

Note from (5.3) that $1/\tau = N \, A \, (K_i/\Gamma)^{\alpha}$. Thus, a rise in the tax rate has two opposing effects on the growth rate. First, by lowering K_i/Γ (See (5.4)), it raises the marginal productivity of capital and hence affects the growth rate positively. This effect is captured by the term $\tau^{1-\alpha/\alpha}$ in (5.6). Secondly, as of given K_i and Γ, a higher τ lowers the net return from investment in capital accumulation, as shown by the expression $(1 - \tau)$ in (5.6). For low levels of the tax rate, the first effect dominates, while the second effect takes over at higher rates. It is easy to check by differentiating (5.6) with respect to τ that the growth maximising tax rate is $\tau^* = 1 - \alpha$. Consequently, the maximum rate of growth for the Private Economy is

$$g^* = \frac{\alpha \, (A^{1/\alpha} \, N^{1 \, \alpha/\alpha} \, \alpha \, (1 - \alpha)^{1-\alpha/\alpha}) - \rho}{\theta}. \tag{5.7}$$

At this value of τ, the size of the government is $\Gamma/Y = 1 - \alpha$, which has the implication that it satisfies a natural condition for efficient resource allocation at each point of time. To appreciate this fact, differentiate Y in (5.2) with respect to Γ and use $\Gamma/Y = 1 - \alpha$ to get

$$\frac{\partial Y}{\partial \Gamma} = (1 - \alpha) \, A \, N \, K_i^{\alpha} \, \Gamma^{-\alpha}$$

$$= (1 - \alpha) \frac{Y}{\Gamma}, \quad \text{using (5.2)}$$

$$= 1. \tag{5.8}$$

Thus, the instantaneous marginal benefit of a unit of Γ is unity.[4] On the other hand, the instantaneous social marginal cost of a unit of Γ is measured by a unit withdrawal of Y from consumption and/or capital formation. Comparing with (5.8), we see that the marginal social cost and return are equated, thereby guaranteeing the aforementioned static efficiency condition.

Despite the distortion introduced by the proportional tax rate therefore, the growth maximising tax rate satisfies an efficiency property, given the assumed Cobb-Douglas form of the technology. This leads us to expect that the growth maximising tax rate may have other optimality properties too. To verify this intuition, we move on to the alternative policy objective for the government, viz. maximisation of welfare. Under balanced growth, $c_i(t) = c_{i0}\, e^{gt}$. Consequently, using

$$c_i + \dot{K}_i = (1 - \tau)\, Y_i,$$

$$c_i(t) = K_{i0}\, e^{g\,t} \left(\frac{(1 - \tau) Y_{i0}}{K_{i0}} - g \right). \tag{5.9}$$

As was the case in Section 3.2.7, the Private Economy is in perpetual balanced growth equilibrium and no out of balanced growth dynamics is warranted by the model. This can be seen from the fact that Y_{i0}/K_{i0} has a fixed known value, so that c_{i0} is uniquely known once K_{i0} is specified.

Next, integrating the welfare function, note that along a balanced growth path, the household's welfare equals (except for a neglected constant term)

$$U = \frac{c_{i0}^{1-\theta}}{1 - \theta} \frac{1}{\rho - (1 - \theta)g}. \tag{5.10}$$

Use (5.1) and (5.5) to see that

$$(1 - \tau)\frac{Y_i}{K_i} = \frac{g\theta + \rho}{\alpha}.$$

---

[4]It is important to note that the marginal benefit has no intertemporal connotation. If Γ were an accumulable input, then an extra unit of Γ would raise marginal productivity forever, as was the case in Section 2.1.1. In the present exercise, however, Γ is a pure flow that is instantaneously used up. We shall present a different view of the nature of infrastructure in Section 5.4.

Moreover, substituting for $(1-\tau)Y_i/K_i - g$ in (5.9), it follows that

$$c_{i0} = K_{i0}\left(\frac{\rho}{\alpha} - \left(1 - \frac{\theta}{\alpha}\right)g\right).$$

Substituting for c_{i0} in (5.10),

$$U = \frac{K_{i0}^{1-\theta}}{1-\theta}\frac{(\rho/\alpha - (1-\theta/\alpha)g)^{1-\theta}}{\rho - (1-\theta)g}. \tag{5.11}$$

Differentiating with respect to g and using

$$\frac{\rho}{\alpha} - \left(1 - \frac{\theta}{\alpha}\right)g > \rho - (1-\theta)g > 0,$$

we conclude that U is increasing in g. This means that, as conjectured, a growth rate maximising tax rate is also welfare maximising in the Private Economy. [5]

PROPOSITION **5.1** *A perpetually maintained proportional tax rate on output determines the balanced growth rate for the infrastructure driven Private Economy. A balanced growth rate maximising tax rate exists. For the Cobb-Douglas production structure, a growth rate maximising tax rate maximises the aggregate welfare for the Representative Household. So long as the tax rate is held constant, the economy does not exhibit out of balanced growth dynamics.*

5.2.2 Command vs. Private Economy

As with our earlier exercises, we proceed now to isolate the external effects in the Private Economy. This calls for a reintroduction of the Command Economy.idcommand ecom. The social planner would view the aggregate production function as

$$Y = \sum Y_i$$

$$= A\left(\frac{\Gamma}{K_i}\right)^{1-\alpha}(N\,K_i). \tag{5.12}$$

---

[5]Barro (1990) shows that this result does not hold for a general production function. Futagami et al (1993) prove a similar result for a two-sector stock version of the Barro model.

Two facts should be noted about this representation of the function. First, along any balanced growth path, Γ/K_i is a constant. Since the omniscient planner is aware of this fact, he will calculate the *social* marginal product of capital as $\partial Y/\partial(NK_i) = A\ (\Gamma/K_i)^{1-\alpha}$. Thus, the social marginal product of K_i exceeds the private marginal product $\alpha\ A\ (\Gamma/K_i)^{1-\alpha}$. Secondly, the former is only a gross measure of productivity of capital. For, the constancy of Γ/Y implies that a unit increase of Y requires Γ to be increased by Γ/Y units. Thus, out of each unit of extra Y brought forth by increased K_i, the planner must divert a fraction Γ/Y towards the maintenance of Γ/Y. Therefore, the *net* social marginal product of capital is $(1-\Gamma/Y)\ A\ (\Gamma/K_i)^{1-\alpha}$ Manipulating (5.2) now, express $A\ (\Gamma/K_i)^{1-\alpha}$ as $A^{1/\alpha}\ N^{1-\alpha/\alpha}\ (\Gamma/Y)^{1-\alpha/\alpha}$ and the *net* social marginal product of capital as $A^{1/\alpha}\ N^{1-\alpha/\alpha}(1-\Gamma/Y)(\Gamma/Y)^{1-\alpha/\alpha}$. Taking these facts into account, the equilibrium rate of growth for the Command Economy is

$$G^{\cdot} = \frac{A^{1/\alpha}\ N^{1-\alpha/\alpha}\ (1-\Gamma/Y)(\Gamma/Y)^{1-\alpha/\alpha} - \rho}{\theta}, \qquad (5.13)$$

if Γ/Y is the size of the government. Recall now the efficiency condition $\Gamma = (1-\alpha)\ Y$, which the planner would necessarily satisfy. Using this knowledge, we conclude that the Command Economy growth rate is

$$G^* = \frac{A^{1/\alpha}\ N^{1-\alpha/\alpha}\ \alpha\ (1-\alpha)^{1-\alpha/\alpha} - \rho}{\theta}, \qquad (5.14)$$

As expected, $G^* > g^*$. One may explain this phenomenon by the fact that the planner, being aware of the constancy of Γ/Y, internalises the *social* marginal productivity of capital, which the private entrepreneur cannot. The result is that the gross marginal product of capital for the social planner equals its average productivity $A\ (\Gamma/K_i)^{1-\alpha}$, whereas for the private entrepreneur, it equals the marginal product $\alpha\ A\ (\Gamma/K_i)^{1-\alpha}$. Under concavity, the former exceeds the later.[6]

It is important to find out if there is any other tax regime that can sustain G^* within the market framework. Barro and Sala-i-Martin show that a lump sum tax on the household achieves the objective. Suppose then that the sole intervention by the government in the market economy takes the form of a lump sum tax equal to Δ at each point of time. Then, the household's budget constraint reduces to

$$c_i + \Delta_i + \dot{K}_i = Y_i.$$

---

[6]It may be shown now that the welfare maximising tax rate for the Command Economy also equals $1-\alpha$.

Since the entire income Y_i accrues to the household, Δ_i may also be viewed as a lump sum consumption tax. There is no wedge now between the value of the firm's output and the household's income. Thus, the demand rate of growth is given by

$$
g_{lump}^d = \frac{\partial Y_i / \partial K_i - \rho}{\theta},
$$

$$
= \frac{\alpha \, A \, (\Gamma / K_i)^{1-\alpha} - \rho}{\theta},
$$

where the subscript '*lump*' indicates that the tax is lump sum. We have already seen (while deriving (5.13)) that

$$
A \, (\Gamma / K_i)^{1-\alpha} = A^{1/\alpha} \, N^{1-\alpha/\alpha} \, (\Gamma / Y)^{1-\alpha/\alpha}.
$$

Hence, by choosing $\Gamma = \sum \Delta_i = (1 - \alpha) \, Y$, the expression for g_{lump}^d reduces to G^*.

PROPOSITION **5.2** *The Command Economy grows faster than the Private Economy. The growth rate for the Command Economy can be decentralised by means of a lump sum tax.*

5.3 Growth, Public Input and Congestion

Barro and Sala-i-Martin (2003) extend their model of the previous section to consider the possibility that the available infrastructure might cause congestion as aggregate output rises relative to a fixed level of infrastructure. The congestion might show up as aggregate output Y rises with increases in K_i in the face of a given level of Γ. In this case, the rise in output will be constrained by the scarcity of Γ relative to Y. A production function that captures this property is

$$
Y_i = A \, K_i \, f\left(\frac{\Gamma}{Y}\right), \tag{5.15}
$$

where $f' > 0$, $f'' < 0$ and $Y = \sum Y_i$. The functional form implies the property noted above. As K_i rises, output Y_i rises linearly as of given Γ / Y. However, Y increases with Y_i, which depresses Y_i unless Γ increases.

5.3.1   The Private Economy: Proportional Tax

With reference to the previous exercises, it is straightforward to see that the Private Economy's growth rate is

$$g = \frac{A\,(1-\tau)\,f(\tau) - \rho}{\theta},\qquad(5.16)$$

where τ stands for the proportional tax rate, or, what amounts to the same thing, the size of the government Γ/Y, and the market rate of interest equals the tax distorted private marginal product of capital $(1-\tau)Af(\tau)$. If the government chooses a tax rate to maximise the rate of growth of the Private Economy, then the optimal tax rate τ^* satisfies

$$f(\tau) = (1 - \tau)\,f'(\tau).\qquad(5.17)$$

Condition (5.17) in turn implies that the natural condition of static efficiency, viz. $\partial Y/\partial \Gamma = 1$ is satisfied. To check this, note that

$$\frac{\partial Y}{\partial \Gamma} = A\,K\,\frac{f'(\tau)}{Y}\left\{1 - \tau\,\frac{\partial Y}{\partial \Gamma}\right\},$$

where $K = NK_i$. Solving this equation for $\partial Y/\partial \Gamma$,

$$\frac{\partial Y}{\partial \Gamma} = \frac{f'(\tau)}{f(\tau) + \tau\,f'(\tau)},$$

which, under condition (5.17), yields $\partial Y/\partial \Gamma = 1$.

5.3.2   Command Economy Optimum

Given any size of the government Γ/Y, the planner would, using arguments for the no congestion case, choose the growth rate

$$G = \frac{A\,(1-\Gamma/Y)\,f(\Gamma/Y) - \rho}{\theta}.\qquad(5.18)$$

A minimal condition of optimality that the planner should satisfy is $\partial Y/\partial \Gamma = 1$. On the other hand, this would mean that the optimal value of Γ/Y for the Command Economy is the solution τ^* to (5.17). That is, the Command Economy will choose the growth rate of the Private Economy corresponding to the optimal proportional tax rate. The interesting feature of this result (which depends crucially on the fact that (5.15) is linear in K_i for fixed Γ/Y is that the proportional tax distorted growth rate for the Private Economy is the best growth rate from the Command Economy's point of view also.

Indeed, quite opposite to the no congestion model, the Command Economy growth rate is not decentralisable with a lump sum tax. Under a lump sum tax, the Private Economy will grow at the rate

$$g^d_{lump} = \frac{A\ f(\Gamma/Y) - \rho}{\theta}. \tag{5.19}$$

Comparing equations (5.18) and (5.19), it is straightforward that if the value of Γ/Y is chosen to satisfy the efficiency condition (5.17), the Private Economy will grow at a rate that is higher than the optimal rate chosen by the Command Economy. In other words, unlike the case without congestion, the Private Economy will grow at an excessively high rate under lump-sum taxes if it has to satisfy the condition of efficient resource allocation, viz. $\Gamma/Y = \tau = \tau^*$. The Command Economy solution is therefore not decentralizable by means of a lump sum tax. Alternatively, with a lump sum tax, the Private Economy *might* succeed in growing at the Command Economy's optimal growth rate $G = A\ (1 - \tau^*)\ f(\tau^*) - \rho/\theta$, but in order to do so, (5.19) shows that it must choose a value of $\Gamma/Y \neq \tau^*$. It may grow at the optimal *rate*, but to do so, resources will have to be allocated suboptimally. (This can happen, for example, if the levels of capital and Γ are higher and that of c lower than warranted.)

PROPOSITION **5.3** *In the Barro-Sala-i-Martin economy with congestion, the optimal growth path is decentralizable through proportional taxation. A lump-sum tax does not share this decentralization property.*

5.4   Growth with Stock Infrastructure

For most developing economies, infrastructure, viewed as stocks of public capital, constitutes a major constraint on growth. Shortage of infrastructure causes congestion and, as a result, a strong tendency for diminishing returns to capital in industry. The low rate of return so generated acts as a disincentive to investment. This implies a low rate of labour absorption, thus causing the vicious circle of poverty to perpetuate.

Infrastructure though is a bulky commodity, such as an airport, that calls for large investments of capital and long gestation lags to be created. Moreover, the service flows generated by infrastructure are often characterized by public good features, viz. non-rivalry and non-excludability, though the extent to which these characteristics are present could vary across services. Both the bulkiness as well as the public good properties act on the other hand as disincentives to private participation in its provision. Thus, while private capital is averse to penetrating industrial activities on account of insufficient infrastructure, it is wary of creating the necessary infrastructure for itself at the same time. It is precisely for this reason that one expects the government, which is not guided by any obvious (economic) profit motive, to play a major role in the accumulation of infrastructure.

This provides the broad outline of the theoretical problem to be discussed below. The model to be used will of course represent an abstraction, emphasizing certain features of reality and ignoring others. So, it is best not to interpret it as *the* representative model for any particular developing economy, even though it will be utilized to arrive at analytical conclusions about growth strategies.

5.4.1   The Model of a Mixed Economy

There are two sectors of production, denoted Y and G. Sector Y produces a (Solow (1956) type) consumption-cum-investment good Y. The output of sector G, written $\dot{G}$, is identically the same as investment in public capital or infrastructure. Commodity Y is produced under competitive conditions and investment in G is under government control. In this sense, the model represents a Mixed Economy. Both outputs are produced with the help of the services of private and public capital as well as semi-skilled labour, denoted by K, G and L respectively.

There is a surplus of semi-skilled workers available in unlimited amounts at a subsistence wage rate $\bar{w}$, *á la* Lewis (1954). Thus, by assumption, the absolute size of employable labour is very large. It is this fact rather than the precise rate of population growth that will motivate the modelling strategy to follow. Hence, the analysis will emphasize absolute magnitudes in preference to per capita values of variables. The government views accumulation of industrial capital as an important vehicle for employment generation. This is captured by assuming labour to be complementary with private capital. Thus, we may suppose that $L_i/K_i = \lambda = constant$, $i = y, g$ where y and g index the Y and G-sectors respectively.

Commodity Y is produced under competitive conditions. The services of G are supplied free of user charge. The government finances its purchases of private capital by imposing a lump-sum tax T on sector Y, which could vary across time points in the spirit of the discussion of such levies in Barro (1990) and Barro and Sala-i-Martin (2004). The entire tax revenue is spent on purchasing K at the market rate of interest. Thus, the government does not directly organize the production of infrastructure stocks. Instead, as is often the case for both developed as well as developing economies, it floats tenders to contract out production of infrastructure stocks (such as bridges or highways) to private capitalists. Note, however, that the demand for capital is restricted by the government's budget constraint. Hence, capital may not earn its marginal product in the G-sector, a potential source of inefficiency in the economy. Another inefficiency will arise from the shadow price for G underlying the lump-sum tax for the private sector.

Labour and capital being complementary, the single notation K may be employed to denote the joint input of the two factor services. Given this convention, technologies in the two sectors are represented by neoclassical production functions satisfying the Inada conditions. In particular, we write

$$
\begin{aligned}
Y &= G f_y(k_y) \\
&= G A_y k_y^\alpha, \ 1 > \alpha > 0; \quad (5.20) \\
\dot{G} &= G f_g(k_g) \\
&= G A_g k_g^\beta, \ 1 > \beta > 0, \quad (5.21)
\end{aligned}
$$

where $k_i = K_i/G$ is the factor intensity and K_i the capital allocation in the i-th sector, $i = y, g$.

Profit in the Y-sector is given by

$$
\Pi_y = Y - (r + \bar{w}\lambda)K_y - T. \quad (5.22)
$$

As with the joint input K, let us use r *wlog* to denote the term $r + \bar{w}\lambda$. Given the meaning assigned to r, the necessary *foc* for profit maximization is

$$
r = f_y'(k_y),
$$

$$= \alpha A_y k_y^{\alpha-1}. \tag{5.23}$$

It will be assumed that at each point of time the government fixes T at a level consistent with competitive shares. In other words,

$$\frac{T}{Y} = 1 - \alpha. \tag{5.24}$$

Since T is a lump sum, profit maximization ensures that irrespective of the quantum of K_y, the entire existing supply of the free input G will be used up by the Y-sector. The G-sector, though, is not a profit maximizer and is *assumed* to employ G to capacity. The value of the marginal product of G in sector Y is

$$q = (1 - \alpha) f_y(k_y). \tag{5.25}$$

Thus, in view of (5.24) and the fact that the Y-sector employs the entire available supply of G, it follows from Euler's Theorem that

$$T = qG. \tag{5.26}$$

However, q is merely an effective price underlying T. It may appear that (5.26) guarantees productive efficiency. This is not the case, since efficiency calls for the effective price to equal the *social* marginal productivity of the public good G. This matter will be taken up below.

Full employment of capital services implies that at each point of time t,

$$k(t) = k_y(t) + k_g(t), \tag{5.27}$$

where $k = K/G$. Moreover, appealing to (5.26) and (5.25), the government's budget constraint is written

$$\begin{aligned} rk_g &= \frac{T}{G} \\ &= q_y \\ &= (1 - \alpha) f_y(k_y). \end{aligned} \tag{5.28}$$

Dividing (5.28) by r, substituting from (5.23) and adding k_y to both sides, we have

$$k = \frac{k_y}{\alpha},$$

$$\text{or,} \quad k_g = \frac{1-\alpha}{\alpha} k_y. \qquad (5.29)$$

The savings rate at each t is chosen optimally by a dynastic household. As before, the latter is endowed with the welfare function

$$W = \int_0^\infty \frac{C(t)^{1-\sigma}}{1-\sigma} e^{-\rho t} \, dt, \qquad (5.30)$$

where $C(t)$ represents aggregate consumption[7] at point of time t, the constant ρ a positive discount parameter and $0 < \sigma \neq 1$ the elasticity of instantaneous marginal utility.[8] A large value of σ indicates a sharp fall in marginal utility in response to a rise in consumption. The household maximizes (5.30) subject to the instantaneous budget constraint

$$C + \dot{K} = rK. \qquad (5.31)$$

The solution to this problem leads to the choice of a demand rate of growth equal to

$$\frac{\dot{C}}{C} = \frac{r - \rho}{\sigma}. \qquad (5.32)$$

5.4.2   Existence of a Balanced Growth Equilibrium

We may now set out a reduced system of equations based on the above specifications. Define a new variable $x = C/G$. Then, (5.32) and (5.21) give rise to

---

[7] We do not follow our earlier practice of defining instantaneous utility as a function of per capita consumption. This re-emphasizes the Lewis feature of *unlimited* supply of workers.

[8] When $\theta = 1$, the function reduces to $\int_0^\infty \ln C(t) \, e^{-\rho t} d\,t$.

$$\dot{x} = x \left\{ \frac{r - \rho}{\theta} - f_g(k_g) \right\}. \tag{5.33}$$

Next, (5.31) and (5.21) yield

$$\dot{k} = k \left\{ r - \frac{x}{k} - f_g(k_g) \right\}. \tag{5.34}$$

At each t, equations (5.23), (5.27), (5.29), (5.33), and (5.34) are 5 equations in the 5 unknowns $k_y(t)$, $k_g(t)$, $r(t)$, $\dot{x}(t)$ and $\dot{k}(t)$ given $k(t)$ and $x(t)$. Thus, with the evolution of $k(t)$ and $x(t)$, the variables $\dot{k}$ and $\dot{x}$ keep changing. Sustainable balanced growth refers to a situation where the growth rates of all variables especially $C(t)$, $K(t)$ and $G(t)$ are constants and equal to one another, so that $\dot{k} = \dot{x} = 0$. Let us denote q^m to be the balanced growth rate if it exists. We shall proceed now to prove that it does, but a caveat is in order.

A Restriction on g^m: Assuming balanced growth, the chosen form of W implies that a necessary condition for the convergence of the integral is[9]

$$\rho > (1 - \theta)g^m. \tag{5.35}$$

PROPOSITION **5.4** *The economy is characterized by a unique balanced growth path involving a positive balanced growth rate.*

Proof: Using (5.32) and (5.23),

$$k_y = \left(\frac{g^m \theta + \rho}{\alpha A_y} \right)^{1/\alpha - 1}.$$

On the other hand, (5.21) yields

$$k_g = \left(\frac{g^m}{A_g} \right)^{1/\beta}.$$

---

[9]Refer to problem 2 below. Notice that the restriction (5.35) is vacuous for $\theta > 1$.

Dividing out, we have

$$\frac{k_g}{k_y} = \left(\frac{g^m}{A_g}\right)^{1/\beta} \left(\frac{\alpha A_y}{g^m \theta + \rho}\right)^{1/\alpha - 1}.$$

Note, however, that (5.29) requires

$$\frac{k_g}{k_y} = \frac{1 - \alpha}{\alpha}.$$

Equating the *RHS*'s of the last two equations, we see that the equilibrium balanced growth rate must satisfy

$$\left(\frac{g^m}{A_g}\right)^{1/\beta} \left(\frac{g^m \theta + \rho}{\alpha A_y}\right)^{1/1 - \alpha} = \frac{1 - \alpha}{\alpha}. \tag{5.36}$$

The *LHS* of (5.36) may be denoted by $\Gamma(g^m)$. The function is easily verified to be convex and monotone increasing. Moreover, $\Gamma(g^m) \to 0$ as $\gamma^m \to 0$ and $\Gamma(g^m) \to \infty$ as $\gamma^m \to \infty$. It follows therefore that there is a positive, unique solution g^m to (5.36).

The corresponding value k_g^m of k_g follows from (5.21) and the value k_y^m of k_y follows from (5.29). Equation (5.27) implies a consistent value of $k = k^m$ that is constant over time. Solving for r^m from (5.23), equation (5.34) determines the associated value of x.

Figure 5.3 will illustrate this solution. For the present, however, Figure 5.1 provides an alternative depiction of the equilibrium. Equation (5.33) implies, using $\dot{x} = 0$, that $k = k_g^m$ solves

$$f_y'(k^m - k_g) = \rho + \theta \, f_g(k_g) \tag{5.37}$$

in equilibrium. The *LHS* of this equation is monotone increasing in k_g, approaches $f_y'(k^m)$ as $k_g \to 0$ and ∞ as $k_g \to k_m$. The *RHS* is a concave, monotone increasing function, approaching ρ as $k_g \to 0$ and $\rho + \theta \, f_g(k^m)$ as $k_g \to k^m$. The uniqueness result of the preceding proposition along with the shape of f_y' for $k_g \cong k^m$ guarantees that the solution k_g^m to (5.37) is unique and that $\rho + \theta\ f_g(k_g) > f_y'(k^m - k_g)$, $\forall\ k_g < k_g^m$. This representation will have an important bearing on the proof of Proposition 3 below.

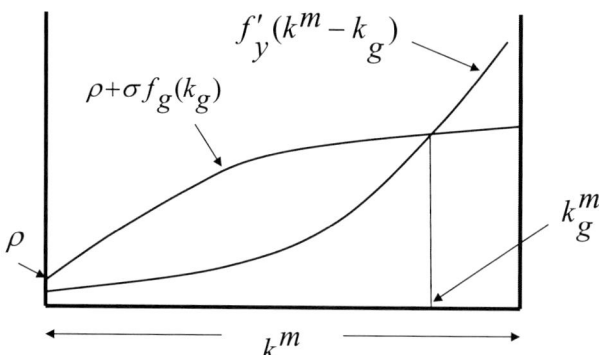

Figure 5.1: Equilibrium Capital Allocation in Stock Infrastructure Model

Proposition 5.1 determines the balanced growth values of the different variables and, in particular, of the variable $k = K/G$. If the economy starts out with these values, then it remains in balanced growth equilbrium forever. However, there is no guarantee that the exogenously given values K_0 of K and G_0 of G at $t = 0$ will conform to the balanced growth equilibrium value of k. If it does not, it will be necessary to verify if the equations of motion governing the economy will move towards the balanced growth equilibrium. In other words, it is necessary to prove that the balanced growth equilbrium of Proposition 1 is stable.

5.4.3 Stability

It is possible to prove a local stability result for the model described so far. (See Dasgupta (1999)). For the present exposition, however, we shall prove a simpler stability result by restricting attention to the case $\theta = 1$. As noted, this reduces the instantaneous household utility function to $ln\ C$.

PROPOSITION **5.5** *The unique balanced growth path is locally saddle point stable.*[10]

---

[10]See Chiang (1984) for a definition of saddle point stability.

Proof: Writing $\omega = x/k$, it follows now from (5.33) and (5.34) that

$$\dot{\omega} = \omega(\omega - \rho). \tag{5.38}$$

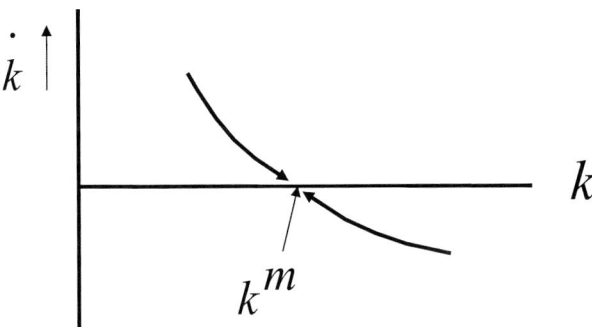

Figure 5.2: Stability of Equilibrium

Under balanced growth, we have $\omega = \rho$, or, $x = \rho k$. This is a familiar relationship between consumption and asset size for a logarithmic utility function. Moreover, (5.38) shows that, any other choice leads ω to move away from balanced growth equilibrium. On the other hand, the choice of $\omega = \rho k$ keeps $x/k = constant$ forever. However, although it is feasible to choose $\omega = \rho k$ at each point of time, this does not ensure that the system as a whole is in balanced growth equilibrium, for the choice does not imply that x and k are constants, as balanced growth requires. Given the constancy of x/k, however, analysing the stability of the balanced growth path boils down to studying any one of the two equaions (5.33) and (5.34). We confine our attention to the latter. Towards this end, rewrite (5.34) as

$$\dot{k} = k\left\{f_y'(k_y) - \omega - f_g(k - k_y)\right\}.$$

Differentiating this equation in the neighbourhood of the balanced growth equilibrium value of k and taking note of (5.29), we see that

$$\frac{d\dot{k}}{dk} = \{\alpha f_y''(k_y) - (1 - \alpha)f_g'(k_g)\}.$$

The RHS of the equation is strictly negative. Hence $d\dot{k}/dk < 0$ implies that the growth path is saddle point stable.

Figure 5.2 illustrates the stability of the balanced growth equilibrium path. Where have we arrived? Our results show that it is possible to organize economic activities with the private sector in charge of production of consumer goods and accumulation of physical capital under competitive conditions and the government sector accumulating public infrastructure. Both private and public capital stocks tend to grow at the same constant rate in the economy given sufficient time. This means in particular that the demand for labour in both sectors grows at the same constant rate as the rate of growth of capital stocks. Consequently, the economy is expected to absorb over time its stock of surplus labour and reduce the extent of the problem we highlighted earlier.

There is a difficulty with the growth path, however, that was ignored so far. In terms of resource allocation, the path is inefficient. It is, as already emphasized above, inefficient on two counts. First, the shadow price underlying the lump sum tax paid by the Y-sector equals the private marginal product of G. This falls short of its social marginal product, given that G is a pure public good. An omniscient government could of course charge a price equal to the social marginal product of G to the private producers, but this by itself cannot solve the inefficiency problem. The government's demand for K still remains constrained by the size of its budget, and hence the G-sector may not satisfy required marginal conditions.

We proceed therefore to study the optimal path for the Command Economy and compare it with the inefficient path derived in this section.

5.4.4 Command Economy vs. Mixed Economy

As before, the welfare function of the planner is identically the same as that of the Household. The planner's problem is solved by maximizing the current value Hamiltonian

$$H = \frac{C^{1-\sigma}}{1-\sigma} + \eta[A(\phi K)^\alpha G^{1-\alpha} - C] + \xi[B((1-\phi)K)^\beta G^{1-\beta}], \quad (5.39)$$

where ϕ is the share of K used in the Y-sector, $1-\phi$ the share in the G-sector and η and ξ are the costate variables associated with the stocks of K and G. The balanced growth solution for this problem may be called the Command Equilibrium and the associated rate of growth denoted g^c. The first order optimality conditions for the maximization of H are

$$\frac{\partial H}{\partial C} = 0 \tag{5.40}$$

$$\frac{\partial H}{\partial \phi} = 0 \tag{5.41}$$

$$\dot{\eta} = -\frac{\partial H}{\partial K} + \eta \rho \tag{5.42}$$

$$\dot{\xi} = -\frac{\partial H}{\partial G} + \xi \rho. \tag{5.43}$$

Conditions (5.40) through (5.43), along with the transversality conditions

$$\eta(t)e^{-\rho t} \to 0 \text{ as } t \to \infty$$

and

$$\xi(t)e^{-\rho t} \to 0 \text{ as } t \to \infty,$$

are a necessary characterization of the optimum path solving the planner's problem.

The above equations are manipulated to produce

$$\left(\frac{g^c}{B}\right)^{1/\beta}\left(\frac{\sigma g + \rho}{\alpha A}\right)^{1/(1-\alpha)} = \frac{1-\alpha}{\alpha}\frac{\beta g^c}{\rho + (\sigma - (1-\beta))g^c}. \tag{5.44}$$

The LHS of this equation is identically the same as the function $\Gamma(g^c)$ of (5.36). The RHS, which differs from the RHS of (5.36), will be denoted by $\Psi(g^c)$. Equation (5.44) has a solution $g^c = 0$. This will be ignored as suboptimal, since it implies that the marginal utility of investment in infrastructure is non-positive.

We proceed now to discuss the existence of a positive solution g^c to the planner's problem and compare the balanced growth path for the Command Economy with that for the Mixed Economy of the previous section.

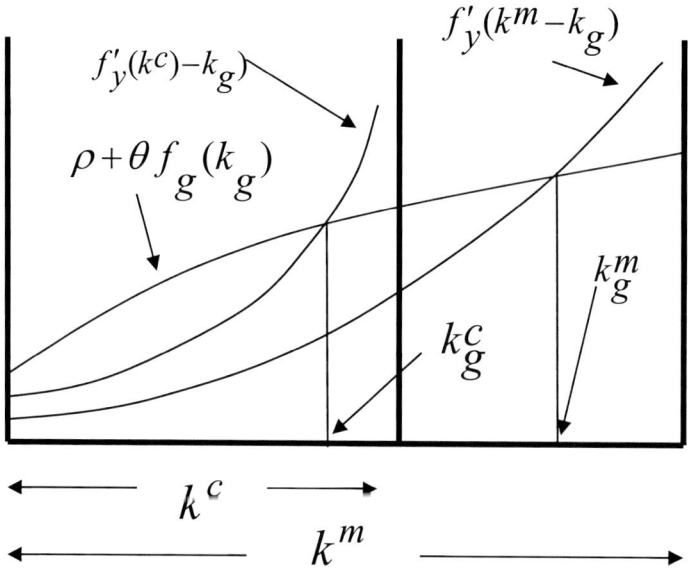

Figure 5.3: Comparison of Mixed Economy and Command Economy

PROPOSITION **5.6** (1) *A strictly positive solution for the Command Economy's growth rate exists and the growth rate achieved by the Mixed Economy exceeds that of the Command Economy.* (2) *The overall capital-infrastructure ratio chosen by the Command Economy under balanced growth is smaller than the one chosen by the Market Economy.*

Proof: (See Figure 5.3) The function $\Psi(g)$ has the following easily verifiable properties:

$$\Psi'(g^c) = \frac{1-\alpha}{\alpha} \frac{\beta\rho}{(\rho + (\sigma - (1-\beta))g^c)^2} > 0$$

and

$$\Psi'(g^c) \to \frac{(1-\alpha)}{\alpha}\beta > 0 \text{ as } g^c \to 0.$$

On the other hand, the function $\Gamma(g^c)$ satisfies the property that

$$\Gamma'(g^c) \to 0 \text{ as } g^c \to 0.$$

Thus, for g^c arbitrarily close to zero, $\Psi(g^c) > \Gamma(g^c)$. Next, by Proposition 5.4, $g^m > 0$ exists. Now, for any $g^c > 0$, (5.35) implies that

$$\Psi(g^c) < \frac{(1-\alpha)}{\alpha}.$$

The inequality holds in particular for $g^c = g^m$. Hence, (5.36) implies that $\forall\, g^c \geq g^m$, $\Psi(g^c) < \Gamma(g^c)$. The continuity of $\Psi(g^c)$ and $\Gamma(g^c)$ implies now from the Intermediate Value Theorem that $\exists\, g^c > 0$ satisfying (5.44) and that $0 < g^c < g^m$. This proves the first part of the proposition.

To prove the second part, let k^m and k^c denote the overall K/G ratios chosen by the two systems under balanced growth. Similarly, let k_g^m and k_g^c be the corresponding ratios used by the G-sector. Further, $f_y'(k^m - k_g^m)$ and $f_y'(k^c - k_g^c)$ are the marginal products of capital in the Y-sector under the two systems.

Suppose that $k^c \geq k^m$. Then,

$$f_y'(k^m - k_g^m) \geq f_y'(k^c - k_g), \quad \forall k_g \leq k_g^m, \tag{5.45}$$

with strict inequality for $k^c < k^m$.

We know that

$$\rho + \theta\, f_g(k_g) \;>\; f_y'(k^m - k_g), \quad \forall k_g < k_g^m, \text{ from (5.37)},$$

$$>\; f_y'(k^c - k_g), \quad \forall k_g < k_g^m, \text{ from (5.45)}.$$

In other words,

$$\rho + \theta\, f_g(k_g) > f_y'(k^c - k_g), \quad \forall k_g < k_g^m.$$

In fact, the inequality must hold for $k_g = k_g^m$, or else the uniqueness of the market solution would imply $k^c = k^m$ and the two systems will grow at the same rate, violating $g^c < g^m$. Hence, we may write the above inequality as

$$\rho + \theta\, f_g(k_g) > f_y'(k^c - k_g), \quad \forall k_g \leq k_g^m. \tag{5.46}$$

Let us now write the condition for the Command Economy's balanced growth equilibrium:

$$\frac{f'_y(k^c - k^c_g) - \rho}{\theta} = f_g(k_g)$$

$$\text{or,} \quad f'_y(k^c - k^c_g) = \rho + A_g(k^c_g)^\beta. \tag{5.47}$$

Comparing (5.47) with (5.46), it follows that $k^c_g > k^m_g$. Since the balanced growth rage g for any system is $\dot{G}/G = k_g$, it follows that $g^c > g^m$, contradicting our earlier conclusion.

Hence, $k^c < k^m$.

The intuition underlying Proposition 3 is straightforward. The Command Economy internalises the externality associated with G, which leads it to choose a higher value of equilibrium G/K, or a lower value of k. At this lower k, every feasible choice of k_g is associated with a larger value of the marginal product of capital in the Y-sector compared to the Mixed Economy. This means that the k_g solving (5.47) must be smaller than the k_g solving (5.37). Consequently, the Command Economy balanced growth rate is smaller than that of the Mixed Economy.

5.4.5   A Policy Question

As far as balanced growth is concerned, the economy can choose to grow at either of the two growth rates, g^m and g^c. Which one should appeal to policy makers? The answer is not simple. The Command Economy solution obviously yields more welfare, as measured by the value assumed by W. This follows since it does not suffer from any of the inefficiencies of resource allocation characterizing the Mixed Economy.idmixed economy. It also involves a higher equilibrium stock of infrastructure relative to private capital. But its rate of growth falls short of the rate achieved by the Mixed Economy and the latter maintains, for any given level of infrastructure, a larger stock of private capital. The higher growth rate implies a higher rate of growth of employment, since $K/L = constant$. The higher stock of K implies, moreover, that the size of the employed labour force too is larger. Thus, not only does the manufacturing sector grow faster, the policy would also seem to address the problem of unemployment in a more satisfactory way compared to the Command Economy.

The policy choice then reduces to a simple question: Higher employment growth or higher welfare? The answer to the question turns out to be a simple one. We are concerned here with a model of surplus labour. The rise in aggregate utility that welfare improvement entails does not percolate down to the population in the presence of unemployment, since large masses of the work force are deprived of the purchasing power necessary to enjoy the improved welfare. On the other hand, a policy of higher employment has the advantage of equipping more people with the means of claiming a share in the *GDP*. Consequently, a democratically elected government would necessarily consider the policy of employment improvement to be more attractive to the one that raises aggregate utility over time without delivering the goods produced to the multitudes.

Even otherwise, recent experience has taught us the practical difficulties associated with planning. The disadvantages of excessive centralization more than outweigh the attraction of higher utility. In other words, the Command solution is hard to implement. In this connection, Dasgupta (2001) proves a decentralization result, in the spirit of the second fundamental theorem of welfare economics, which suggests a way of supporting the Command Solution. The solution requires the planner to *administer* the rate of interest at the optimal level, impose optimal taxes on both production sectors and offer subsidies to the household to maintain the equilibrium. Though theoretically interesting, the strategy is certainly less practical than leaving the rate of interest to adjust to the free market for capital services.

Judged from this point of view, recent policies followed by the Indian economy would appear to have an appeal. At a more practical level, one might even be tempted to argue that while unemployment is to a large extent a measurable variable, welfare expressed in terms of a utility function is hardly observable. It is probably for this reason that all recent debates centre on the rate of growth concept. The higher the rate of growth of an economy, the more successful it is judged to be. It might even appear from some discussions that the objective of policy should be the maximization of the growth rate. One can easily see through the fallacy of this viewpoint, since the highest growth rate corresponds to a path of pure capital accumulation, which involves no consumption at any point of time!

The phenomeonon reported here is amplified when the economy is opened up to international trade. As shown by Dasgupta and Shimomura (2006), the movement from autarky to free trade without foreign direct investment can be growth, and hence, employment enhancing.

However, growth rates of capital, infrastructure and employment improve dramatically when foreign capital is allowed free entry. On the other hand, the rate of growth of consumption expenditure takes a dip raising questions about the overall welfare effect.

Before ending, a caveat is in order regarding the conclusions of the model. The endogenisation of the growth rate in the model depended crucially on the availability of a large surplus of unemployed work force. It is this assumption that allowed us to fix the wage rate at a subsistence level and treat capital and labour as a joint input. With balanced growth at a rate higher than an exogenously imposed rate of growth of labour, however, the surplus will be eliminated in finite time. Once this happens, the specifications of the model will call for change, thereby altering the conclusions we reached. Our analysis can be interpreted therefore to rest on the premise that the unemployed labour force is so large that the time required to reach full-employment, even if finite, is itself quite long. Under such circumstances, the optimal paths calculated are normally close to the ones that would have emerged from the corresponding long but finite horizon exercises, particularly so in the presence of discounting.

Summary

1. The chapter has dealt with the links between infrastructure development and growth.

2. It starts off with a model (due to Barro (1990) and Barro and Sala-i-Martin (2003))of flow infrastructure, where infrastructure, like environment, is a pure public good. Infrastructure is financed by the government with the help of a proportional tax on output and provided free of user charge to household producers.

3. The model does not involve any out of steady state dynamics and the economy is perpetually on the balanced growth path.

4. The rate of endogenous growth depends on the tax rate and the welfare optimizing tax rate is found to be the same as the growth rate maximizing tax rate. The result may not hold except for Cobb-Douglas production functions.

5. The Command Economy exercise for this model exhibits a rate of growth that is higher than the Private Economy and the higher rate of growth is shown to be decentralizable with the help of a lump-sum tax

on households.

6. Barro and Sala-i-Martin extend the model to one involving congestion that could arise if infrastructure does not grow at the same rate as output. A growth rate maximizing tax rate leads to socially optimal allocation of resources.

7. The Command Economy's growth rate is equal to the growth rate of the proportional tax distorted Private Economy growth rate. In fact, a lump-sum tax fails to decentralize the Command Economy growth rate.

8. Dasgupta (1999 and 2004) considers a stock version of the infrastructure led growth model for a Lewis (1954) type developing economy with unlimited supply of labour. As with the flow infrastructure models, infrastructure is treated as a pure public good.

9. The economy is mixed, with the private sector accumulating capital and producing the consumption good and the government accumulating infrastructure. In the presence of two distinct types of capital, the model calls for a stability analysis. A unique balaced growth path is shown to exist. When the instantaneous utility function is logarithmic, the balanced growth path is globally stable.

10. The Command Economy exhibits a smaller balanced growth rate compared to the Mixed Economy. On the other hand, the Command Economy internalizes the externalities produced by infrastructure, thereby leading to a larger value of infrastructure relative to private capital. Besides, the Command Economy also gets rid of distortions produced by the proportional tax rate on profits in the Private Economy used to finance infrastructure accumulation by the government.

11. The model ends up with a question relevant for developing economies saddled with unemployment problems. Since the Mixed Economy grows faster than the Command Economy, from the political economy point of view, the Private Economy is likely to perform better than the welfare maximizing Command Economy. The higher growth rate for the Private Economy, on the other hand, leads to a larger rate of labour absorption, thereby making it the preferred alternative.

Problems

1. A necessary condition for the Private Economy version of the Barro and Sala-i-Martin model to exist was seen to be $\rho + (\theta - 1)g > 0$. Since g is an endogenously determined variable, the condition needs to be

restated in terms of the exogenous parameters of the model. Can you find a sufficient condition for the existence of a meaningful solution that involves the parameters of the model alone?

2. Suppose that the proportional tax rate of Section 5.2 were to be imposed on interest income rather than on output. Would the results for the model be affected by this change?

3. (Based on Barro and Sala-i-Martin (1992)). Change the production function of Section 5.3 to one where congestion is caused by disproportionate changes in Γ/K rather than Γ/Y. How would the results of Section 5.3 be affected on account of the reformulation?

4. Solve problem 1 once again for the stock infrastructure model with reference to condition (5.35).

5. (Based on Dasgupta (2001)) Since the model of Section 5.4 involves a pure public good (services of infrastructure) entering the production of two different commodities, the marginal productivities of infrastructure will be different for the two sectors. Under the circumstances, can you construct a scheme for decentralizing the Command Economy solution?

6. Read Dasgupta (1999) for a local stability version of Proposition 5.5 based on the utility function (2.18).

7. Read Futagami et al (1993).

8. Read Dasgupta and Shimomura (2006) for an open economy version of the model of Section 5.4.

9. Read Guha et al (2006) for the relationship between the number of firms and growth for the model of Section 5.4.

Chapter 6

Technical progress as a Conscious Economic Activity-II

6.1   Resource Allocation for Technological Advancement

Chapter 4 developed models to show how human capital formation might influence the growth rate of an economy. We move on now to our next theme, the link between economic growth and knowledge accumulation. In other words, this chapter will view knowledge itself as a form of capital. In Solow's aggregate growth model, diminishing returns implied that increases in physical capital relative to effective labour lead to declining growth rates of output and physical capital itself till, in the long run, capital and effective labour grow at equal rates, or, what comes to the same thing, per capita capital, output etc. grow at the same rate as the exogenously specified rate of growth of technology. In the language of supply and demand, the supply rate of growth turns out to be perfectly inelastic to interest rate changes, thereby making the equilibrium growth rate impervious to changes in demand forces. Chapters 3 and 5 suggested ways of separating the growth rate of capital from exogenous factors by introducing either learning by doing induced changes in effective factor supply (Arrow, d'Autume and Michel, Frankel, Romer) or allowing for growth in endogenously provided infrastructure (Barro and Sala-i-Martin, Dasgupta). In these cases too, diminishing returns ensured the equality of the rates of growth of physical capital and effective labour or infrastructure (when a balanced growth path exists). However, the rates of growth of the latter were not exogenously specified. Supply side considerations nailed down the equilibrium rate of interest, or alternatively, the marginal productivity of capital, independently of the economy's rate of growth. Consequently, Solow's zero elastic supply curve was replaced by one that was infinitely elastic and changes in demand parameters began to influence the equilibrium rate of growth even in the absence of supply shifts.

Both Chapter 2 and Chapter 3, however, were concerned with extreme forms of the supply curve. Accordingly, Chapter 4 considered more moderately behaved supply responses. This involved the introduction of two sectors of production, the first of which produced final goods as in Solow, while the second was concerned exclusively with the activity of accumulation and determined the supply rate of growth as a function of the factor intensity ruling in that sector. The latter changed with variations in factor prices, in particular the rate of interest. Consequently, the supply rate of growth was neither infinitely elastic nor perfectly inelastic.

Rebelo II and the Lucas models represented particularly clear versions of the new approach. The distinctive feature of these models lay in the AK feature of the second sector. We justified this assumption in the Rebelo II case by interpreting K as a mixture of physical and human capital. As far as Lucas was concerned, no defence was provided for the assumption at all. In both cases, however, the AK assumption led to an upper bound on the economy's achievable rate of growth. We choose this fact as a point of departure and move on to the next stage of our investigation.

An often ignored, though vitally important, factor of production is the stock of knowledge at the disposal of any society.[1] Knowledge in this context refers of course to familiarity with productive techniques, in particular the latest advances in that area. Countries that have discovered better ways of carrying out production are obviously well-equipped to break through growth barriers. Moreover, at any point of time, the total knowledge in existence resembles a *stock*. Quite obviously, like any other stock, knowledge too grows over time. Consequently, it has features similar to capital. Unlike other forms of capital though, the stock of knowledge can grow in two different ways. First, it grows through dissemination across persons, i.e., the learners. Second, it grows in the shape of new knowledge, when improved upon through research. We

---

[1]Romer (1986) may be the earliest model to recognise this feature of knowledge.

may refer to these two forms of knowledge generation as quantitative and qualitative expansion respectively.

Technologically speaking, both forms of knowledge enhancement involve two basic factors of production, the existing stock of knowledge (as incorporated in the pages of a book for example) and labour. As far as quantitative expansion goes, the application of human effort to master it is not likely to give rise to diminishing returns. The reason for this lies in the fact that the body of knowledge incorporated in the book counts as knowledge only if the latter is studied by a student. Two students (with similar capability) studying the book produce then twice as much knowledge. Three students multiply the knowledge threefold. Viewed this way, the technology for knowledge *dissemination* would appear to display constant returns to labour as of a fixed pool of knowledge. That is to say, the technology is endowed with an AK structure.[2]

Moving over now to the second aspect of knowledge accumulation, i.e., qualitative expansion, it would appear that no clear boundary separates it from quantitative expansion. The understanding that the reading of a book generates may not be limited to the exact content of the book studied. Each individual reading the book is likely to interpret it in his own way and each new way of understanding existing phenomenon counts as new knowledge. Of course, full-fledged knowledge creation involves more than application of labour on a given volume of knowledge. Indeed, a series of discoveries, hence new bits of knowledge or intermediate products, separate the starting point of a research endeavour from its destination. However, this fact is likely to be suppressed in any vertically integrated representation of the knowledge technology. As a result, from the point of view of technology specification, there may be little to distinguish between the two forms of knowledge expansion.

Thus, Romer (1990) and Grossman and Helpman (1991b) assume the creation of new knowledge to be linear in the use of human capital (or labour in general) as of a given stock of knowledge. However, with respect to the use of human capital and existing knowledge taken together, the technology is taken to display increasing returns. The linearity assumption lends justification to the AK format, so long as the stock of knowledge in use is held fixed. At the same time, the replacement of the technology of human capital creation by the one for new knowledge creation rids the model economy of the earlier noted unde-

---

[2]Note that this channel of knowledge expansion is not clearly distinguishable from growth in human capital. Although Lucas analysed the matter, existing knowledge did not play any role in the creation of new human capital. As such, the assumption of a linear technology for human capital accumulation had an ad hocness about it.

sirable feature of the Rebelo II and Lucas models, viz. the technological upper bound on the achievable growth rate (See Chapter 4). As will be apparent from the following sections, the rate of growth of knowledge accumulation will, in principle, be unbounded above. The existing *level* of human capital will put temporary bounds on this growth rate. But a growth in human capital will relax the bound. In other words, Romer and Grossman and Helpman trace back the bound on economic growth to scarcity of resources rather than to a technological constraint.

For Romer, each new addition to the knowledge stock helps to produce a novel input which in turn helps to raise the productivity in the final goods sector. By contrast, Grossman and Helpman build models to highlight the role played by knowledge capital in giving rise to consumption variety. The first part of the present chapter will discuss Romer's work. This will be followed up by a presentation of a model of brand proliferation due to Grossman and Helpman.

6.2 Description of the Romer Economy

Technological progress in Romer's model shows up in the form of specialised inputs used for producing final goods.[3] The production function is given by

$$Y = T_y^\alpha \int_0^A x(i)^{1-\alpha} di, \qquad (6.1)$$

where T_y represents human capital employed in producing Y, $x(i)$ the quantity of the ith variety of specialised input used in the production of Y and A the cardinality of a continuum of existing varieties. Specialised inputs are indexed according to the chronological order of their appearance. The proximate object of research is the ith design or idea,[4] whose concrete embodiment is the input $x(i)$. Progress in research, i.e., knowledge accumulation, implies an increase in the value of A and along with it, an expansion in the size of the set of ideas as well as that of the set of specialised inputs.

That (6.1) captures the notion of specialisation may be appreciated from the following considerations. Assuming all $x(i)$'s to be used at the

---

[3]Following an idea of Ethier (1982), the function is a reinterpretation of the Dixit-Stiglitz (1977) preference function for variety.

[4]The words 'design', 'idea', 'knowledge' etc. will be used synonymously in what follows.

same level, say x, the production function reduces to

$$Y = T_y^\alpha A x^{1-\alpha}. \tag{6.2}$$

Given x, the marginal return to variety is measured by

$$\frac{\partial Y}{\partial A} = T_y^\alpha x^{1-\alpha}.$$

In other words, there are constant returns to variety, given the level of $x(i)$. As opposed to this, the marginal return to an increase in x, given that variety is fixed at A, behaves as follows:

$$\frac{\partial Y}{\partial x} = T_y^\alpha A(1-\alpha)x^{-\alpha} > 0$$

$$\frac{\partial^2 Y}{\partial x^2} = T_y^\alpha A(-\alpha)(1-\alpha)x^{-\alpha-1} < 0.$$

Thus, given A, there are decreasing returns to a mere increase in the quantity in which the different inputs are employed. In other words, specialisation offsets the tendency for diminishing returns associated with an intensive use of existing inputs.

The production of $x(i)$ is thought of as a two stage (but not necessarily vertically integrated) process. The lower stage consists of the creation of a design, i.e., the task of 'hitting an idea'. Human capital is an essential input in this process and calls for a once for all payment to the inventor. At the higher stage, non-specialised or raw capital (Solow's K) is converted to specialised $x(i)$ by means of a fixed coefficient production function, each unit of $x(i)$ requiring ζ units of raw capital.

6.2.1 The Private Economy

When used for producing new designs, the design for a specialised input is nonexcludable, since it can be copied relatively costlessly. It is also nonrival, since two research processes based on the *same* idea can be simultaneously operated. Unlike rival inputs, there is no sense in which the two processes can be viewed as employing two *pieces* of the same idea. Being both nonrival and non-excludable, a design has the required characteristics of a pure public good when used as an input for producing new designs. All existing designs may be freely employed by competing researchers to produce new designs or knowledge.

Free availability of knowledge, however, could act as a disincentive for research as a privately organised activity. Romer's Private economy resolves the difficulty by looking at the market for the special input based on any particular design or idea as a monopolistically competitive organization backed by patent laws. There are two ways in which an existing design may be utilised. First, as already explained, any idea can be utilised to create newer ideas through further research. Second, it may be used to produce the specialised input based on it. The patent laws inhibit free access to a design by a non-patent holder in the second of these activities. However, the laws cannot preclude the free use of an existing idea to churn out new ones. Thus, putting the two uses of a design together, a patent accords to a design the status of a *partially* excludable commodity. The total body of knowledge incorporated in the stock of existing ideas (of size A) is a free input into new research, but the use of each individual design is excludable in producing the corresponding input.

Social Accounts for the Romer Model			
Sector	Output	Input	Market Structure
Final Goods	Y	$T_y, \quad x(i)$, $i \in (0, A]$	Competitive
Inter-mediate Goods	$x(i)$, $i \in (0, A]$	$K, \quad i^{th}$ design, $i \in (0, A]$	Monopoly
Research	$\dot{A}$	$T_A, \quad A$	Competitive

As the above scheme demonstrates, the economy consists of three parts: a perfectly competitive sector producing Y; for each i, a monopolist producing $x(i)$ by means of a non-sector specific capital good K, which (as in Solow) is physically the same as Y; and a competitive sector producing research ideas or designs with the aid of human capital T_A and the stock A of 'ideas'.

The household H faces the instantaneous budget constraint

$$C(t) + \dot{A}(t) = W_T + r \, \mathcal{A}(t),$$

where W_T represents aggregate wages of human capital[5] and $\mathcal{A}(t)$ stands for the aggregate value of assets held by H. More precisely, $\mathcal{A}(t)$ stands

---

[5]Note the difference between Rebelo II and the present model as far as the returns to human capital goes.

for the aggregate value of equity (or, shares in profits of monopoly firms) and $K(t)$ at each t. In equilibrium, H must be supposed to be indifferent between the two forms of assets. Hence, r is the common rate of return from the two types of assets. Subject to the above constraint, H maximises

$$\int_0^\infty \frac{C^{1-\theta} - 1}{1 - \theta} e^{-\rho t} dt.$$

As before, the exercise gives rise to the standard demand curve, i.e.,

$$g_C^d(r) = \frac{r - \rho}{\theta},$$

The equations characterising the production sectors will be derived under the assumption that the economy satisfies standard market equilibrium conditions at each t. In particular, the following should be satisfied:

(i) $\mathcal{A}(t) = P_A + K(t) \ \forall \ t$, where P_A is the price of a monopoly firm producing x;
(ii) demand for $x(i)$ = supply of $x(i) \ \forall \ i$;
(iii) sectoral as well as the aggregate demands for human capital equal their supplies.

The final good Y being produced under perfect competition, the wage rate w_T^y of human capital in this sector equals its marginal product:

$$w_T^y = \alpha T_y^{\alpha-1} \int_0^A x(i)^{1-\alpha} di. \tag{6.3}$$

In what follows, Y will act as the numéraire. The inverse derived demand function for the input $x(i)$ is

$$p(i) = (1 - \alpha) T_y^\alpha x(i)^{-\alpha} \tag{6.4}$$

where $p(i)$ is the price paid per unit use of $x(i)$.

The raw capital congealed in $x(i)$ is borrowed from H. If $x(i)$ is infinitely lived, there is an interest cost per period to be incurred by its producer for infinite time. Alternatively, $x(i)$ could also be looked upon as a consumable input, reproduced in each period. In this case too, there is an infinite stream of interest payments.[6] A patent holder of the

---

[6]The input $x(i)$ does not undergo obsolescence in Romer. Given the nature of the production function, there will always be positive demand for it by the competitive producers of Y. Obsolescence related problems are recognised by Aghion and Howitt (1992) and Young (1993). Chapter 7 will investigate these problems.

i^{th} idea is the monopolist supplier of $x(i)$ who earns an infinite stream of profits. The stream is discounted using the prevailing market rate of interest r on K, which is viewed as the minimal acceptable return on investment. This is justified, as already argued above, by the fact that H must be indifferent between ownership rights over K and ownership rights over monopoly firms in equilibrium. Potential monopolists compete for the difference between the present value of the stream and the once for all payment for the design. This raises or depresses the price of the design, till the cost is equalised with the benefit.

The instantaneous profit of a monopoly producer of $x(i)$ is given by

$$\pi(i) = p(i)x(i) - r\zeta x(i), \tag{6.5}$$

where $\zeta x(i)$ is borrowed from the households. Using (6.4), hence the second of the equilibrium conditions noted above, the maximisation of (6.5) yields an expression for $p(i)$ that depends only on r for each i:

$$p = p(i) = \frac{r\zeta}{1-\alpha}. \tag{6.6}$$

Combining this with (6.4), $x(i)$ is independent of i. Thus, the value of $x(i)$ will be denoted simply by x. Hence, (6.3) reduces to

$$w_T^y = \alpha T_y^{\alpha-1} A x^{1-\alpha}. \tag{6.7}$$

The value of $\pi(i)$ is also dependent on r alone:

$$\pi = px - r\dot{\zeta}x = \frac{r\zeta}{1-\alpha}x - r\zeta x = \alpha px \tag{6.8}$$

and the infinite stream of π, discounted at the market rate of interest, equals

$$\int_0^\infty e^{-rt}\pi dt = \frac{\pi}{r}$$

$$= \frac{\alpha px}{r}$$

$$= \frac{\alpha(1-\alpha)T_y^\alpha x^{1-\alpha}}{r}. \tag{6.9}$$

Since P_A is none other than the investment in research by prospective monopolists competing for the right to produce $x(i)$, no arbitrage requires that in equilibrium it be equal to the discounted infinite stream of monopoly profits in (6.9). Hence,

$$P_A = \frac{\alpha(1-\alpha)T_y^\alpha x^{1-\alpha}}{r}. \tag{6.10}$$

This, along with a second no arbitrage condition to be specified below, will yield the supply rate of balanced growth for the Romer economy.

The technology for research is given by

$$\dot{A} = aAT_A \tag{6.11}$$

where a is a positive constant and T_A the human capital employed in producing new ideas (i.e., $\dot{A}$). The production function captures the idea discussed in the introductory section. Given A, production of new knowledge is linearly related to T_A, though there are increasing returns to simultaneous variations in A and T_A. On the other hand, the sector is perfectly competitive. Since the production function is homogeneous of degree 2 in A and T_A, payment of factors according to their marginal productivity will over-exhaust the output value. This is avoided however, A being a free input into the research process by the assumption of partial excludability. There is thus no difficulty in paying T_A according to the value of its marginal productivity. The value of the marginal product of T_A is $P_A aA$.

With reference to Sections 4.2.2 and 4.3.1, balanced growth imposes the following two conditions on the Romer model:

$$\frac{\dot{K}}{K} = \frac{\dot{A}}{A} = constant$$

and

$$\frac{T_y}{T_A} = constant.$$

Equating the wages of human capital w_T^A in research to the value of its marginal product and using (6.10),

$$w_T^A = P_A aA = \frac{\alpha(1-\alpha)T_y^\alpha x^{1-\alpha}}{r} aA. \tag{6.12}$$

A second no arbitrage requirement calls for equality of wages received by human capital in the final good sector and the research sector, i.e., $w_T^y = w_T^A = w_T$. Hence, using (6.7) and (6.12) and cancelling terms,

$$T_y = \frac{r}{a(1-\alpha)}. \tag{6.13}$$

Substituting (6.13) into (6.11) and recalling that $T_y + T_A = \bar{T}$, i.e., the third of the equilibrium conditions listed earlier,

$$\frac{\dot{A}}{A} = a\left(\bar{T} - \frac{r}{a(1-\alpha)}\right). \tag{6.14}$$

The last step in the derivation of the supply rate function is to identify it with (6.14). Going back to (6.2), at any fixed value of r,

$$
\begin{aligned}
Y &= T_y^\alpha A x^{1-\alpha} \\
&= T_y^\alpha A^\alpha A^{1-\alpha} x^{1-\alpha} \\
&= T_y^\alpha A^\alpha (Ax)^{1-\alpha} \\
&= (AT_y)^\alpha K^{1-\alpha} \frac{1}{\zeta^{1-\alpha}},
\end{aligned}
\tag{6.15}
$$

where $K = \zeta A x$ is the aggregate value of raw capital embodied in the specialised inputs when the rate of interest is fixed at r.[7] Now, K/A, being equal to ζx, is a constant given r. Using (6.15),

$$
\frac{C}{K} + \frac{\dot{K}}{K} = \frac{1}{\zeta^{1-\alpha}} T_y^\alpha \left(\frac{A}{K} \right)^\alpha.
\tag{6.16}
$$

Given r, the value of T_y is fixed. Hence, the RHS of (6.16) is a constant. This implies that the rates of growth of A, C, K and Y are the same in balanced growth. Thus, (6.14) is equivalently rewritten as

$$
g_C^s(r) = a \left(\bar{T} - \frac{r}{a(1-\alpha)} \right).
\tag{6.17}
$$

As with Rebelo, this is a declining function of r. The intersection $g_C^d(r)$ with $g_C^s(r)$ determines the equilibrium rate of interest (r^*) and rate of growth (g^*) as before. The dynamic equilibrium is shown in Figure 6.1.[8] The diagram clarifies that a positive rate of growth is achievable in equilibrium only if $\bar{T}$ is large enough.[9] Romer argues on the basis of this observation that a minimum size of the stock of human capital is a necessary precondition for growth. The difference between rich nations and the poor may be explained therefore in terms of the differences in the size of human capital in these societies.[10]

Romer's findings for the private economy may now be summarised.

---

[7] It is of interest to note that (6.15) reduces the output of Y to a function of K and *augmented human capital* AT_y as opposed to Solow's K and AL.

[8] As should be obvious, the Romer balanced growth equilibrium fixes the value of K/A. Consequently, as with the Rebelo I (1991) and Lucas (1988) models, a detailed analysis of the stability of the balanced growth path is called for. A nontrivial analysis of this issue may be found in Arnold (2000).

[9] To be precise, the condition is $a(1-\alpha)\bar{T} > \rho$.

[10] As is obvious, $\bar{T}$ acts as a shift variable in Romer's model. The remaining models

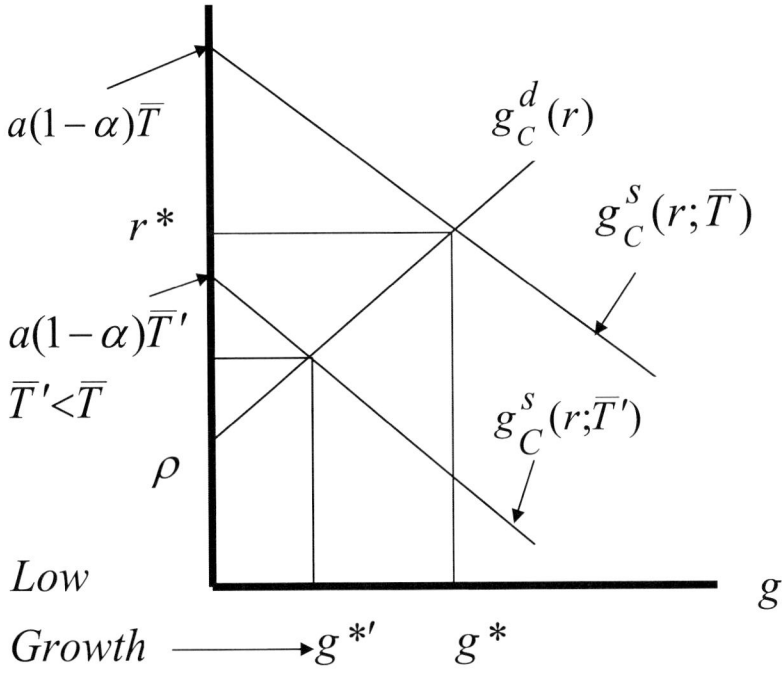

Figure 6.1: Equilibrium of the Romer Economy

PROPOSITION **6.1** *When technical progress assumes the form of specialised inputs into the productive process, the equilibrium growth rate of an economy can be sustained by a combination of perfectly competitive and monopolistically competitive markets, the latter backed by a*

---

to be presented below in this chapter and the next are characterised by similar shift variables. Jones (1995) questioned the empirical validity of this result and offered an alternative model to be discussed below in Chapter 8. Peretto (1998) too offered the following criticism against models involving shift variables affecting the rate of growth. Since a rise in $\bar{T}$ raises the rate of balanced growth in the economy, with population growing exponentially over time, Romer's model predicts the rate of growth of the economy to rise exponentially over time. The criticism has been handled by later researchers (such as Segerstrom (1998), who suggested, along with Jones (1995) that productivity of research falls with a rise the stock of knowledge. These developments have been neatly summarised in Dinopoulos & Sener (2003).

legal structure recognising patent rights.

6.2.2   Inefficiencies in the Private Economy

The existence of a monopoly sector in the Romer model is a potential source of inefficiency in resource allocation. A second reason for inefficiency may be traced back to a possible divergence between the social marginal productivity of knowledge and the price paid by the market for a unit of knowledge. We take these up in turn restricting the discussion to balanced growth equilibrium paths only.

Monopoly and Inefficiency For the purpose of the discussion that follows, we shall express all prices in some abstract unit of account instead of choosing Y as the numéraire good. Under balanced growth, $T_y/x = \lambda$ say $=$ *constant*. Consequently, the total cost of producing Y is

$$
\begin{aligned}
C_1(Y) &= w_T^y T_y + pAx \\
&= (w_T^y \lambda + pA)x \\
&= \left(\frac{w_T^y \lambda + pA}{\lambda^\alpha A} \right) Y.
\end{aligned}
\tag{6.18}
$$

The corresponding marginal cost is

$$
\begin{aligned}
C_1'(Y) &= \left(\frac{w_T^y \lambda + pA}{\lambda^\alpha A} \right) \\
&= \left(\frac{w_T^y \lambda + (r\zeta/1-\alpha)A}{\lambda^\alpha A} \right),
\end{aligned}
\tag{6.19}
$$

using (6.6).

Consider now an alternative way of producing Y by vertically integrating the Y-sector with monopolistic intermediate goods sector. In this enlarged Y-sector, the final output may be viewed as being produced by means of T_y and K. We may, however, eliminate T_y by noting that $Y = AT_y^\alpha x^{1-\alpha} = (T_y^\alpha x^{-\alpha})\, Ax = \lambda^\alpha Ax$. Since $K = \zeta Ax$, we obtain

$$
Y = \left(\frac{\lambda^\alpha}{\zeta} \right) K,
$$

which reduces Y to a function of K alone. Using this function, the total K required to produce Y is

$$K = \left(\frac{\zeta}{\lambda^\alpha}\right) Y.$$

Hence, the aggregate cost of producing Y is

$$C_2(Y) = \left(\frac{r\zeta}{\lambda^\alpha}\right) Y, \tag{6.20}$$

so that the marginal cost is

$$C_2'(Y) = \left(\frac{r\zeta}{\lambda^\alpha}\right). \tag{6.21}$$

Comparing (6.19) and (6.21), it is clear that in the presence of the monopoly producers of the intermediate good, the marginal cost of producing Y is higher. Since the Y-sector is perfectly competitive, the price q of its product in the chosen unit of account is

$$q = C_1'(Y)$$
$$> C_2'(Y),$$

where $C_2'(Y)$ may be interpreted as the true marginal cost of producing Y. This explains the monopoly-induced inefficiency in the model.

Divergence between Private and Social Marginal Product of A

Given the balanced growth equilibrium path of A and the fact that $Y = AT_y^\alpha x^{1-\alpha}$ along this path, raising A marginally at any point of time increases the output of Y by $T_y^\alpha x^{1-\alpha}$ forever. Consequently, the social marginal productivity of A is

$$MP_A^s = \int_0^\infty e^{-rt} T_y^\alpha x^{1-\alpha}\, dt$$
$$= \frac{T_y^\alpha x^{1-\alpha}}{r}.$$

The market, however, does not ensure this return for a unit of knowledge creation. In fact, knowledge cannot be directly sold to the final users (i.e., Y producers) of the produce of knowledge (i.e., x). Instead, the market pays P_A for a unit of knowledge, where

$$P_A = \int_0^\infty e^{-rt}\pi \, dt$$

$$= \int_0^\infty e^{-rt}\{(1-\alpha)T_y^\alpha x^{1-\alpha} - r\zeta x\} \, dt$$

$$< MP_A^s,$$

We therefore conclude that

PROPOSITION **6.2** *The Private economy for the Romer model is characterised by inefficiencies induced by* (a) *monopoly pricing of intermediate products and* (b) *divergence between the social and private marginal product of knowledge.*

6.2.3   The Command Economy

We end up our discussion of Romer's problem by comparing the Private Economy's growth rate with the Command Economy's growth rate. Given the inefficiencies noted in the last section, we expect the Command economy to correct the inefficiencies and grow faster.

Solving (2.39) and (6.17), the equilibrium balanced growth rate for Romer's Private economy is

$$g^* = \frac{(1-\alpha)a\bar{T} - \rho}{1 - \alpha + \theta}. \tag{6.22}$$

For the purpose of the present discussion, however, we normalise the stock of human capital to unity, i.e., $\bar{T} = 1$ and rewrite the growth rate as

$$g^* = \frac{(1-\alpha)a - \rho}{1 - \alpha + \theta}. \tag{6.23}$$

To solve for the Command Economy's growth rate, let δ denote the share of human capital used in the Y-sector. Further, the planner is assumed to produce Y in a vertically integrated fashion by internalising the intermediate good sector. This eliminates the inefficiency caused by the monopoly sector. Thus, the production function for Y reduces to

$$Y = \zeta^{\alpha-1}(A\delta)^\alpha K^{1-\alpha}$$

and the planner's optimisation problem is written

$$\text{Maximise} \int_0^\infty \frac{C^{1-\theta} - 1}{1 - \theta} e^{-\rho t} dt$$

subject to

$$\dot{K} = \zeta^{\alpha-1}(A\delta)^\alpha K^{1-\alpha} - C$$

$$\dot{A} = a(1 - \delta)A.$$

The problem is solved by setting up the Hamiltonian function

$$\mathcal{H} = \frac{C^{1-\theta} - 1}{1 - \theta} + \xi\{\zeta^{\alpha-1}(A\delta)^\alpha K^{1-\alpha} - C\} + \eta a(1 - \delta)A$$

and appealing to the conditions set out in Section 4.2.4. Equating the derivative of $\mathcal{H}$ with respect to C to zero and differentiating further, we have

$$-\theta\frac{\dot{C}}{C} = \frac{\dot{\xi}}{\xi}. \tag{6.24}$$

Equating the derivative with respect to δ to zero,

$$\alpha\xi\zeta^{\alpha-1}(A\delta)^{\alpha-1} K^{1-\alpha} = \eta a. \tag{6.25}$$

Finally, the condition governing the evolution of the co-state variable η is

$$\frac{\dot{\eta}}{\eta} = -a + \rho. \tag{6.26}$$

Denote the Command economy balanced growth rate by G^*. Differentiating (6.25) and using $\dot{C}/C = \dot{K}/K = \dot{A}/A$ under balanced growth, we have

$$\frac{\dot{\eta}}{\eta} = \frac{\dot{\xi}}{\xi}$$

$$= -\theta G^*. \tag{6.27}$$

Eliminating $\dot{\eta}/\eta$ from (6.27) and (6.26),

$$G^* = \frac{a - \rho}{\theta}. \tag{6.28}$$

Comparing (6.23) and (6.28), we conclude $G^* > g^*$. Hence, the intuition stated at the beginning of the section is justified.

PROPOSITION **6.3** *The Command economy for the Romer model corrects for monopoly induced inefficiencies and internalises the intertemporal externalities associated with knowledge capital to achieve a faster balanced growth rate compared to the Private economy.*

This completes our discussion of the Romer model.

6.3   Brand Proliferation: Grossman and Helpman

Romer's work constitutes an important move towards capturing the role of knowledge capital in economic growth. Grossman & Helpman (1991b) represents another instance of a similar attempt. For Romer, knowledge accumulation was geared towards reducing the cost of producing the final good. Cost reduction was effected through an increase in the variety of inputs used, as of a given level of intensity of each type of input. To appreciate this fact, note that according to the cost function (6.18), the average cost of production falls with a rise in A. This resulted in a sustained quantitative expansion of the output of the final goods sector. As opposed to this, Grossman & Helpman were concerned with a rise in the number of varieties constituting a final goods basket, i.e., product innovation (rather than Romer's process innovation). The ensuing scenario was described as one involving brand proliferation.[11]

An enlargement in the size of the 'vector' of final products involves the invention of new varieties of goods. With no (Romer like) reduction in cost of production, however, and as of a given size of the labour force, the expansion in the set of goods can take place only at the expense of a reduction in the size of individual components in the basket. For a meaningful growth model, the rise must more than compensate for the fall. Grossman and Helpman ensured this by appealing to the positive impact of increasing variety on utility. As will be argued in the sequel (See Section 6.3.4), aggregate utility will grow if the rate of growth in variety more than balances off the rate of fall in individual components in the consumption basket. The associated growth process must therefore imply a growth in utility, rather than a growth in output as such.

---

[11]This is only one type of product innovation considered by the authors. The next chapter will introduce a second type, viz. the quality ladder model involving improvements in the qualities of a well-defined set of commodities.

Given the focus on utility enhancement through increase in consumption variety, it is natural that the exercise abstracts from the role of intermediate inputs altogether. There is of course a Romer type Research sector that produces blueprints of new varieties of final goods either with the help of human capital alone, or with human capital and the existing stock of knowledge. The blueprint is then purchased by a patent protected monopolist, who produces the commodity by means of human capital. For neither productive activity is it necessary to employ physical capital. Hence, growth in the Grossman-Helpman economy is driven entirely by the accumulation of knowledge capital. The model, in other words, is an abstraction designed to single out the role of knowledge capital in producing economic growth. We shall present two versions of the model, depending on the nature of technology characterising the Research sector. In one version, technology is a private commodity, to which no one other than the patent holder has access. The second is a Romer type world where the research sector, though not the final goods sector, has free access to the stock of blueprints discovered till date.

At the analytical plane, the model to be presented involves generalisations in two directions. The first one comes up when knowledge is a private commodity. As we shall observe, this rules out the existence of a balanced growth equilibrium. Consequently, we will need to appeal to the notion of a perfect foresight equilibrium, as was the case for the Romer (1986) paper. It is for the case of public knowledge capital, however, that the more interesting of the generalisations show up. The economy in this instance will be capable of exhibiting a balanced growth equilibrium. Yet, the dynamic equilibrium for the case will not be representable as the supply-demand cross of our previous chapters. The underlying reason may be explained as follows. The household's dynamic optimisation exercise will lead it to choose a rate of growth of the commodity basket over time. We noted above that a growth in the basket has at least two components of change: a change in the size of the 'vector' and a change in the individual components of the vector. A further complication will come up on account of the fact that we shall be generally concerned with the *value* of the changing basket along the balanced growth path. Thus, a third variable will appear in the shape of a commodity price. Consequently, the demand rate of growth will be a composite of three rates of change, the rate of change of the quantity of each commodity in the basket, the rate of change of the 'number of elements' in the basket and the rate of change of the price of each commodity. Like Romer (1990), however, the supply rate of growth will involve the growth in the set of ideas, i.e., the cardinality of the aforementioned basket. Consequently, it will not be possible for us to equate the supply and the demand rates as before.

Put differently, the earlier exercises involved two equations. The first expressed the demand rate of growth of consumption as a function of the rate of interest. The second gave the supply rate of growth of consumption (which was identically the same as the supply rate of growth of ideas in Romer (1990)) as a function of the rate of interest. Equating the supply and the demand rates, we were left with two equations in two variables, the equilibrium growth rate and the rate of interest. Conceptually therefore, the system was solvable. As opposed to this, the model to be presented now will give rise to a composite of demand growth rates. Though the supply side will be less complicated, the resultant system will no longer be a system of two equations in two unknowns. Hence, we shall need to dispense with the simple demand supply device to determine the growth rate of the system. The matter will be elaborated further when the occasion arises below (in Sections 6.3.2 and 6.3.4).

We move on now to a description of the basic details of the economy.

6.3.1   Description of the Economy

We begin with a description of agent H's behaviour, which breaks up into a static and a dynamic part. There is a continuum of imperfectly substitutable commodities consumed at any moment of time. The cardinality of the set of commodities is $A(t)$ at the point of time t. The static problem consists of finding the demand functions of H for each commodity in the basket available at any given t. The amount of the jth type demanded is $x(j)$, with $j \in (0, A(t)]$. Dropping t for convenience and following Dixit and Stiglitz (1977), instantaneous utility (or, felicity) is defined over the composite commodity

$$D = \left(\int_0^A x(j)^\alpha dj \right)^{1/\alpha}, \ 0 < \alpha < 1, \tag{6.29}$$

so that the elasticity of substitution between any pair of commodities is a constant $\epsilon = 1/(1 - \alpha)$. The instantaneous utility function is $ln\ D$, which the household maximises subject to

$$E = \int_0^A p(j)x(j)dj, \tag{6.30}$$

where $p(j)$ is the price paid for commodity j.[12] We have so far followed the convention of choosing the output of the final good sector as the numéraire. In the present set up, however, there is an evolving variety of final goods, so that there is no obvious candidate for a numéraire. To preserve symmetry therefore, we shall suppose that all price variables for the economy are expressed in some exogenously specified unit of account. The *FOC* for the problem is

$$\frac{x(j)^{\alpha-1}}{x(k)^{\alpha-1}} = \frac{p(j)}{p(k)}. \tag{6.31}$$

Thus, the static demand function is given by

$$x(j) = \frac{x(k)}{p(k)^{1/(\alpha-1)}} p(j)^{1/(\alpha-1)}$$

$$= \frac{\int_0^A p(k)x(k)dk}{\int_0^A p(k)p(k)^{-1/(1-\alpha)}dk} p(j)^{-1/(1-\alpha)}$$

$$= \frac{\int_0^A p(k)x(k)dk}{\int_0^A p(k)^{1-\epsilon}dk} p(j)^{-\epsilon}. \tag{6.32}$$

The coefficient of $p(j)^{-\epsilon}$ admits an economic interpretation. To do so, we associate with the composite commodity an efficient price p_D by imagining D to be produced with the help of the intermediate products $x(j)$ under perfect competition. Profit from production is

$$p_D \left[\int_0^A x(j)^{\alpha}dj\right]^{1/\alpha} - \int_0^A p(j)x(j)dj.$$

Maximization of profit yields

$$p_D\left[\int_0^A x(j)^{\alpha}dj\right]^{1-\alpha/\alpha} x(j)^{\alpha-1} = p(j). \tag{6.33}$$

which reduces to identically the same *FOC* as (6.31). Manipulating (6.31), we have

$$\left(\int_0^A x(j)^{\alpha}dj\right)^{(1/\alpha)-1} = \frac{\left(\int_0^A p(j)^{\alpha/(\alpha-1)}dj\right)^{1-\alpha/\alpha}}{p(k)^{-1} x(k)^{-(1-\alpha)}}.$$

---

[12]The choice of the utility function *ln D* may be viewed as a special case of the function $(D^{1-\theta} - 1)/1 - \theta$, obtained by choosing $\theta = 1$. Whether the results reported below generalise to arbitrary positive values of θ need to be verified carefully.

Using this in (6.33), we get

$$p_D = \left(\int_0^A p(j)^{\alpha/\alpha-1} dj \right)^{-(1-\alpha)/\alpha} \tag{6.34}$$

$$= \left(\int_0^A p(j)^{1-\epsilon} dj \right)^{1/(1-\epsilon)}. \tag{6.35}$$

Equations (6.34) and (6.35) are alternative expressions of the efficiency price attached to D. Competitive pricing also implies that $p_D \, D = \int_0^A p(j)x(j)dj = E$. Hence, (6.32) may be replaced by

$$x(j) = \frac{p_D D}{p_D^{1-\epsilon}} p(j)^{-\epsilon} \tag{6.36}$$

$$= \frac{E}{p_D^{1-\epsilon}} p(j)^{-\epsilon}. \tag{6.37}$$

When the composite good is large compared to any individual component $x(j)$, the demand for the latter may be assumed to be a function of $p(j)$ alone, for $p(j)$ will have negligible influence on D or p_D. Thus, (6.36) and (6.37) can be treated in the standard manner as downward falling functions of $p(j)$ alone. This completes the description of the household's static problem.

The dynamic problem involves characterising the optimal time path of E (alternatively, p_D and D). To do this, we take account of the fact that the household's income flows from two sources. The first is $w\bar{T}$, the income from human capital, where $\bar{T}$ is assumed to be a constant across t. The second is the profit income from ownership of monopoly firms producing the different $x(j)$'s. Denote the aggregate value of shares in firms' profits by $\mathcal{A}$.[13] The dynamic maximisation problem is written

---

[13] In Romer, $\mathcal{A}$ stood for the aggregate value of shares in profits *and* physical capital held by the monopoly firms. The latter disappears in Grossman and Helpman, since physical capital plays no role at all.

$$\text{Maximise} \qquad \int_0^\infty \ln D \, e^{-\rho t} dt$$

$$\text{subject to } \dot{\mathcal{A}} \;=\; w\bar{T} + r\mathcal{A} - p_D D,$$

where r stands for the rate of return, to be called interest, paid on $\mathcal{A}$. The by now standard procedure leads to the following first order condition describing the optimal path of E:

$$\frac{\dot{E}}{E} \;=\; \frac{\dot{D}}{D} + \frac{\dot{p_D}}{p_D}$$

$$\;=\; r - \rho. \qquad\qquad (6.38)$$

This expression obviously corresponds to the demand rate of growth for the economy. At the cost of repetition, it is worth emphasising that the demand rate of growth subsumes three explicit rates of growth, of x, of A and of p.

As before, the economy must be in equilibrium at each t. Thus, the following should be satisfied:

(i) $\mathcal{A}(t) = p_A(t) \, A(t) \; \forall t$, where p_A is the value of each monopoly firm;
(ii) demand for $x(j) = $ supply of $x(j) \; \forall \; j$;
(iii) return to human capital in the manufacturing sector $=$ return to human capital in the research sector;
(iv) sector wise as well as aggregate demands for human capital equal supplies at each t.

Keeping these conditions in mind, we proceed to a discussion of each atomistic monopoly firm's instantaneous profit maximisation problem. For all j, production of a unit of $x(j)$ requires a unit of human capital. Thus, the profit function of the jth firm is given by

$$\pi(j) \;=\; p(j)x(j) - wx(j)$$

$$\;=\; \frac{E}{p_D^{1-\epsilon}} \, p(j)^{1-\epsilon} - w \, \frac{E}{p_D^{1-\epsilon}} \, p(j)^{-\epsilon}.$$

Maximisation leads to

$$p(j) \;=\; -\frac{\epsilon}{1-\epsilon} \, w$$

$$= \frac{w}{\alpha}, \tag{6.39}$$

so that prices of all $x(j)$'s are equal. Substituting for $p(j)$ in $\pi(j)$, we conclude that

$$\pi(j) = \frac{E}{p_D^{1-\epsilon}} \, p^{-\epsilon} \, (p - w)$$

$$= \frac{E}{p_D^{1-\epsilon}} \left(\frac{w}{\alpha}\right)^{1-\epsilon} (1 - \alpha)$$

$$= \frac{E}{\int_0^A (w/\alpha)^{1-\epsilon} dj} \left(\frac{w}{\alpha}\right)^{1-\epsilon} (1 - \alpha)$$

$$= \frac{(1 - \alpha) \, E}{A}. \tag{6.40}$$

Thus, at any t, the value of an existing monopoly firm is

$$p_A(t) = \int_t^\infty e^{-\int_t^s r(\tau)d\tau} \, \pi(s) \, ds$$

$$= \int_t^\infty e^{-\int_t^s r(\tau)d\tau} \frac{(1 - \alpha)E(s)}{A(s)} \, ds. \tag{6.41}$$

We move on now to alternative descriptions of the research sector. The first treats knowledge as a private commodity, while the second adopts the Romer (1990) viewpoint.

6.3.2　Research Without Public Knowledge

The technology for research is given by

$$\dot{A} = a \, T_A, \tag{6.42}$$

where T_A represents human capital employed in research and a is a constant. Like Romer, there is perfect competition in the research sector. Since the value of a unit of A, i.e., the value of $\dot{A}$, is p_A, the research firm's profit is $p_A \dot{A} - wT_A = (p_A a - w) T_A$. Consequently, profit maximisation implies

$$p_A a - w \leq 0, \text{ if } \dot{A} \geq 0$$

$$= 0, \text{ if } \dot{A} > 0. \tag{6.43}$$

Similar to the Romer (1986) exercise[14], the model does not allow for a balanced growth equilibrium path. This follows from the third of the market equilibrium conditions, viz. the condition for equilibrium in the market for human capital. To appreciate this, denote the total demand for human capital for producing final goods by T_x. Since all brands carry the same price p and there are A brands, the quantity produced of each brand is E/Ap (from the second equilibrium condition above). Thus, $T_x = A\,(E/Ap) = E/p$ and the market for human capital is in equilibrium if

$$
\begin{aligned}
\bar{T} &= T_A + T_x \\[2mm]
&= \frac{1}{a}\,\dot{A} + \frac{E}{p}.
\end{aligned}
\qquad (6.44)
$$

If $\dot{A}/A = \text{constant} > 0$, as required by balanced growth, then (6.44) will be violated from some finite t onwards. As asserted therefore, the model cannot display balanced growth equilibrium. For the model to work, one must follow Romer (1986) to generalise the condition of dynamic equilibrium.

> **Definition:** For the Grossman-Helpman model, a *perfect foresight* equilibrium path of $\{A(t)\}_0^\infty$ satisfies the condition that it is realised if expected.

We proceed now to characterise the dynamic path followed by the economy in perfect foresight equilibrium. First, let us derive the path governing the behaviour of A. Equations (6.42) and (6.41) imply that the wage rate in the research sector is

$$
p_A(t)\,a = \left(\int_t^\infty e^{-\int_t^s r(\tau)d\tau} \frac{(1-\alpha)E(s)}{A(s)}\, ds \right) a, \qquad (6.45)
$$

if $\dot{A}(t) > 0$. No arbitrage requires the wage rate in the manufacturing sector (given by (6.39)) to be equalised with the wage rate in the research sector. Using $T_x = E/p$, (6.39) and (6.45), the no arbitrage condition is written

$$
\begin{aligned}
\alpha\,p(t) &= \frac{\alpha\,E(t)}{T_x(t)} \\[3mm]
&= \left(\int_t^\infty e^{-\int_t^s r(\tau)d\tau} \frac{(1-\alpha)E(s)}{A(s)}\, ds \right) a.
\end{aligned}
$$

---

[14]See Chapter 3, Section 3.2.8

Hence,

$$T_x(t) = \frac{\alpha}{1-\alpha} \frac{E(t)}{\int_t^\infty e^{-\int_t^s r(\tau)d\tau} \, (E(s)/A(s)) \, ds} \frac{1}{a}. \tag{6.46}$$

From (6.42), (6.44) and (6.46),

$$
\begin{aligned}
T_A(t) &= \frac{1}{a} \, \dot{A}(t) \\[2mm]
&= \bar{T} - T_x(t) \\[2mm]
&= \bar{T} - \frac{\alpha}{1-\alpha} \frac{E(t)}{\int_t^\infty e^{-\int_t^s r(\tau)d\tau} \, (E(s)/A(s)) \, ds} \frac{1}{a}.
\end{aligned}
$$

$$\tag{6.47}$$

The differential equation (0.47) governs the motion of A when all the four conditions of equilibrium stated above are satisfied. For the path to constitute a dynamic equilibrium one needs further that it be consistent with the demand rate of growth of E, viz. (6.38). Accordingly, substituting $E(s) = E(t) \, e^{\int_t^s (r(\tau)-\rho)d\tau}$ in (6.47), we conclude that the dynamic equilibrium path of A must satisfy[15]

$$\frac{1}{a} \, \dot{A}(t) = \bar{T} - \frac{\alpha}{1-\alpha} \frac{1}{\int_t^\infty e^{-\rho(s-t)}(1/A(s)) \, ds} \frac{1}{a}. \tag{6.48}$$

Let us simplify (6.48) by defining a new variable

$$\kappa(t) = \int_t^\infty e^{-\rho(s-t)} \frac{1-\alpha}{A(s)} \, ds, \tag{6.49}$$

which, from (6.41) expresses p_A in units of E. Then, (6.48) $\Rightarrow$

$$\dot{A} = \begin{cases} a\bar{T} - \alpha/\kappa, & \text{if } \dot{A} > 0 \\ 0 & \text{otherwise .} \end{cases}$$

---

[15]Note that the expression for $\dot{A}(t)$ does not depend upon $r(\tau)$, which cancels out so long as the utility function has the assumed logarithmic form. This prevents the determination of an equilibrium (path for the) rate of interest in the model. Alternatively, dynamic long run equilibrium can hold for any exogenous specification of the interest rate. While we do not fix the rate of interest at any arbitrary level, the Grossman-Helpman approach involves pegging $r = \rho$.

Note that $\dot{A} > 0 \Rightarrow w = p_A a$, or, $p_A = w/a = \alpha p/a$, from (6.39). On the other hand, (6.44) shows that $p > E/\bar{T}$ when $\dot{A} > 0$. Thus, $p_A = \alpha p/a > \alpha E/a\bar{T}$, or, $\kappa > \alpha/a\bar{T} = \bar{\kappa}$, (say). In other words, $\dot{A} > 0 \Rightarrow \kappa > \bar{\kappa}$. Conversely, let $\kappa > \bar{\kappa}$, or, $p_A > \alpha E/a\bar{T}$. Since, $w \geq p_A a$, we have $\alpha p/a = w/a \geq p_A > \alpha E/a\bar{T}$. Hence, $p > E/\bar{T}$, or, $\dot{A} > 0$. Consequently, $\dot{A} > 0$ iff $\kappa > \bar{\kappa}$. Thus, the equation describing the equilibrium dynamics of $\dot{A}$ is finally written

$$\dot{A} = \begin{cases} a\bar{T} - \alpha/\kappa, & \text{if } \kappa > \bar{\kappa} \\ 0 & \text{otherwise .} \end{cases} \tag{6.50}$$

Since (6.50) involves the variable κ, we need a second differential equation characterising changes in u over time. This is found by differentiating $\kappa(t)$ in (6.49).[16]

$$\dot{\kappa} = \rho\,\kappa - \frac{1-\alpha}{A}. \tag{6.51}$$

Thus,

$$\dot{\kappa} > 0 \Leftrightarrow \kappa > \frac{1-\alpha}{A\rho}$$

$$\dot{\kappa} = 0 \Leftrightarrow \kappa A = \frac{1-\alpha}{\rho}$$

$$\dot{A} > 0 \Leftrightarrow \kappa > \bar{\kappa}.$$

According to the definition of a perfect foresight equilibrium, note that the path of $\{\kappa(t)\}_0^\infty$ implied by an expected path of $\{A(t)\}_0^\infty$ via (6.49) must be realised, since $\{A(t)\}_0^\infty$, if expected, is realised by definition. The reader is encouraged to infer the nature of the perfect foresight paths by drawing a phase diagram based on the following observations. (Figure 3.1 of Grossman and Helpman (1991), constructed for a choice of numéraire different from ours, will provide further illumination.) There are two cases to consider.

Case 1: $A_0 < \bar{A} = (1-\alpha)/\bar{\kappa}\rho$. If κ_0 is too small, A is ultimately a constant (since $\kappa < \bar{\kappa}$) along this path. If this is a perfect foresight path, then agents are aware that $A(s) = constant \ \forall \ s > t_0$. Hence, by (6.49), they expect $\kappa(s) = constant \ \forall \ s > t_0$. But κ is continually declining along the path. Hence, the expected κ is not realised, a contradiction.

---

[16]This qualifies as the Fisher equation.

If on the other hand, κ_0 is too large, then both κ and A diverge along a typical path. Hence, $1 - \alpha/A \downarrow 0$. This means, agents must ultimately expect κ to decline, once again a contradiction. Thus, a perfect foresight path beginning from $A_0 < \bar{A}$ can only converge to $(\bar{A}, \bar{\kappa})$.

Case 2: $A_0 > \bar{A}$. The only feasible perfect foresight paths in this region stay put on a stationary point vertically above A_0 on the curve defining the locus of points satisfying $\dot{\kappa} = 0$.

6.3.3   Efficiency Questions

There are two potential sources of distortions in the model. The first is static in nature and arises from monopoly pricing. The distortion would actually materialise if the monopoly sector had an interface with a (say) competitive manufacturing sector (as in Romer (1990). However, this is not the case in the Grossman and Helpman model. Consequently, monopoly power can cause distortions to the extent that it varies across monopoly firms. As we saw, however, all manufacturing firms enjoyed the same degree of monopoly, viz. $1/\alpha$. This means that the ratio of prices charged by the monopoly firms will uniformly equal the ratio of marginal costs $(w/w = 1)$. In other words, no distortion would arise on account of monopoly.

Two other sources of market failure remain, both dynamic in nature. To begin with, entrepreneurs do not internalise the extra utility accruing to H due to the appearance of new variety, as of a given E. Secondly, and once again as of given E, profits $((1 - \alpha)E/A)$ of incumbent entrepreneurs fall as A rises. New entrants fail to internalise this. The external economy and the diseconomy cancel out however, thus eliminating distortions altogether. We show this below.

The aggregate welfare at t may be written as

$$U_t = \int_0^\infty e^{-\rho(s-t)} \ln \left(\frac{E}{p_D} \right) ds, \quad \text{since } E = p_D D$$

$$= \int_t^\infty e^{-\rho(s-t)} \ln \left(\frac{E}{w} \right) ds - \int_t^\infty e^{-\rho(s-t)} \ln \left(\frac{p_D}{w} \right) ds,$$

$$(6.52)$$

expressing expenditure and prices in T units. We assume a marginal increase in variety at t, causing a parallel shift in the path of A, thereby leaving $\dot{A}$ unchanged at all $s > t$. Each individual firm's profit in wage unit being $\pi/w = (1-\alpha)(E/w)/A$, aggregate profit is $A\pi/w$. Hence, the effect of a small rise in A is $\pi/w + Ad(\pi/w)/dA$ at all $s > t$. The first term represents the gain to the innovating firm at the margin, while the second represents a fall in the profits of existing firms. The discounted value of the stream of gains is exactly offset by the cost of innovation along the equilibrium path. Hence, there is no net social gain or loss associated with the additional A alone. Thus, the aggregate social effect on profit is $A\,d(\pi/w)/dA = -(1-\alpha)(E/w)/A + (1-\alpha)d(E/w)/dA$.

Consider the macro identity $E + Savings = w\bar{T} + \Pi$, where Π stands for aggregate profit at any instant of time. In the Grossman & Helpman set up, real savings (i.e., savings in wage units in the present exercise) are equal to real investment in the research sector. The latter equals $T_A = \dot{A}/a$. Hence, $E/w = \bar{T} + \Pi/w - \dot{A}/a$. Consequently, given that $\dot{A}$ is unchanged at all $s > t$,

$$\frac{d(E/w)}{dA} = \frac{d(\Pi/w)}{dA}, \; \forall \, s > t$$

$$= -(1-\alpha)\frac{E/w}{A} + (1-\alpha)\frac{d(E/w)}{dA},$$

i.e.,

$$\frac{d(E/w)}{dA} = -\frac{1-\alpha}{\alpha}\frac{E/w}{A}. \tag{6.53}$$

With this expression in hand, we may proceed to calculate the effect of the proposed change on (6.52). It is not hard to show that

$$\frac{dU_t}{dA} = \int_t^\infty e^{-\rho(s-t)}\frac{1}{E/w}\frac{d(E/w)}{dA}ds + \int_t^\infty e^{-\rho(s-t)}\frac{1-\alpha}{\alpha}\frac{1}{A}ds.$$

Equation (6.53) implies that the last expression is zero. Thus, the consumers' surplus effect is exactly destroyed by the profit destruction effect. In other words, there is no dynamic distortion in the model. Thus, the Command economy will not be able to improve upon the Private economy path.[17]

PROPOSITION **6.4** *When all knowledge is privately owned, the brand proliferation model displays a zero growth, perfect foresight equilibrium in the long run. The Private economy equilibrium is socially optimal. The equilibrium may be realised instantaneously or asymptotically, depending on initial conditions.*

---

[17]The reader should verify the truth of the above intuitive argument by working out the algebra for the Command economy via the Hamiltonian approach.

6.3.4   Research with Public Knowledge

In this case, (6.42) is replaced by (6.11). Consequently, (6.43) and (6.44) change to

$$p_A a A - w \;\; \leq \;\; 0, \text{ if } \dot{A} \geq 0$$

$$= \;\; 0, \text{ if } \dot{A} > 0. \tag{6.54}$$

and

$$\bar{T} = \frac{1}{a} \frac{\dot{A}}{A} + \frac{E}{p}. \tag{6.55}$$

Equation (6.55) demonstrates immediately that the model will permit balanced growth equilibrium, i.e., a positive constant value of $\dot{A}/A$. The remainder of the section will derive the equilibrium balanced growth rate. Proceeding as in Section 6.3.2, but taking account of (6.11), we see that (6.48) changes to

$$\frac{1}{a} \frac{\dot{A}(t)}{A(t)} \;\; = \;\; \bar{T} - T_x(t)$$

$$= \;\; \bar{T} - \frac{\alpha}{1-\alpha} \frac{1}{\int_t^\infty e^{-\rho(s-t)}(1/A(s)) \; ds} \frac{1}{aA(t)}. \tag{6.56}$$

Under balanced growth, $\dot{A}/A = g$ (say). Thus, $A(s) = A(t) \; e^{g(s-t)}$. Consequently, the integral in the extreme right hand denominator of (6.56) is written

$$\left(\int_t^\infty e^{-\rho(s-t)}(1/A(s)) \; ds \right)$$

$$\times a A(t) \;\; = \;\; a \int_t^\infty e^{-\rho(s-t)}(1/A(s))$$

$$\times (A(t) \; e^{g(s-t)}) \; e^{-g(s-t)} \; ds$$

$$= \;\; a \int_t^\infty e^{-\rho(s-t)}(1/A(s))$$

$$\times A(s) \; e^{-g(s-t)} \; ds$$

$$= \;\; a \int_t^\infty e^{-(\rho+g)(s-t)} \; ds$$

$$= a/(\rho + g).$$

Substituting the above in (6.56),

$$\frac{1}{a} \frac{\dot{A}(t)}{A(t)} = \frac{1}{a} g$$

$$= \bar{T} - \frac{\alpha}{1 - \alpha} \frac{\rho + g}{a}. \tag{6.57}$$

We argued in Section 6.3.2 that (6.48) captured the motion of A in a dynamic equilibrium. The arguments apply *mutatis mutandis* to (6.57) also. Consequently, the solution $g = g^*$ to (6.57) represents the equilibrium balanced growth rate for the economy.[18] Solving, we get

$$g^* = a \, (1 - \alpha) \, \bar{T} - \alpha \, \rho. \tag{6.58}$$

It is clear that no positive balanced growth equilibrium is possible if

$$\frac{\rho}{1 - \alpha} > \frac{a\bar{T}}{\alpha}.$$

The above inequality admits the following interpretations. (i) A high ρ ⇒ present consumption is preferred to future consumption, hence low rate of growth; (ii) a high α ⇒ high substitutability between $x(j)$'s, low preferences for variety, hence low growth rate; (iii) a low value of 'a' implies low productivity in research, hence low growth rate.

Balanced growth is not characterised by constant growth in the output of the final goods sector. Indeed, as opposed to previous exercises, the final goods sector does not produce a single commodity. With the total stock of human capital fixed, the output x of each monopoly firm falls as the number A of firms rises. The latter increase, however, more than compensates for the former fall, so that $ln \, D$ rises with $\dot{D}/D > 0$. To prove this, observe that p/E is constant under balanced growth. This follows from (6.55), since $g = constant$. Next, by definition, $E = Apx$. Thus, $E/p = Ax$, or, $\dot{A}/A = -\dot{x}/x$, since $E/p = constant$. Now, $D = (\int_0^A (x^\alpha dj))^{1/\alpha} = A^{1/\alpha} x$. Therefore, $\dot{D}/D = ((1 - \alpha)/\alpha) \, \dot{A}/A > 0$, as claimed. Welfare increases through variety expansion, even though consumption of each type of 'x' declines.[19]

---

[18]We may view (6.57) to be a generalisation of the requirement that the demand and the supply rates of growth be equal.

[19]Grossman and Helpman argue further that the balanced growth path is the only possible perfect foresight path for the economy.

6.3.5 The Command Economy

From our discussion of the private knowledge case, it is straightforward that there will be no inefficiency caused by monopoly. However, the research sector will now generate a non-internalisable externality as in the Romer model. This will be reflected in the growth rate chosen by the Command economy.

The Command Economy's problem (like most of our earlier exercises) consists of a static and a dynamic exercise. The static exercise consists of allocating a given total of human capital, say χ, across the existing brands $[0, A]$. Formally, the planner maximises

$$D = \left(\int_0^A (x(j))^\alpha dj \right)^{1/\alpha}$$

subject to $\qquad \int_0^A x(j)dj \leq \chi.$

Since $0 < \alpha < 1$, optimality requires equal distribution, χ/A across all brands. This implies in turn that $D = \chi\, A^{1-\alpha/\alpha}$.

Given this information, the dynamic problem is stated as

Maximise

$$\int_0^\infty e^{-\rho t} \ln D \, dj = \int_0^\infty e^{-\rho t} \left(\ln \chi + \frac{1-\alpha}{\alpha} \ln A \right) dj$$

subject to

$$\frac{1}{a} \frac{\dot{A}}{A} + \chi = \bar{T}. \tag{6.59}$$

In what follows, we shall restrict our attention to balanced growth paths only. Thus, by assumption, T_A and χ are constants. The problem is solved by setting up the Hamiltonian

$$\mathcal{H} = \left(\frac{1-\alpha}{\alpha} \ln A + \ln \chi \right) + \xi(\bar{T} - \chi)\, a\, A. \tag{6.60}$$

The *FOC*'s are

$$\frac{1}{\chi} = \xi\, a\, A, \tag{6.61}$$

$$\dot{\xi} = -\frac{1-\alpha}{\alpha} \frac{1}{A} - \xi\, a\, (\bar{T} - \chi) + \rho\, \xi, \tag{6.62}$$

$$e^{-\rho t} \xi \quad \to \quad 0 \text{ as } t \to \infty. \tag{6.63}$$

Notice that under the assumption of balanced growth, (6.61)

implies that ξA is a constant. Hence, (6.63) may be rewritten as

$$e^{-\rho t} \xi A \to 0 \text{ as } t \to \infty. \tag{6.64}$$

Equations (6.61), (6.62) and (6.64) are now used to derive the balanced growth rate for the Command economy. Define a new variable $M = \xi A$, so that $\dot{M}/M = \dot{\xi}/\xi + \dot{A}/A$. Then, using the constraint in (6.59), equation (6.62) reduces to

$$\dot{M} = \rho M - \frac{1-\alpha}{\alpha}, \tag{6.65}$$

while (6.64) is rewritten as

$$e^{-\rho t} M \to 0 \text{ as } t \to \infty. \tag{6.66}$$

The solution to (6.65) (under the constraint (6.66)) is[20]

$$M(t) = \frac{1-\alpha}{\alpha \rho} = constant. \tag{6.67}$$

Thus, by definition of M and (6.61), $\chi = \alpha \rho / a (1 - \alpha)$. Hence, using the constraint for (6.59), the growth rate G^* for the Command economy is

$$
\begin{aligned}
G^* &= \frac{\dot{A}}{A} \\
&= a \bar{T} - a \chi \\
&= a \bar{T} - \frac{\alpha \rho}{1 - \alpha} \\
&= \frac{1}{1 - \alpha}(a (1 - \alpha) \bar{T} - \alpha \rho).
\end{aligned} \tag{6.68}
$$

Comparing with (6.58), we see that $G^* > g^*$, as expected.[21]

---

[20]The equation is solved as follows. Multiplying both sides by the integrating factor $e^{-\rho t}$, we get $\dot{M} e^{-\rho t} - \rho M e^{-\rho t} = -(1 - \alpha/\alpha) e^{-\rho t}$. Integrating out, $M e^{-\rho t} = (1 - \alpha/\alpha) e^{-\rho t}/\rho + constant$. Using (6.66), the result follows.

[21]While this completes our discussion of the brand proliferation model of Grossman and Helpman, it would be in the interest of the reader to follow up the original reference for details of the model's policy implications.

PROPOSITION **6.5** *When knowledge is a free good in research, the brand proliferation model displays a positive balanced growth equilibrium. The Private economy equilibrium is socially sub-optimal and grows at a smaller balanced rate than the Command economy.*

We have now introduced ourselves to two classic works on knowledge capital accumulation and growth. While they bring out some special points of interest regarding knowledge capital, there are other important features of knowledge that they ignore. One of the vital aspects of knowledge capital they do not pay attention to is the fact that research on knowledge accumulation is normally characterised by uncertainty of arrival of new ideas. The other side of the coin is that the arrival of new knowledge often renders existing knowledge obsolete. We consider these issues in Chapter 7 of this book.

Summary

1. The chapter has dealt with the links between knowledge-based specialization and growth.

2. It starts off with Romer's (1990) treatment of specialized inputs. Specialization prevents the law of diminishing returns to capital accumulation from setting in.

3. Specialization, however, calls for research and the latter uses human capital as well as existing knowledge as inputs.

4. Existing knowledge is a pure public good, available free of cost to all researchers. It is both non-excludable as well as non-rival in use.

5. The output of research is new knowledge, which, from the point of view of production, constitutes an abstract design. At the concrete level, new specialized inputs are based on new designs. Patent laws surrounding the design, or the produce of research, ensure that research is incentive compatible.

6. The patent laws introduce a monopoly structure into the model with each specialized input being produced by a monopolist. The activity of research as well production of final goods are carried out with the help of perfectly competitive markets.

7. Inefficiencies arise in the Private Economy on account of the presence of monopolies and a divergence between private and social marginal

productivities of knowledge. The Command Economy removes these inefficiencies and leads to a higher rate of growth for the economy.

8. Unlike Lucas and Rebelo (Chapter 4), the stock of human capital is fixed for Romer. It is the ultimate constraint on the achievable rate of growth for the economy. The rate of growth will be raised if the stock of human capital is increased. Thus, in Romer's work, growth is constrained, not by technology (as in Lucas), but by the scarcity of human capital.

9. The Grossman and Helpman model of Section 6.3 is yet another instance of the link between human capital, variety and growth. Unlike Romer, however, Grossman and Helpman introduce variety in the final consumption basket or brand proliferation.

10. There are two different forms of the technology of research. The first involves knowledge as a private good and the second treats it to be a public good as in Romer. In the first case, the perfect foresight equilibrium for the model involves a zero rate of growth in the long run. The Private Economy is socially optimal despite the presence of monopolies. In the second case, the model displays a positive balanced growth equilibrium. The Private Economy is sociall suboptimal and grows at a smaller rate than the Command Economy.

Problems

1. (Based on Barro and Sala-i-Martin (2003)). Replace (6.1) by

$$Y = T_y^\alpha \left(\int_0^A x(i)^\sigma \right)^{1-\alpha/\sigma} di,$$

where $0 < \sigma < 1$ and work out the Romer model. How would you interpret the parameter σ?

2. Draw a phase diagram to analyse the stability properties of the model of Section 6.3.2. Is this model capable of balanced growth?

Chapter 7

Research and Uncertainty

7.1 Uncertainty and Obsolescence

The preceding chapter attempted to capture an important aspect of reality, the role of knowledge capital accumulation in economic growth. Both models viewed new pieces of knowledge to be determinate outputs of a research technology. However, the assumption of a deterministic output flow from a research activity, though admissible as a first approximation, must ultimately be dispensed with in the interest of realism. A second defect of the earlier models lies in the fact that each new invention brings about a novel product that keeps contributing to either productivity or utility forever. Once again, the nature of competition in the actual world appears to be far more drastic. More often than not, the appearance of a new technique (Romer's intermediate input) renders many of the existing technologies obsolete.[1]

This chapter will present two models, due to Aghion and Howitt (1992, 1998) and Grossman and Helpman (1991a, 1991b) respectively, which attempt to fill out the lacuna. Although the two models address similar issues, they differ in their analytical structures. The Aghion and Howitt exercise is closer to the Romer (1990) model, while the Grossman and Helpman model has several features resembling their

---

[1]The idea that new products and/ideas render older ones extinct goes back to Domar (1946) and Schumpeter (1934), who pointed out the inevitability of any exercise in economic growth to be associated with a simultaneous process of destruction of existing facilities prior to maturity. The fact that market competition does not internalise the capital losses implies that an increase in the growth rate is not unambiguously welfare improving.

own deterministic exercise considered in the last chapter.

7.2 Aghion and Howitt: Description of the Economy

Structurally, the Aghion and Howitt work shares features of the Romer (1990) as well as the Grossman and Helpman (1991b) worlds. As far as similarity with the latter goes, Aghion and Howitt rely entirely on knowledge capital as the engine of growth, thus abstracting from physical capital. However, the concrete form in which new knowledge manifests itself assumes the form of a Romer type of intermediate input that improves the productivity of the competitive final goods sector and is itself produced by a monopolist. Unlike the Romer exercise though, the arrival of each new variety renders any existing variety obsolete.[2] Consequently, the form of the production function (6.1) loses relevance. The productivity increase brought about by each new generation of intermediate input is therefore assumed to be exogenously given. Unlike the Solow model, this does not determine the rate of growth of the economy in balanced growth, since the arrival of new inputs follows a stochastic path. As a result, the concept of rate of growth of the economy is replaced by its expected rate of growth. The latter is endogenously determined.

The endogenous determination of the expected rate of growth is explained as follows. The blueprint for each new variety of input is a product of research in Romer-Grossman-Helpman fashion. The novel feature introduced is that the arrival rate of blueprints is a stochastic variable, with the probability of success in research rising with a rise in labour input. The desire to advance the flow of profits in the intermediate input sector induces a *potential* monopolist to raise the demand for research labour (say, indirectly, by offering a higher price for the blueprint or, directly, by running a research firm where it offers higher wages). As against this, there is a disincentive for the *potential* monopolist to encourage research. He realises that once current research is successful and he actually sets up a monopoly firm, he will be threatened with extinction by potential rivals engaged in or supporting research on the next generation of the input. So, the lure of profits

---

[2]The reason underlying obsolescence is that new inputs involve higher productivity. Aghion and Howitt also consider the possibility of simultaneous use of different varieties, i.e., of non-drastic innovations. See Young (1993) for a non-stochastic version of the problem.

affects labour input into research positively, while the risk of survival implied by future competition exerts a negative pressure on research. The equilibrium employment of research labour is determined in standard neoclassical manner by balancing the pain against the pleasure. Once this is known, the probability of success is solved for using the distribution governing the arrival rate of ideas and this in turn determines the expected growth rate of the economy.

7.2.1   The Private Economy: Drastic Innovation

In this section, we shall restrict attention to the case of drastic innovations, i.e., to the case where the arrival of new technology makes old technology infeasible. The possibility of non-drastic innovations will be considered subsequently. Time is denoted by the continuous variable t and the chronological order of new inventions by the discrete variable τ. The time distance separating the $\tau-th$ from the $\tau+1-th$ invention will be referred to as the $\tau-th$ *time interval*. The time point t at which the $\tau-th$ invention occurs is not known with certainty. Hence, the length of the $\tau-th$ time interval is a stochastic variable. The variable x_τ denotes the specialised input used during the $\tau-th$ time interval, while the research to develop a blueprint for x_τ is undertaken during the interval $\tau-1$. Similarly, $x_{\tau+1}$ is researched during the $\tau-th$ time interval and used during interval $\tau+1$ and so on.

As in Romer, there are three sectors of production, a competitive final good sector, a monopolistic intermediate good sector and a competitive research sector. The final good is produced according to[3]

$$Y = Ax^\alpha, \ 0 < \alpha < 1, \tag{7.1}$$

where A is a productivity parameter whose level is determined by the generation of x in use. Thus, x_τ is associated with A_τ, $x_{\tau+1}$ with $A_{\tau+1}$, etc. Further, $A_{\tau+1} = \gamma A_\tau$, $\gamma > 1$, where γ is a nonstochastic variable. If successive generations of the inputs were to be available in a *deterministic* chronological sequence, the economy's growth rate would be fairly transparent. However, as noted already, the arrival time of a new input is a stochastic variable.

The entire quantum of Y is consumed (as in Rebelo II), so that there is no direct savings out of Y. Nevertheless, savings occurs since the level of Y depends on that of x and the latter is determined by the

---

[3]The presentation of this section depends on Aghion and Howitt (1998). A somewhat more general treatment may be found in Aghion and Howitt (1992).

allocation of human capital to the production of x. The larger (smaller) the allocation in favour of x, the larger (smaller) is current consumption. Thus, a decision to produce less of x amounts a decision to save more.

The input x_τ is produced by means of human capital, but the latter has a competitive use in research also. A fixed quantity $\bar{T}$ of skilled labour is allocated between these alternative uses. (In Romer, it is allocated between research and the final good). The two activities involving labour use will be described in turn and it is simpler to begin with x_τ. Any x is produced by the linear technology:

$$x_\tau = T_x^\tau, \tag{7.2}$$

where T_x^τ stands for labour used in producing x_τ. As with Romer, the producer of x_τ is a monopolist, with the price p_τ of x_τ satisfying the inverse demand relationship

$$p_\tau = \alpha \, A_\tau \, x_\tau^{\alpha-1}. \tag{7.3}$$

The equilibrium condition for this sector is found by maximising profit

$$\pi(x_\tau) = \alpha \, A_\tau \, x_\tau^{\alpha-1} \, x_\tau - w_\tau \, x_\tau,$$

for which the FOC is

$$w_\tau = A_\tau \, \alpha^2 \, x_\tau^{\alpha-1}. \tag{7.4}$$

The corresponding optimal choice of x_τ is

$$\operatorname*{argmax}_{x_\tau} \pi(x_\tau) = \left(\frac{\alpha^2}{w_\tau / A_\tau} \right)^{1/1-\alpha}. \tag{7.5}$$

The above may be expressed as a functional relationship

$$
\begin{aligned}
x_\tau &= \tilde{x}\left(\frac{w_\tau}{A_\tau} \right) \\
&= \tilde{x}(\omega_\tau), \tag{7.6}
\end{aligned}
$$

where $\omega_\tau = w_\tau / A_\tau$. An increase in ω_τ lowers x_τ, hence the demand for T_x^τ. On the other hand, the inelastic supply of human capital is assumed to be $\bar{T}$ at each t. The availability of labour for the research sector rises therefore as ω_τ goes up. Thus, $\bar{T} - \tilde{x}(\omega_\tau)$ may be interpreted as the residual supply of labour for the research sector after ensuring equilibrium for the x-sector. We denote $\bar{T} - \tilde{x}(\omega_\tau)$ by $T_A^s(\omega_\tau)$ and show it as the upward rising curve in Figure 7.1. The intercept of the curve on the vertical axis is given by $\alpha^2/\bar{T}^{1-\alpha}$. At any ω_τ rate below this, $\bar{T}$ is entirely devoted to producing x_τ. (T_A^τ refers to an *equilibrium* value of T_A to be explained below.)

Using (7.4), the expression for profit is rewritten

$$\pi(x_\tau) = ((1-\alpha)/\alpha)\, \omega_\tau\, x_\tau. \tag{7.7}$$

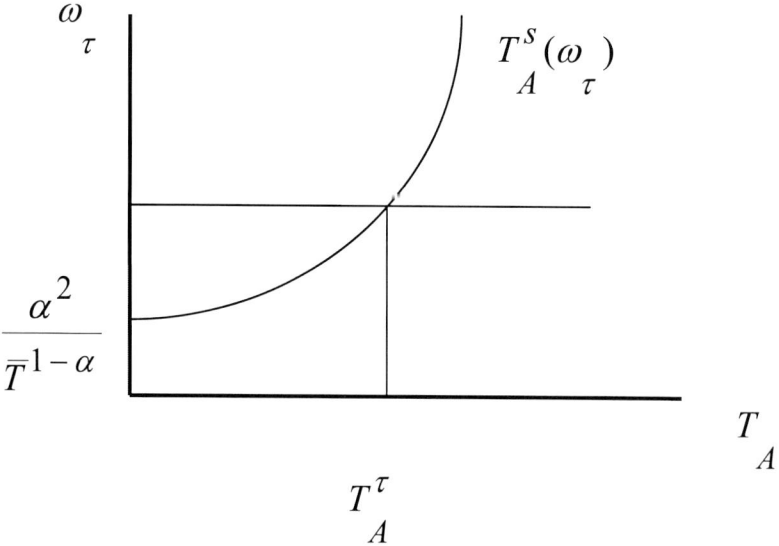

Figure 7.1: Supply Curve of Research Labour in the Aghion-Howitt Economy

Further, productivity adjusted profit is $\tilde{\pi}(\omega_\tau) = \pi(x_\tau)/A_\tau$, which falls as ω_τ rises (using (7.5)). This function will appear once again in the discussion of equilibrium for the research sector. The equilibrium in question will be determined once we have specified the demand function for research labour. This will be done in two steps. The first step consists of assigning a value to the research product, while the second involves writing down the condition of profit maximisation in that sector.

Towards the first step, we begin by noting a crucial difference between (6.11) and the specification of the research technology in the Aghion and Howitt model. The models of Chapter 6 visualised a non-stochastic link between human capital input and the rate of flow of ideas. Consequently, the equilibrium allocation of human capital to the research sector determined the supply rate of growth of the economy. The present set up specifies the common rate of growth of productivity associated with any new idea exogenously. Equilibrium labour allocation in the research sector merely helps to fix the probability of arrival of a new idea and hence the expected rate of growth of the economy. Keeping this in mind, let us denote the price of the $\tau+1-th$ innovation, i.e., the *idea* behind the specialised input $x_{\tau+1}$, by $V_{\tau+1}$. (Recall that the research labour force of interval τ is engaged developing the said idea.)

No arbitrage will require $V_{\tau+1}$ to be equal to the discounted present value of the stream of expected profit for the monopoly firm using $x_{\tau+1}$ in the $\tau+1-th$ interval. In order to calculate the expected profit, let T_A^τ be the level of human capital employed during the $\tau-th$ interval for developing the blueprint for the product $x_{\tau+1}$. Similarly, $T_A^{\tau+1}$ is the level of human capital employed in research during the $\tau+1-th$ interval for developing the blueprint for the product $x_{\tau+2}$.

We shall assume the probability of success at any point of time t (in the $\tau-th$ interval) to be λT_A^τ, $\lambda > 0$. The assumption is governed by the following considerations. First, the specification is based on the assumption that the flow of ideas follows a Poisson process. Thus, let us consider the following Poisson distribution

$$f(n) = \frac{e^{-\lambda t} (\lambda t)^n}{n!}, \quad n = 1, 2, 3, \cdots$$

governing the number of arrivals (n) of a random variable (more concretely, the number of ideas or blueprints) during a time interval $[0, t]$, where λ stands for the parameter of the Poisson distribution. According to this distribution, the probability of zero arrival during $[0, t]$ is $e^{-\lambda t}$. Consequently, the probability of at least one arrival during $[0, t]$ is $1 - e^{-\lambda t}$. The latter yields the density function $\lambda e^{-\lambda t}$, which stands for the probability that the waiting time for an arrival is *exactly* t. As $t \to 0$, we obtain the probability of instantaneous arrival as λ.

Suppose now that researches carried out by distinct researchers are statistically independent processes. In particular, let X_1 and X_2 be random variables governed by two independent Poisson processes with instantaneous arrival rates λ_1 and λ_2. The probability that at least one success will occur is $\lambda_1 + \lambda_2$. The Aghion and Howitt model assumes that $\lambda_1 = \lambda_2 = \lambda$. Thus, when the size of research labour is T_A^τ, the Poisson arrival rate of innovations for the *economy as a whole* is the "sum" of the individual arrival rates, viz. λT_A^τ.

A second characteristic of the distribution is that it views research to be a memoryless process. Thus, firms do not derive any benefit from the experience gained from unsuccessful research efforts, so that newcomers may embark upon a research activity without having gone through any of the earlier stages of research on previous generation ideas. Essentially, one is assuming that it is sufficient for present researchers to study existing specimens of previous generation products to churn out new ideas. In other words, research satisfies the public knowledge assumption of the previous chapter. The same observations will characterise the research sector of the Grossman and Helpman model on Quality Ladders to be discussed subsequently.

The expected profit at any t in the $\tau + 1 - th$ interval is given by $e^{-(\lambda\ T_A^{\tau+1})\ t}\ \pi(x_{\tau+1})$, since $e^{-(\lambda\ T_A^{\tau+1})\ t}$ is the probability of no success till t with respect to research on $x_{\tau+2}$. Let r stand for the prevailing rate of interest, assumed to be an exogenously given constant across time. Then, the discounted present value of expected profit is

$$\int_0^\infty e^{-rt}\ e^{-\lambda\ T_A^{\tau+1}\ t}\ \pi(x_{\tau+1})\ dt \quad = \quad \int_0^\infty e^{-(r+\lambda\ T_A^{\tau+1})\ t} \quad (7.8)$$

$$\times \pi(x_{\tau+1})\ dt \quad (7.9)$$

$$= \quad \frac{\pi(x_{\tau+1})}{r + \lambda\ T_A^{\tau+1}}. \quad (7.10)$$

On account of no arbitrage therefore,

$$V_{\tau+1} = \frac{\pi(x_{\tau+1})}{r + \lambda\ T_A^{\tau+1}}, \quad (7.11)$$

or,

$$r\ V_{\tau+1} = \pi(x_{\tau+1}) - \lambda\ T_A^{\tau+1}\ V_{\tau+1}.$$

The last equation has the following interpretation. The opportunity cost of investing in the research product is $r\ V_{\tau+1}$. On the other hand, the monopolist purchasing the blueprint for $x_{\tau+1}$ earns $\pi(x_{\tau+1})$ at each instant and suffers the uncertainty of capital loss due to the possible arrival of $x_{\tau+2}$, the next generation input. The probability of this event is $\lambda\ T_A^{\tau+1}$, so that the expected loss is $\lambda\ T_A^{\tau+1}\ V_{\tau+1}$. The RHS of the above equation captures the monopolist's expected net return at each t. Opportunity cost then is equated to the expected marginal gain.[4]

---

[4]Compare with the interpretation of (2.9).

Equation (7.11) completes the first step towards specifying the demand function for L_A^τ in the research sector in the interval τ.

The second step in deriving the demand for research labour during τ involves noting that it is the product of research labour T_A^τ that is priced $V_{\tau+1}$. The probability of success at any t in τ being $\lambda\, T_A^\tau$, the associated expected revenue of research firms is $\lambda\, T_A^\tau\, V_{\tau+1}$ and expected profit is therefore given by $\lambda\, T_A^\tau\, V_{\tau+1} - w_\tau\, T_A^\tau$. The corresponding *FOC* for expected profit maximisation by research firms is

$$w_\tau = \lambda\, V_{\tau+1}. \tag{7.12}$$

We may combine (7.11) and (7.12) to get

$$
\begin{aligned}
\omega_\tau &= \frac{\lambda}{A_\tau}\, V_{\tau+1} \\[2mm]
&= \lambda\, \frac{\pi(x_{\tau+1})/A_\tau}{r + \lambda\, T_A^{\tau+1}} \\[2mm]
&= \frac{\lambda\,(A_{\tau+1}/A_\tau)\,\tilde{\pi}(\omega_{\tau+1})}{r + \lambda\, T_A^{\tau+1}}.
\end{aligned}
$$

In other words,

$$\omega_\tau = \lambda\, \frac{\gamma\, \tilde{\pi}(\omega_{\tau+1})}{r + \lambda\, T_A^{\tau+1}}. \tag{7.13}$$

This fixes ω_τ, given $\omega_{\tau+1}$ and $T_A^{\tau+1}$ and defines, finally, an infinitely elastic demand curve for T_A^τ at the fixed ω_τ.[5] The equilibrium value of L_A^τ in interval τ occurs where $T_A^{\tau\,s}(\omega_\tau)$ intersects the horizontal demand curve. See Figure 7.1, which may now be reinterpreted to show the equilibrium pair (ω_τ, T_A^τ), given $(r, \omega_{\tau+1}, T_A^{\tau+1})$.

The equilibrium allocation of human capital helps to fix an expected growth rate of the Y-sector. To explain the nature of this expected rate, note that the flow of Y during two successive innovations is

$$
\begin{aligned}
Y_\tau &= A_\tau\, x_\tau^\alpha \\[2mm]
Y_{\tau+1} &= A_{\tau+1}\, x_{\tau+1}^\alpha \\[2mm]
&= \gamma\, A_\tau\, x_{\tau+1}^\alpha.
\end{aligned}
$$

---

[5] See Aghion and Howitt (1992) for a more general demand curve.

Since τ is a discrete variable, the rate of growth of Y is $ln\, Y_{\tau+1} - ln\, Y_\tau$. To get a handle on this expression, we may divide up the analysis into two parts. The first relates to the special case where the equilibrium human capital allocation derived above repeats across time. In this case, x_τ as well as T_A^τ would be constants for all τ and a state parallel to the balanced growth equilibrium of earlier chapters will emerge, with important variables like Y_τ, π_τ, w_τ growing at the same rate as the rate of growth of A_τ. In the second case, the equilibrium is non-repetitive.

Repetitive Equilibrium

In this case, $w_\tau = w$ and $T_A^\tau = T_A$ (say) $\forall\ \tau$. As a result, (7.13) is replaced by

$$w = \lambda\, \frac{\gamma\, \tilde{\pi}(w)}{r + \lambda\, T_A}$$

$$- \;\; w_d(T_A; r), \qquad\qquad (7.14)$$

The function $w_d(T_A; r)$ may be interpreted to yield the demand price of research labour as a function of the quantity T_A. Similarly, the monotonic property of $\tilde{x}(w)$ and

$$T_A^s(w) = \bar{T} - \tilde{x}(w)$$

may be used to write the supply price as a function of the quantity T_A. Thus,

$$w = w_s(T_A), \qquad\qquad (7.15)$$

The function $w_d(T_A; r)$ is decreasing and $w_s(T_A)$ increasing in T_A. The repetitive equilibrium $(\hat{T}_A, \hat{w})$ occurs at the intersection of these two curves. Plugging the equilibrium values back in (7.14) and recalling (7.7),

$$w = \frac{\lambda\, \gamma\, .\, ((1-\alpha)/\alpha)\, .\, w\, .\, (\bar{T} - \hat{T}_A)}{r + \lambda\, \hat{T}_A},$$

or,

$$\frac{\lambda\, \gamma\, ((1-\alpha)/\alpha)\, (\bar{T} - \hat{T}_A)}{r + \lambda\, \hat{T}_A} = 1. \qquad\qquad (7.16)$$

For the repetitive equilibrium, we have $x_\tau = $ constant, so that $Y_{\tau+1} = \gamma\, Y_\tau$. Thus, $ln\, Y$ increases by $ln\, \gamma$ each time an innovation occurs. Suppose that during a unit interval of time, there has occurred $\epsilon(t)$ innovations. Then, during this interval, $ln\, Y$ rises by $\epsilon(t)\, ln\, \gamma$ and

$$ln\, Y(t+1) - ln\, Y(t) = \epsilon(t)\, ln\, \gamma.$$

The probability of $\epsilon(t)$ innovations occurring in the unit interval is $((\lambda\, T_A)^{\epsilon(t)} e^{-\lambda\, T_A}/\epsilon(t)!)$. The mean of this distribution is $\lambda\, T_A$. Hence,

$$E[\ln\, Y(t+1) - \ln\, Y(t)] = \lambda\, T_A\, \ln\, \gamma$$

and the expected rate of growth of the Y-sector is

$$g(r) = \lambda\, T_A\, \ln\, \gamma, \qquad (7.17)$$

where the dependence on r arises from (7.14). With a rise in r, the discounted stream of profits falls (as per (7.11)), $w_\tau = \lambda\, V_{\tau+1}$ falls, x rises and T_A falls according to (7.14). Thus, $g(r)$ falls with r. With reference to earlier exercises, we may identify this relationship as the supply rate curve, since its derivations involve only profit maximisation by the firms.

The natural question to ask is whether one can superimpose a demand curve on the supply curve following our adopted procedure. As far as preferences go, the representative household is assumed to maximise

$$U = \int_0^\infty Y(t)\, e^{-rt} dt. \qquad (7.18)$$

This function is significantly different from (2.1). In particular, instantaneous utility is now a linear function of consumption. An important role played by this deviation from (2.1) will be discussed below in connection with the nature of capital markets that may sustain the equilibrium over time. As we have already seen, the level of Y is determined at best as a random variable. Hence, the only sensible maximand for the household is the expected value of U in (7.18). On the other hand, this requires knowledge of the distribution governing the arrival of ideas. This knowledge, however, is restricted to the firm sector alone, since it depends on the equilibrium level of human capital employment in research. Normally, the household is not expected to be able to internalise this knowledge. Thus, the model as posed leaves the demand curve unsolved for.[6] As a result, the equilibrium rate of interest cannot be endogenously determined and continues to be an exogenously specified variable.

---

[6] An alternative procedure, one followed by Grossman and Helpman and to be discussed in Section 7.3 below, is to pose the household's demand problem in nominal terms by solving for the growth rate of optimal expenditure on consumption. In this case, random changes in the level of Y cause proportionate changes in its price, leaving the non-stochastically determined expenditure term unaffected.

PROPOSITION **7.1** *In the presence of obsolescence with new ideas arriving according to a stochastic law, supply forces determine an expected
rate of growth for the economy even when the allocation of human capital to the different sectors of production is invariant over time. This rate
of growth is a monotone decreasing function of the exogenously specified
interest rate prevailing in the market.*

Non-repetitive Equilibrium

In case of a non-repetitive equilibrium, we shall have an infinite se-
quence $\{(\cdots,(\omega_{\tau-1},T_A^{\tau-1}),(\omega_\tau,T_A^\tau),(\omega_{\tau+1},T_A^{\tau+1}),\cdots\}$ satisfying (7.13).
This sequence constitutes a perfect foresight equilibrium in the sense
that its expectation leads to its fulfilment. To understand the nature of
the path followed by the sequence, note that a rise in equilibrium $T_A^{\tau+1}$
causes equilibrium $x_{\tau+1}$ and therefore equilibrium $\hat{\pi}(\omega_{\tau+1})$ to fall. Equation (7.13) implies then a corresponding fall in equilibrium w_τ, a rise in

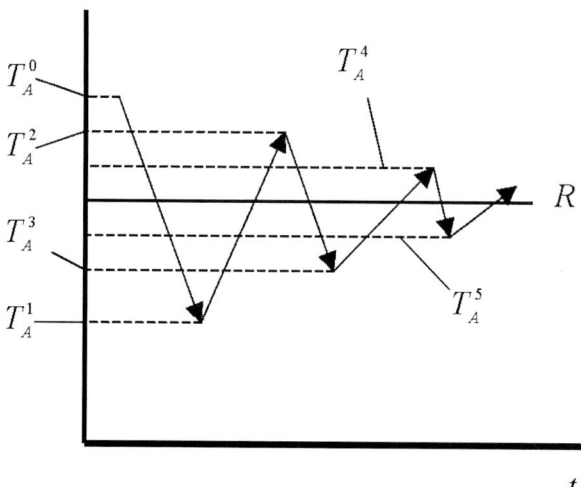

Figure 7.2: A Non-repetitive perfect foresight equilibrium path for the
Aghion-Howitt Economy

x_τ and finally a fall in T_A^τ also. Hence, there is a monotone decreasing
function $T_A^\tau = \psi(T_A^{\tau+1})$ connecting consecutive pairs $(T_A^\tau, T_A^{\tau+1})$. Depending on the slope of the function ψ, alternative scenarios emerge.
One such, a converging sequence to the repetitive equilibrium, is depicted by Figure 7.2. (See Figure 2.3 in Aghion and Howitt (1998)

for more insight into the nature of perfect foresight equilibria.) The perfect foresight equilibrium portrayed by the diagram may be understood as follows. The expectation of T_A^2 gives rise to the employment of $T_A^1 = \Psi(T_A^2)$. Similarly, the expectation of T_A^1 causes $T_A^0 = \Psi(T_A^1)$. The sequence of T_A^τ so generated, when read forwards (following the direction of the arrowheads) converges to a repetitive equilibrium at the level R. Another interesting special case arises when $T_A^0 = \psi(T_A^1)$ and $T_A^1 = \psi(T_A^0)$. If both $T_A^0 > 0$ and $T_A^1 > 0$, then research employment fluctuates without any tendency for convergence. The reader is encouraged to prove that if either T_A^0 or T_A^1 is zero, then the economy is caught in a zero growth trap.

7.2.2 The Private Economy: Non-drastic Innovation

In the drastic innovation case, the incumbent monopolist is not constrained by competition from the holders of previous patents. Non-drastic innovation, by contrast, refers to the case where the incumbent's pricing policy is constrained by the threat of undercutting by past monopolists. In the non-drastic case, the need to keep competitors out leads a monopolist to charge less than in the case of drastic innovation. This means that in both cases, two vintages of intermediate products do not coexist.

We shall derive first a necessary and sufficient condition under which innovation will be drastic. The previous patent holder will stay out of the market if he is allowed a maximum profit of zero. This will be possible if the price of the product is driven down to the average cost of production. Given (7.2), it follows that the price should equal w_τ. The corresponding cost of producing Y by means of the previous generation $x_{\tau-1}$ will be denoted by $C_{\tau-1}(w_\tau, Y)$. Since, $Y = A_{\tau-1}\, x_{\tau-1}^\alpha$ when the previous patent holder supplies x, it follows that

$$
C_{\tau-1}(w_\tau, Y) = w_\tau\, x_{\tau-1}
$$

$$
= w_\tau \left(\frac{Y}{A_{\tau-1}} \right)^{1/\alpha}. \tag{7.19}
$$

The innovation will be drastic if unconstrained monopoly pricing by the latest generation x producer leads to a cost of production of Y that is lower than $C_{\tau-1}(w_\tau, Y)$. Let us calculate this cost. The solutions for x and π in the drastic case are given by (7.5) and (7.7). Further, using

(7.3), the price charged by the monopolist causing drastic innovation is

$$p_\tau = \frac{w_\tau}{\alpha}. \tag{7.20}$$

Hence, the cost function for Y when x_τ replaces $x_{\tau-1}$ is

$$
\begin{aligned}
C_\tau(p_\tau, Y) &= p_\tau\, x_\tau \\[2mm]
&= \frac{1}{\alpha}\, w_\tau \left(\frac{Y}{A_\tau}\right)^{1/\alpha}. \tag{7.21}
\end{aligned}
$$

According to the argument developed above, the innovation is drastic *iff*

$$C_\tau(p_\tau, Y) \le C_{\tau-1}(w_\tau, Y)$$

or, after manipulation,

$$\gamma \ge \alpha^{-\alpha}. \tag{7.22}$$

Alternatively, the innovation is non drastic *iff*

$$\gamma < \alpha^{-\alpha}. \tag{7.23}$$

In this case,

$$C_\tau(p_\tau, Y) > C_{\tau-1}(w_\tau, Y),$$

which suggests that the latest product must be charged a price $\tilde{p}$ lower than p_τ so that $C_\tau(p_\tau, Y)$ falls to

$$C_\tau(\tilde{p}, Y) = C_{\tau-1}(w_\tau, Y).$$

The above equation reduces to

$$\tilde{p}\left(\frac{Y}{A_\tau}\right)^{1/\alpha} = w_\tau \left(\frac{Y}{A_{\tau-1}}\right)^{1/\alpha},$$

or,

$$
\begin{aligned}
\tilde{p} &= \gamma^{1/\alpha}\, w_\tau \\[2mm]
&< \frac{1}{\alpha}\, w_\tau, \text{ given (7.23)}.
\end{aligned}
$$

The corresponding level of profit earned is

$$
\begin{aligned}
\tilde{\pi}_\tau &= \tilde{p}\,\tilde{x}_\tau - w_\tau\,\tilde{x}_\tau \\[2mm]
&= (\gamma^{1/\alpha} - 1)\, w_\tau\,\tilde{x}_\tau \\[2mm]
&> 0,
\end{aligned}
$$

where $\tilde{x}_\tau$ maximises $A_\tau \, x^\alpha - \tilde{p} \, x$. For the repetitive equilibrium case, (7.16) is replaced by

$$\frac{\lambda \, \gamma \, (\gamma^{1/\alpha} - 1) \, \tilde{x}}{r + \lambda \, \tilde{T}_A} = 1. \tag{7.24}$$

7.2.3   The Private Economy: Capital Markets

A problem associated with the uncertain nature of research output is that wages to be paid to human capital may not be coterminous with the arrival of revenue even in the repetitive equilibrium case discussed above. Under the circumstance, the financing of wage payment to research workers would appear to pose a problem. The form of the welfare function (7.18), however, simplifies the problem.

To appreciate this, note that according to (7.12), $w_\tau = \lambda \, V_{\tau+1}$ stands for the expected wage rate of a researcher at each t in the τ-th interval. Thus, aggregate expected wages equal $V_{\tau+1}$ itself when $1/\lambda$ workers are employed. On the other hand, $V_{\tau+1}$ is also the discounted present value of the expected flow of profits to the monopoly firm in possession of $x_{\tau+1}$. According to (7.18), researchers would be indifferent between an expected payment of $V_{\tau+1}$ *now* and the expected flow of returns from an investment of $V_{\tau+1}$ calculated at the rate of interest r.[7] Thus, one may view the Aghion-Howitt world to be organised according to the following plan. At each instant of time, the owners of an existing monopoly firm consume the profit and non-research workers consume the wages. Research workers are treated as potential owners of the monopoly firm that will be set up once they innovate successfully. Consequently, they are indifferent between the expected value of current wages and the expected value of the profit stream.

The above arrangement is equivalent to a perfect credit market where the return to capital loaned out will be equalised with the market rate of interest r.[8]

---

[7] As per (7.18), the household is indifferent between a unit of consumption at t_0 and $e^{r \, (t_1 - t_0)}$ units of consumption at t_1.

[8] Note, however, treating r as the market rate of interest leaves open the question of its determination. In our earlier models, the equilibrium rate of interest was determined endogenously with the equilibrium rate of balanced growth. See remarks at the end of our discussion of the Repetitive Equilibrium. Problems related to capital market imperfections are discussed by Aghion and Howitt (1998), King and Levine (1993).

7.2.4   The Command Economy: Repetitive Equilibrium

In his optimisation exercise, the social planner is in a position to internalise the probability of arrival. Consequently, in a repetitive equilibrium, he will maximise the expected value of U, i.e.,

$$
\begin{aligned}
E\, U &= \int_0^\infty e^{-rt}\, (E\, Y(t))\, dt \\[2mm]
&= A_0\, x^\alpha \int_0^\infty e^{-rt}\, \left(\sum_0^\infty \frac{e^{-\lambda\, T_A\, t}\, (\lambda\, T_A\, t)^\tau}{\tau!} \right) \gamma^\tau\, dt \\[2mm]
&= A_0\, x^\alpha \int_0^\infty e^{-(r-\lambda\, T_A\, (\gamma-1))t}\, dt \\[2mm]
&= \frac{A_0\, (\bar{T} - T_A)^\alpha}{r - \lambda\, T_A\, (\gamma - 1)}.
\end{aligned}
\tag{7.25}
$$

The derivation of (7.25) uses the fact that

$$
\sum_{\tau=0}^\infty \frac{(\lambda\, T_A\, \gamma\, t)^\tau\, e^{-\lambda\, T_A\, t}}{\tau!} = e^{-\lambda\, T_A\, t} \sum_{\tau=0}^\infty \frac{(\lambda\, T_A\, \gamma\, t)^\tau}{\tau!}
$$

$$
= e^{\lambda\, T_A\, (\gamma-1)\, t}.
$$

The planner maximises (7.25) *wrt* T_A, the *FOC* for which reduces to

$$
1 = \frac{\lambda\, (\gamma - 1)\, (1/\alpha)\, (\bar{T} - T_A^*)}{r - \lambda\, T_A^*\, (\gamma - 1)},
\tag{7.26}
$$

where T_A^* stands for the optimal choice by the planner. Comparison with (7.16) as well as (7.24) reveals that the planners choice of T_A^* may be lower than $\hat{T}_A$ or $\tilde{T}_A$. Consequently, the expected rate of growth in the Command economy could fall short of that achieved by the Private economy. (See (7.17).) The result is reminiscent of our findings in Chapter 3 in connection with the Quality of life model. Aghion and Howitt explain it by noting that the planner is likely to internalise the profits/ losses of an incumbent monopolist on account of early arrival of the next generation input in calculating the social gain from innovation. This could cause him to reduce the equilibrium input into the research sector. The Private economy on the other hand, will not internalise the losses arising from obsolescence and might end up growing faster. The penultimate line of (7.25), however, suggests an alternative interpretation of the result, one that is comparable to the intuition underlying the Quality of life model, or indeed, any model of optimum growth. As we can see, the expression involves a trade-off between consumption (the term $A_0 \, x^\alpha$) and rate of growth (the term $e^{\lambda \, T_A \, (\gamma-1)}$). The planner's choice of T_A^* balances off one against the other. The Private economy, as we have seen, engages in no optimisation exercise at all as far as the household's welfare goes. Profit maximisation by the firms, without reference to the growth consumption trade-off incorporated in the welfare function, can therefore give rise to excessive growth and sub-optimal consumption.

PROPOSITION **7.2** *The Command economy for the Aghion and Howitt model internalises losses on account of excessive growth, arising either due to losses from obsolescence or consumption, and may end up growing at a rate lower than the Private economy.*

7.3 Quality Ladders - Grossman and Helpman: Description of the Economy

The second model we proceed to discuss in this chapter goes back to Grossman and Helpman. They called it the Quality ladder model and meant it to complement their Brand proliferation model of the previous chapter. This model bears to the Aghion and Howitt exercise roughly the same relationship that the Brand proliferation model bore to the Romer (1990) model. Thus, the intermediate input sector is avoided, new ideas being incorporated directly in final products. Moreover, as against the Aghion and Howitt model, the final goods sector manufactures a fixed set of commodities, represented by a continuum of size unity. Each commodity j in the set $(0, 1]$, however, faces a random prospect of quality upgradation at each point of time.[9] Thus, a commodity can be improved in a discrete sequence of endlessly many vertically differentiated varieties. The τ-th quality of product j is indicated by a quantitative index A_j^τ, $\tau = 1, 2, \cdots$, with $A_j^{\tau+1} = \gamma \, A_j^\tau$, independent of j and τ.

---

[9]Quality upgradation is to be understood as new innovative goods replacing old ones and offering more services per unit of expenditure on them. '$\cdots$ a compact disc player would be regarded as a superior version of the phonograph. [The] treatment abstracts from the obvious reality that these, like most, sophisticated products are distinguished by more than a single characteristic $\cdots$' Grossman and Helpman (1991b), Chapter 4, p. 85.

We shall further normalise $A_j^0 = 1$, $\forall j$ and denote by x_j^τ the level of consumption of the A_j^τ-th variety of commodity j.

In case of Aghion and Howitt, we argued that there was no point in solving the household's dynamic optimisation exercise, since the household is not in a position to internalise the uncertainty associated with the emergence of new intermediate inputs. In the Quality ladder model, however, this problem is avoided by posing the household's choice problem with reference to its "expenditure" on the fixed set of final goods. Each commodity in the set is viewed as an imperfect substitute of each other. However, given any commodity in the set, a unit of quality incorporated in any specific variety of it is a perfect substitute of a unit of quality in any other. Define the composite commodity index[10] as

$$ln\ D(t) = \int_0^1 ln\ \sum_\tau A_j^\tau\ x_j^\tau\ dj. \tag{7.27}$$

The linear term $\sum_\tau A_j^\tau\ x_j^\tau$ confirms our observation above that a unit of A_j^τ is a perfect substitute for a unit of $A_j^{\tau'}$, $\tau \neq \tau'$. The corresponding welfare function is assumed to be

$$U = \int_0^\infty e^{-\rho\ t}\ ln\ D(t)\ dt, \tag{7.28}$$

---

[10]Writing $\sum_\tau A_j^\tau\ x_j^\tau = X(j)$ for simplicity, this may be seen as a special case of (6.29) obtained by letting $\alpha \to 0$. Rewrite (6.29) as

$$D^\alpha = \int_0^1 X(j)^\alpha\ dj,$$

$$\text{or, } D^\alpha - 1 = \int_0^1 X(j)^\alpha\ dj - 1,$$

$$\text{or, } \frac{D^\alpha - 1}{\alpha} = \int_0^1 \frac{X(j)^\alpha - 1}{\alpha}\ dj,$$

$$\text{or, } lim_{\alpha \to 0} \frac{D^\alpha - 1}{\alpha} = \int_0^1 \lim_{\alpha \to 0} \frac{X(j)^\alpha - 1}{\alpha}\ dj,$$

$$\text{or, } ln\ D = \int_0^1 ln\ X(j)\ dj.$$

The form $(X(j)^\alpha - 1)/\alpha$ is reminiscent of (2.18). With $\alpha \to 0$, we can see that the elasticity of substitution between commodity pairs is unity. Thus, as noted above, any two commodities in the set $(0, 1]$ are imperfect substitutes.

As in the case of Chapter 6, we choose to represent prices in some abstract unit. Denoting total expenditure on manufactured products by the household at any instant by E, it is easy to see (by maximising (7.27) subject to an appropriate budget constraint) that expenditure is distributed uniformly across all commodities. Moreover, the cardinality of the set of commodities being unity, the expenditure on each variety is E.

We may note trivially that the household will spend only on that variety of a commodity which yields the maximum quality per unit of expenditure. Let $\hat{\tau}$ be that variety and p_j^τ be the price of variety τ. Then the household's demand function for commodity j at any instant is given by

$$x_j^\tau = \begin{cases} E/p_j^\tau, & \text{if } \tau = \hat{\tau} \\ 0 & \text{otherwise} . \end{cases}$$

The above function assumes the absence of a tie between two different varieties of j.[11]

The above constitutes a solution to the household's static optimisation problem. To solve the dynamic optimisation exercise, we begin by constructing a price index for the composite product $[x_j^{\hat{\tau}}]_0^1$. We proceed as in Chapter 6 by viewing D as a production function and maximising profits for a competitive producer of the product. Using (7.27), the production function is written in explicit form as

$$D = e^{\int_0^1 \ln A_j^{\hat{\tau}} \, x_j^{\hat{\tau}} \, dj}.$$

The competitive producer maximises $p_D \, D - \int_0^1 p_j^{\hat{\tau}} \, x_j^{\hat{\tau}} \, dj$, where p_D is the price of the composite good D. The *FOC* for this problem is

$$p_D \left(e^{\int_0^1 \ln A_j^{\hat{\tau}} \, x_j^{\hat{\tau}} \, dj} \right) \frac{1}{x_j^{\hat{\tau}}} = p_j^{\hat{\tau}} \, \forall \, j.$$

Applying logarithm to both sides and simplifying

$$p_D = e^{\int_0^1 \ln (p_j^{\hat{\tau}})/(A_j^{\hat{\tau}}) \, dj}.$$

Given this expression, the household's dynamic optimisation problem is solved precisely the same way as in Section 6.3 and the solution is identical with (6.38).

We may proceed now to a discussion of the producers' behaviour.

---

[11] The reason underlying this fact will be evident once we explain the nature of oligopolistic competition underlying the manufacturing sector.

7.3.1   Manufacturing and Research Sector

Let us begin with producers of the final goods. Parallel to Chapter 6, each variety of a product j requires a unit of human capital to be produced. Thus, the marginal cost of production equals the wage rate w irrespective of variety as well as product type. Each industry j is characterised by oligopolistic competition. The outcome of the competition, however, is that there is effectively a single producer in industry j producing the latest variety of the product.[12] Imagine first that there are multiple producers producing a particular variety of the product. There are two possibilities here. First, one is a successful innovator and the other is an imitator. Price competition will drive the price down to marginal cost (i.e., the wage rate). The innovator's profit will be zero and the imitator, who will have an imitation cost in addition to the cost of production, will earn negative profit. The latter, therefore, cannot survive. The second case involves two simultaneous innovators. This possibility has very low probability. To see this, assume that the probability of success[13] in research during an interval dt is $\lambda\, T_{A_j}^{\tau}\, dt$ if T_{A_j} units of labour are employed to carry out research. When simultaneously running research projects are characterised by two statistically independent probability distributions, the probability of joint occurrence of two successes is $(\lambda\, T_{A_j}^{\tau}\, dt)^2$, which is negligibly small (even if the two processes employ different quantities of labour, say $T_{A_{j1}}^{\tau}$ and $T_{A_{j2}}^{\tau}$).

For reasons similar to the ones characterising the case of nondrastic innovation in the Aghion and Howitt model, the market will follow a pricing mechanism that ensures that two producers, one using the latest technology and the other lagging a step behind, cannot coexist. In order to drive the older technology out, the state of the art producer will charge a price marginally below $\gamma\, w$, if w is the ruling wage rate.[14] Consequently, he will earn a profit approximately equal to

$$\pi \;=\; \gamma\, w\, x - w\, x \tag{7.29}$$

$$=\; \left(1 - \frac{1}{\gamma}\right) \gamma\, w\, x$$

---

[12]Refer to the immediately preceding footnote.

[13]The probability distribution is assumed to have the same features as in the Aghion and Howitt model.

[14]The reader should work this out.

$$= \left(1 - \frac{1}{\gamma}\right) p \, x$$

$$= \left(1 - \frac{1}{\gamma}\right) E. \qquad (7.30)$$

It is revealing to note that the successful monopolist will never wish to stay more than one step ahead of the one he ousts. Assume to the contrary that he is two steps ahead. Then, he will charge a price slightly below $\gamma^2 \, w$ and his profit from the new venture will be approximately

$$p \, x - w \, x \;=\; \gamma^2 \, w \, \frac{E}{\gamma^2 \, w} - w \, \frac{E}{\gamma^2 \, w}$$

$$= \left(1 - \frac{1}{\gamma^2}\right) E.$$

Against this, however, he will have to set off the loss he causes to himself by scrapping the previous generation product. Thus, his net return will be

$$\left(1 - \frac{1}{\gamma^2}\right) E - \left(1 - \frac{1}{\gamma}\right) E = \frac{1}{\gamma} \left(1 - \frac{1}{\gamma}\right) E,$$

which falls short of $(1 - 1/\gamma) \, E$ in (7.30).

The industries being symmetric, the employment of human capital in each line of production may be taken to be identical, independent of the generation of the product being researched (i.e., the value of τ). We may therefore denote the value of this variable by $T_A(t)$ at time t. The size of the set of products being unity, $T_A(t)$ stands for the aggregate quantity of human capital employed in research also. In the same vein, $p_j^\tau(t) = p(t) = \gamma \, w(t)$, $\forall \, j$. Thus, total human capital employed in manufacturing is $E(t)/\gamma \, w(t)$. The market for human capital will be in equilibrium at each t if

$$T_A(t) + \frac{E(t)}{\gamma \, w(t)} = \bar{T}, \qquad (7.31)$$

where $\bar{T}$ stands for the fixed quantum of human capital at all t, as in the previous model.

7.3.2   Repetitive Equilibrium

To describe the equilibrium, let us first solve for the value $V(t)$ of a research firm. This is easily done, given our derivation of (7.10). Thus,

$$
\begin{aligned}
V(t) &= \int_t^\infty e^{-\int_t^s r(i)di}\, e^{\int_t^s -\lambda\, T_A(i)di}\, \pi(s)\; ds \\[2mm]
&= \int_t^\infty e^{-\int_t^s (r(i)+\lambda\, T_A(i))di}\, \left(1 - \frac{1}{\gamma}\right)\, E(s)\; ds.
\end{aligned}
$$

$$(7.32)$$

In a repetitive equilibrium, $T_A(t) = T_A \;\forall\, t$. Hence, from (7.31), $E(t)/\gamma\; w(t) = constant$. Following the procedure of Section 6.3.2, substitute $E(s) = E(t)\, e^{\int_t^s (r(\tau)-\rho)d\tau}$ in (7.32) and write $u(t) = V(t)/E(t)$ to conclude

$$
u(t) = \left(1 - \frac{1}{\gamma}\right)\, \int_t^\infty e^{-(\rho+\lambda\, T_A)(s-t)}\; ds.
$$

Thus, in a repetitive equilibrium, u is a constant for all t. Upon differentiation, we obtain

$$
\frac{\dot{u}}{u} = (\rho + \lambda\, T_A) - \left(1 - \frac{1}{\gamma}\right)\frac{1}{u} \qquad (7.33)
$$

Let $\bar{V} = 1/u$, which is a *constant* in repetitive equilibrium. Then, (7.33) reduces to

$$
\begin{aligned}
\dot{\bar{V}}/\bar{V} &= \left(1 - \frac{1}{\gamma}\right)\, \bar{V} - (\rho + \lambda\, T_A) \\[2mm]
&= 0.
\end{aligned}
$$

$$(7.34)$$

Equation (7.31) is rewritten

$$
T_A = \bar{T} - \frac{1}{\lambda\,\gamma}\, \bar{V}, \qquad (7.35)
$$

using (7.12) and the definition of $\bar{V}$. The solution to (7.34) and (7.35) yields the repetitive equilibrium values of T_A and $\bar{V}$.[15]

---

[15]The reader should be able to argue (following Grossman and Helpman (1991a, 1991b)) that the economy jumps to the balanced growth equilibrium solution as in the models of Chapter 3. Grossman and Helpman demonstrate further that any trajectory other than the balanced growth path cannot define a perfect foresight equilibrium.

It is of interest to appreciate the nature of the balanced growth equilibrium. Similar to the Aghion and Howitt model, an industry does not grow in a deterministic fashion. Each industry progresses in random jumps, following a Poisson distribution. By virtue of the law of large numbers though, the ratio of successful industries in the set of all industries at each t is λT_A. As a result, the growth rate g_D of the consumption index D turns out to be a constant. To calculate g_D, denote $A_j^{\hat{t}}(t) = \hat{A}_j(t)$ and $x_j^{\hat{t}}(t) = \hat{x}_j(t)$ and rewrite (7.27) as

$$ln\ D(t) = \int_0^1 ln\ \hat{A}_j(t)\ \hat{x}_j(t)\ dj.$$

Note that $\hat{x}_j(t) = E(t)/p_j(t) = E(t)/\gamma\ w(t)$. Hence,

$$ln\ D(t) = \int_0^1 ln\ \hat{A}_j(t)\ dj + ln\ E(t) - ln\ w(t) - ln\ \gamma.$$

Since $\bar{V} = E/V$, $w = \lambda\ V$ and $\dot{\bar{V}}/\bar{V} = 0$, it follows that $\dot{w}/w = \dot{E}/E$. Consequently,

$$g_D = \frac{d\ ln\ D(t)}{d\ t} = \frac{d}{dt} \int_0^1 ln\ \hat{A}_j(t)\ dj.$$

The expression $\int_0^1 ln\ \hat{A}_j(t)$ may be viewed as the mean of the logarithms of qualities across all products. Consider now the Poisson probability that a given product will take exactly m steps up the quality ladder in an interval $[0, t]$. The set of industries being a continuum, the Law of Large Numbers implies that the probability equals the fraction of industries experiencing m quality improvements in $[0, t]$. Normalising $\hat{A}_j(0) = 1$, it follows that

$$\int_0^1 ln\ \hat{A}_j(t)\ dj = \sum_{m=0}^{\infty} \frac{(\lambda\ T_A\ t)^m\ e^{-\lambda\ T_A\ t}}{m!}\ ln\ \gamma^m$$

$$= ln\ \gamma \sum_0^{\infty} \frac{(\lambda\ T_A\ t)^m\ e^{-\lambda\ T_A\ t}}{m!}\ m.$$

But $\left[\sum_0^{\infty} ((\lambda\ T_A\ t)^m\ e^{-\lambda\ T_A\ t}/m!)\ m \right]$ is the expected number of improvements in $[0, t]$, which in turn equals $\lambda\ T_A\ t$. Thus,

$$\int_0^1 ln\ \hat{A}_j(t)\ dj = \lambda\ T_A\ t\ ln\ \gamma$$

and

$$g_D = \lambda \, T_A \, ln \, \gamma, \tag{7.36}$$

the RHS of which is identically the same as (7.17). As far as the LHS goes, however, the Grossman-Helpman model solves for an equilibrium growth rate that is independent of r, while, as already observed, Aghion and Howitt end up only with a supply side picture. Grossman and Helpman succeed in eliminating the effect of r by incorporating demand factors in the equilibrium solution. Their method depends crucially on two factors. First, they pose the problem of demand in terms of expenditure E, which helps them convert a stochastic exercise to a deterministic one. A second and no less important reason lies in the choice of the logarithmic utility function. This second fact played an important role in the brand proliferation model of Chapter 6 too and was pointed out in the footnote following equation (6.47).[16]

PROPOSITION **7.3** *In the Quality ladder model characterised by a fixed set of final products, with new qualities arriving according to a stochastic law in each line of production, supply as well as demand forces determine an expected rate of growth of the system even when human capital allocation repeats over time. The rate of growth is independent of the rate of interest, but the model does not determine an equilibrium rate of interest for the system.*

This chapter has presented two examples of growth models based on the insight provided by Schumpeter's work. The essence of his idea was that growth inevitably proceeds through a process of "creative destruction" or "business stealing", as the discovery of higher grade products drive out existing ones. There is a significantly large literature on creative destruction led growth. Some of these are summarised in Dinopoulos (1994) and Romer (1994). Apart from the works covered by this book, one of the earliest foundations of Schumpeterian growth theory may be found in Segerstrom, Anant and Dinopoulos (1990). There has been substantial progress in this area of research since then and some of the findings are adequately summarised in Dinopoulos and Sener (2003). Readers interested in finding out more on the subject may refer to this last mentioned work for more recent thoughts.

---

[16]We refrain from proceeding to discuss the direction of divergence between the Private economy growth rate and the Command economy growth rate. Grossman and Helpman arrive at conclusions similar to the ones of Aghion and Howitt and no additional insight can be gained by working through the algebra.

Summary

• Chapter 6 viewed growth as a result of research activity based on human capital. The model of research, however, was deterministic in nature. In reality, research is characterized by uncertainty. This chapter recognized this fact and introduced, following Aghion and Howitt (1992, 1998), an element of randomness in the arrival of ideas. Further, it recognized the fact that older inventions are often made obsolete by the arrival of new ideas thereby making economic growth an instance of what Schumpeter described as a process of economic destruction.

• Each new generation of idea is assumed to arrive with a specified increase in productivity. Nonetheless, the growth is not exogenously known since the date of arrival of each idea is itself unknown. The result, amongst other things, is that a determinstic growt rate is replaced by an expected growth rate.

• The probability of success in research is positively dependent on labour input. The possible arrival of new products and associated profits have a positive effect on labour demand. On the other hand, competition from future researchers bring up risks of obsolescence of currently discovered products. These two effects work in opposite directions to determine the equilibrium employment of research labour. Once this is known, the expected rate of growth is endogenously determined, since the probability of research success depends on equilibrium employment.

• Innovations can be drastic or non-drastic. In the drastic case the new technology renders old ones infeasible. In the non-drastic case new monopolists face the possibility of price competition from earlier monopolists. Equilibrium employment could repeat over time or be non-repetitive. The non-repetitive case introduces alternative possibilities of growth trajectories, including a zero growth rate.

• The Command Economy grows at a lower expected rate since it internalizes the losses that can arise from future innovations.

• Grossman and Helpman introduce a quality ladder model that bears to the Aghion and Howitt model the same relationship as the brand proliferation model of the previous chapter did to the Romer model. Apart from the dependence of the expected rate of growth on the rate of interest in the Aghion and Howitt model, the expressions for the rate of growth turn out to be the same for both models.

Problems

1. (From Barro and Sala-i-Martin (2003)) Suppose that the government prevents research by private agents and carries out all research by itself. What should be the impact of this change on social welfare.

2. (From Aghion and Howitt (1998)) In real life, monopolists already manufacturing existing products carry out research towards quality improvement. The reason underlying this is the monopolists' better acquaintance with the products compared to new entrants. Extend the Aghion and Howitt model to consider this possibility and determine the equation determining the level of research workers in equilibrium.

Chapter 8

Other Major Issues: Growth, Scale Effects and Inequality

8.1 Introduction

The previous chapters covered some of the classic models of endogenous growth theory. While these works strongly influenced the research agenda of growth theory, subsequent work raised major questions relating to these works. One of these arose from a path breaking paper by Jones (1995) in which he questioned the role played by human capital in the models covered under Chapters 6 and 7. The issue in question was that the stock of human capital functioned as a shift parameter in the models (equation (6.11) for Chapter 6 and the Poisson arrival assumption for Chapter 7) and, as will be argued below, Jones questioned the empirical validity of this conclusion. Jones' work generated a series of refinements in endogenous growth theory and Dinopoulos and Sener (2003) offers a lucid summary of these developments. The present chapter will, however, concentrate mainly on Jones' contribution.

Another important issue that was neglected in the earlier chapters was the relation between growth and inequality. This is an issue that policy makers in most developing economies need to face. A very large body of literature has developed in this connection. As with the Jones issue above, the objective of this chapter is somewhat modest. It introduces the reader to two well-known models that studied the link between growth and inequality, those due to Alesina and Rodrik (1994) and Galor and Zeira (1993). Alesina and Rodrik discuss the problem from the point of view of political economy, while Galor and Zeira fall back upon an overlapping generation model where agents are endowed with bequest motives to derive the long run implications for income distribututation. The reader should note that, apart from the Galor and Zeira paper, all the other models covered by the book deal with dynastic set ups. Readers interested in following up the highly interesting area of research on growth and inequality are referred to Aghion et al (1999).

8.2   The Jones Critique

Jones starts off with the observation that most R and D-based models predict scale effects. In other words, if the number of scientists in the R and D sector is doubled, then the per capita growth rate of an economy should also double. He observes that the number of scientists in advance economies has grown substantially over time. But this increase has not been accompanied by a commensurate rise in the rate of long run growth. In particular, the number of engineers and scientists engaged in R and D in the United States has grown from 200,000 in 1950 to around a million in 1987. But the growth rate of the US economy falls far below this five fold rise in human capital. He concludes from this that the models of the last two chapters are inconsistent with observed facts.

To rectify matters, Jones suggests a revised version of the Romer (1990) model, but he concludes from this that the long run growth rate turns impervious once again (as in Solow (1956)) to policy changes. On the other hand, despite the dependence of the growth rate on exogenous factors alone, Jones' model continues to belong to the class of endogenous growth models.

8.2.1   Jones' Critique and Extensions for the Private Economy

The 'scale effects' in Romer's model are summarized in the reduced model involving the pair of equations (6.11) and (6.15). For ease of reference, we rewrite these below in a simplified form:

$$Y \;=\; K^{1-\alpha}(AT_y)^{\alpha} \tag{8.1}$$

$$\frac{\dot{A}}{A} = \delta\, T_A \qquad (8.2)$$

Equation (8.2) implies that a doubling of T_A doubles the rate of growth of knowledge. In equilibrium, T_A is a constant fraction of the total stock of human capital. Thus, a doubling of total T would imply a doubling of the growth rate. This, as already noted, is not supported by data.

In his search for a new model, Jones starts off with an R and D equation that resembles (6.42). We reproduce this below as

$$\dot{A} = \bar{a}\, T_A, \qquad (8.3)$$

which replaces a in (6.42) by $\bar{a}$. The equation states that knowledge accumulation depends on the number of researchers alone (as in the case of the Poisson process of Chapter 7). The next question Jones asks is how should $\bar{a}$ in (8.3) be linked to A itself? Since existing knowledge creates externalities, he assumes as a first approximation that

$$\bar{a} = a\, A^{\phi} \qquad (8.4)$$

When $\phi < 0$, the rate of innovation decreases with the level of knowledge. Jones refers to this as the "fishing out" case. Positive externalities from knowledge emerge only if $\phi > 0$. When $\phi = 0$, one goes back to (6.42), the case of no externalities. Next, he notes that at any point of time, it is possible for duplication and overlapping research, which reduces the effective number of researchers. Suppose then that the effective labour force engaged in research is T_A^{λ}, $0 < \lambda \le 1$. Equations (8.3) and (8.4) reduce to

$$\dot{A} = a\, T_A\, A^{\phi}\, l_A^{\lambda-1}, \qquad (8.5)$$

where the coefficient l_A represents the possibility of duplicaion generated externalities. In the absence of duplications, i.e. in equilibrium, $l_A = T_A$.[1]

Jones' model replicates Romer (1990), except for the new equation (8.5) replacing (6.11). Equation (8.5) is rewritten

$$\frac{\dot{A}}{A} = a\, \frac{T_A^{\lambda}}{A^{1-\phi}}. \qquad (8.6)$$

---

[1] Note that (8.5) reduces to (6.11) when $\phi = 1 = l_A$.

For balance growth, $\dot{A}/A$ is a constant. Hence, this necessitates T_A^λ and $A^{1-\phi}$ to grow at the same rate. This restriction, as we shall see, puts a bound on the growth rate of the system, thereby ridding the Romer (1990) model of its prediction of unlimited growth subject to the availability of human capital. Since T_A^λ and $A^{1-\phi}$ grow at the same rate under balanced growth, it follows that

$$g_A = \frac{\lambda\, n}{1 - \phi},\tag{8.7}$$

where g_A is the balanced growth rate of A, where n is the exogenously specified rate of growth of T.[2] Quite clearly, the balanced growth rate for this economy is impervious to policy innovations, such as taxes and subsidies.

The share of human capital in the R and D sector of the Private Economy is[3]

$$s^{PE} = \frac{L_A}{L}$$

$$= \frac{1}{1 + \psi^{PE}},\tag{8.8}$$

$$\text{where } \psi^{PE} = \frac{1}{1 - \alpha}\left[\frac{\rho(1 - \phi)}{\lambda\, n} + \frac{1}{\theta}\right],$$

where PE stands for the Private Economy and θ has the same interpretation as in Chapter 2. The share of labour in R and D is positively related to the rate of balanced growth $\lambda\, n/(1 - \phi)$. Since the latter depends on exogenously specified parameters, however, it is the value of these parameters that determine the share in question. It would be erroneous to conclude from here that the Jones model is not an exercise in endogenous growth. As with Proposition 3.1, the rate of growth, even if unalterable by policy changes, is nevertheless determined endogenously by solving for the model. A rise in ρ as well as θ too affect the share. But a change in the productivity parameter a cannot affect the share.

---

[2] Problem 1 asks you to prove that $g_A = g_Y = g_C = g_K$.
[3] See Problem 4.

8.2.2   Jones' Command Economy

It is natural to ask how the Command Economy solution will differ from the Private Economy solution for the balanced growth share of human capital. Using the methods employed earlier, it is not difficult to show that

$$s^{CE} = \frac{L_A}{L}$$

$$= \frac{1}{1 + \psi^{CE}}, \tag{8.9}$$

$$\text{where } \psi^{CE} = \frac{1}{\lambda}\left[\frac{\rho(1-\phi)}{\lambda\,n} + \frac{1}{\theta} - \phi\right],$$

The extra term "$-\phi$" in s^{CE} indicates that the Command Economy internalizes the corresponding externality. If $\phi > 0$, s^{CE} tends to rise because private agents do not take into account to external effect of R and D for the future. When $\phi < 0$, the opposite should be the case. The factor $\lambda < 1$ exerts a negative externality that leads the private economy to overinvest in research. Lastly, the monolpoly induced inefficiency impacts the Jones model the same way it impacts the Romer (1990) economy. The relative values of s^{CE} and s^{PE} depend upon the values of the parameters. Interestingly enough though, Jones' calibration exercise involving different plausible values of the parameters leads to the conclusion that the Private Economy underinvests even when the values of ϕ and λ suggest otherwise. Given these calculations, Jones conjectures that the monopoly generated inefficiency effect (discussed in Section 6.2.2) may dominate other external effects in the model.

8.3   Growth and Inequality

This book has so far ignored a vital question that most developing economies are asking. While growth is seen as a sine qua non for development, can it be achieved with a human face? In other words, does growth lead to concentration of wealth and income and more poverty? Conventional economic theory suggests that inequality is beneficial for growth, since it leads to adequate incentives for investment. However, there is no convergence of views on this subject. This section tries to present two models of new growth theory which address this somewhat unsettled question.

8.3.1   Alesina and Rodrik: Political Economy and Growth

Alesina and Rodrik (1994) were amongst the first researchers to draw
attention to the problems of income and wealth inequality associated
with economic growth. They assumed that production is carried out
with the help of public services. The aggregate production is given by

$$y = Ak^{\alpha}\Gamma^{1-\alpha}l^{1-\alpha} \tag{8.10}$$

where k and l are capital and labor services respectively and Γ is the
aggregate level of government spending to support firms' production.[4]
Government expenditure is financed by capital taxation so that

$$\Gamma = \tau k \tag{8.11}$$

where τ stands for the proportional rate of taxation as in (5.3), but
the tax now is imposed on capital services, rather than output. The
assumption of perfect competition yields

$$
\begin{aligned}
r &= \frac{\partial y}{\partial k} \\
&= \alpha A\tau^{1-\alpha} \\
&= r(\tau) \tag{8.12} \\
w &= \frac{\partial y}{\partial l} \\
&= (1-\alpha)A\tau^{1-\alpha}k \\
&= \omega(\tau)k \tag{8.13} \\
&\tag{8.14}
\end{aligned}
$$

where w is the wage rate of unskilled labor and l is normalized to unity.
Net income of capital and labor are then

$$
\begin{aligned}
y^k &= (r(\tau) - \tau)k \\
y^l &= \omega\tau, \tag{8.15}
\end{aligned}
$$

---

[4]Aggregate output, capital etc. are denoted by y, k rather than Y, K etc. The
change is motivated by the scheme chosen by the authors of the work being reported.

with $y^k + y^l + \Gamma = y$. The structure of the model being similar to that of Barro and Sala-i-Martin (See Chapter 5), the economy will display perpetual balanced growth. The tax on capital performs two functions. First, it affects the demand rate of growth by altering the incentive to save. Secondly, it redistributes income from capital owners to workers by improving the marginal productivity of labor through higher government spending. Agents in the economy differ from each other only in terms of their endowments of labor and capital and this alone is the source of inequality in the model. Agents are identified by their relative endowments of labor and capital as captured by the relative factor endowment index

$$\sigma^i = \frac{l^i}{k^i/k}, \quad \sigma^i \in [0, \infty). \tag{8.16}$$

An agent with high σ is capital poor and vice versa. From (8.15), the income of agent i is

$$y^i = \omega(\tau)kl^i + (r(\tau) - \tau)k^i = \omega(\tau)k^i\sigma^i + (r(\tau) - \tau)k^i.$$

Each individual represents a dynastic household and solves for the path of optimal consumption by maximizing

$$\int_0^\infty ln \; c^i e^{(-\rho t)} dt \tag{8.17}$$

$$\text{subject to } \dot{k}^i = \omega(\tau)k^i\sigma^i + (r(\tau) - \tau)k^i - c^i, \tag{8.18}$$

where c^i denotes consumption. Each individual consumer assumes that the paths of r, k and τ are given. The equation of the demand rate curve for each individual is then

$$\frac{\dot{c}^i}{c^i} = (r(\tau) - \tau) - \rho = \gamma\tau, \tag{8.19}$$

which is independent of individual specific parameters. In a balanced growth equilibrium each individual accumulates k^i by choosing $\dot{k}^i/k^i = \gamma(\tau)$. Consequently, the relative factor ownership remains invariant over time, give each τ. Using these facts, it follows that

$$\gamma'(\tau) = \frac{\partial g}{\partial \tau}$$

$$= (1 - \alpha)\alpha A\tau^{-\alpha} - 1 > 0$$

$$\text{if } \tau < ((1 - \alpha)\alpha A)^{1/\alpha}.$$

For small tax rates, the productivity effect of public expenditure dominates and net return to capital increases with τ. For large tax rates, the return falls. Hence, a growth rate maximizing tax rate is easily found and equals

$$\tau^* = (\alpha(1-\alpha)A)^{1/\alpha}.$$

The best tax rate varies with individuals. To see this, we may note that the government, in order to maximize an individual's well-being, should maximize

$$\int_0^\infty \ln c^i e^{(-\rho t)} dt,$$

$$\text{subject to } c^i = (\omega(\tau)\sigma^i + \rho)k^i,$$

$$\frac{\dot{k}^i}{k^i} = \gamma(\tau),$$

$$\frac{\dot{k}}{k} = \gamma(\tau),$$

where the expression for c^i follows from (8.18), (8.19) and the fact that $\dot{k}^i/k^i = \dot{c}^i/c^i$. Solving the problem, individual i's most preferred tax rate, τ^i, is found from

$$\tau^i(-\alpha A(1-\alpha)(\tau^i)^{-\alpha}) = \rho(1-\alpha)\theta^i(\tau^i),$$

where $\theta^i(\tau^i) = \omega(\tau^i)\sigma^i/(\omega(\tau^i)\sigma^i + \rho)$ is the share of labor income in consumption expenditure, which increases in σ^i. The tax rate is a constant over time and rises with σ^i. In other words, relatively capital poor agents choose higher capital tax rates. If $\sigma^i = 0$, i.e. the agent is a pure capital-owner, then $\tau^i = \tau^* = (\alpha(1-\alpha)A)^{1/\alpha}$. That is, a pure-capital owner chooses the maximal growth rate for the economy.

The authors investigate the nature of the tax and growth rates under majority voting. The decision is reached by pair wise comparison under simple majority rule. Using the median-voter theorem, the tax rate τ^m chosen under majority rule is defined implicitly by

$$\tau^m(1 - \alpha A(1-\alpha)(\tau^m)^{-\alpha}) = \rho(1-\alpha)\theta^m(\tau^m), \qquad (8.20)$$

where $\theta^m(\tau^m) = \omega(\tau^m)\sigma^m/(\omega(\tau^m)\sigma^m + \rho)$ is the relative factor endowment of the median voter. Equation (8.20) gives a relationship between the distribution of factor ownership and growth. One expects that in the real world, the median voter's labor-capital share is above the average share, i.e., $\sigma^m - 1 > 0$. The greater the inequality, the larger the difference between the median and the average. Thus, $\sigma^m - 1$ is an index of inequality.

We can rewrite y^i as $(\omega + (r - \tau)(1/\sigma^i))$ $l^i k$. Thus, y^i is inversely related to σ^i. The larger is $\sigma^m - 1$, the larger would be the gap between median and average income. Hence, (8.20) implies that the higher is $\sigma^m - 1$, the lower is the rate of growth of the economy. In other words, the more unequal is the distribution of income and wealth, the lower is the rate of growth of the society.

This result has been a source of much controversy in growth theory since conventional wisdom in economics suggests the opposite relationship.

8.3.2 Galor and Zeira: Long Run Impact of Growth on Inequality

Galor and Zeira (1993) attempt to explain how differences in initial income distributions affect the growth strategies adopted by different economies and study how the chosen growth paths affect in turn the income distributions over time. The basic premise on which their work rests is that levels of skill formation (hence, investment in human capital) have positive implications for growth and that inequalities in inherited wealth in the presence of imperfect capital markets determine individuals' capacities for skill formation. A society that starts off with an unequal wealth distribution (as is the case with underdeveloped economies) tends to move towards unequal distribution of income, whereas a society that has an equal distribution of income tends towards equal distribution of incomes.

The authors consider a small open economy that faces a given world rate of interest r, at which it can borrow or lend in an imperfect capital market. A single good is produced with the help of two different technologies. The efficient technology uses skilled labor L_t^s and capital K_t at time t. The output of skilled labour is denoted by Y_t^s and the technology is given by the concave production function

$$Y_t^s = F(K_t, L_t^s) \tag{8.21}$$

On the other hand, Y_t^n represents the same good produced by means of unskilled labor, L_t^n, and the technology in this case is

$$Y_t^n = w_n L_t^n \tag{8.22}$$

where w_t is the marginal product of unskilled labour.

Unlike the models presented so far, agents live for two periods in the Galor-Zeira world. In the first period they are endowed with unskilled labor, which they use to produce via (8.22) or invest in accumulating skills to be used as input in the production function (8.21). Depending on the way they behaved in the first period, they can be either a skilled or an unskilled worker in the second period. If skilled, their production technology will change to (8.21) in the second period.

All consumption takes place in the second period and the utility function of any agent is

$$u = \alpha \, ln \, c + (1 - \alpha) ln \, b, \tag{8.23}$$

where b stands for bequest. Individuals differ from each other in terms of the bequests from parents.

Capital is mobile and both firms and individuals have access to the international market. However, individuals might default on their debts by relocation, a choice that firms are denied. This asymmetry introduces imperfections in the capital market. In particular, lenders to individuals incur a cost z to keep track of borrowers, while borrowers spend $\beta \, z$, $\beta > 1$ to beat the lenders. Thus, the actual cost of borrowing is higher than the world rate of interest r.

As noted, firms do not have the option of evasion. Consequently, profit maximization leads to the condition

$$F_k(K_t, L_t^s) = r. \tag{8.24}$$

Since r is held constant, constant returns to scale ensures that the capital labor ratio is a constant in this sector. Thus, the wage rate w of skilled labor is a constant too. In the short run, an agent borrowing d pays an interest i_d to cover the lender's search cost z. Under zero cost competitive financial intermediation,

$$d \, i_d = d \, r + z.$$

On the other hand, lenders ensure that

$$d(1 + i_d) = \beta \, z.$$

Solving the two equations, we observe that

$$i_d = i = \frac{1 + \beta \, r}{\beta - 1} \tag{8.25}$$

Each agent supplies exactly one unit of labor in each period of his/her life. If he/she decides to work as an unskilled laborer in the first period, then the lifetime utility is

$$U_n(x) = \ln\left((x + w_n)(1 + r) + w_n\right) + \epsilon, \tag{8.26}$$

where

$$\epsilon = \alpha \, \ln \alpha + (1 - \alpha) \, \ln (1 - \alpha). \tag{8.27}$$

Such a worker makes a bequest of

$$b_n(x) = (1 - \alpha) \left((1 + r)(x + w_n) + w_n\right).$$

To acquire skills, an agent needs to invest $h > 0$ in human capital. Thus, if the agent's inheritance is $x \geq h$ and he decides to invest in human capital, then he is a net lender, enjoys utility equal to

$$U_s(x) = \ln\left(w_s + (x - h)(1 + r)\right) + \epsilon \tag{8.28}$$

and bequeaths

$$b_s(x) = (1 - \alpha)\left(w_s + (x - h)(1 + r)\right) \tag{8.29}$$

An individual who invests in human capital, but inherits $x < h$, is a borrower with corresponding utility and bequest given by

$$U_n(x) = \ln\left(w_s + (x - h)(1 + i)\right) + \epsilon$$
$$\text{and } b_s(x) = (1 - \alpha)\left(w_s + (x - h)(1 + i)\right)$$

Equations (8.26) and (8.28) imply that lenders would prefer to invest in human capital, since human capital earns more than unskilled labor. Borrowers will prefer to invest in human capital if their inheritance is sufficiently high, i.e.,

$$x \geq \frac{1}{1 - r}\left(w_n(2 + r) + h(1 + i) - w_s\right).$$

Consequently, only endowment wise affluent persons have access the choice to accumulate human capital.

The distribution of inherited wealth affects the distribution in the next period also and so on. In particular,

$$x_{t+1} = b_n(x_t)$$

$$= (1 - \alpha)((x + w_n)(1 + r) + w_n), \quad \text{if } x_t < f,$$

$$x_{t+1} = b_s(x_t)$$

$$= (1 - \alpha)(w_s + (x_t - h)(1 + i)), \quad \text{if } f \leq x_t < h,$$

$$x_{t+1} = b_s(x_t)$$

$$= (1 - \alpha)(w_s + (x_t - h)(1 + r)), \quad \text{if } h \leq x_t.$$

These equations determine the path of wealth distribution over time and the authors derive a stationary distribution for the long run. They go on to demonstrate that a Pareto improvement is possible if the government subsidizes higher education by lowering the cost of skill formation. The general conclusion is that a less developed economy converges to an unequal distribution of income, whereas a developed economy converges to an equal distribution.

Summary

1. The chapter was concerned with two important developments in endogenous growth theory. First, it examined critically the scale effect of human capital on growth that we came across in Chapters 6 and 7. Second, it considered two models developed to study the impact of growth on inequality and vice versa.

2. As far as the scale effect goes, the discussion was limited to the Jones (1995) critique of the models of Chapters 6 and 7. Jones starts off with the empirical observation that the size of research labourers does not affect the long run rate of growth of an economy.

3. He questions the manner in which the existing stock of knowledge af-

fects the research sector. In particular, he introduces the possibility that a growth in the knowledge stock could exert positive or negative externalities on research. Besides, he also introduces external diseconomies that could arise on account of duplication of research output. Also, he allows for labour or human capital growth at an exogenously given positive rate in the model. In other respects, his economy resembles Romer (1990).

4. He demonstrates that with these extensions, it is still possible for the Private Economy to grow at a balanced rate provided the parameters of the model are properly chosen. Jones solves for the share of human capital engaged in the research sector when the total supply of human capital is growing at an exogenously given rate. However, he also concludes that the endogenously determined growth rate does not respond to policy tools, such as a tax or a subsidy. His endogenous growth rate is determined somewhat in the manner in which Arrow's Learning by Doing growth rate was determined in Chapter 3.

5. Solving for the relevant variables in the Command Economy, Jones concludes that it is not possible to pinpoint which of the systems grows faster. Even when the knowledge and duplication related externalities suggest that the Private Economy should grow faster, it turns out that it is the Command Economy which dominates. Jones conjectures that the explanation may lie in the strong monopoly generated inefficiencies in the Private Economy.

6. Alesina and Rodrik (1994) analyse the link between income distribution and the rate of growth of the system. The structure of the economy is borrowed from Barro and Sala-i-Martin (1990 and 2003). However, agents are not identical and differentiated from one another according to their ownership of capital and labour. A proportional tax is imposed on capital services to finance a pure public input that enters as an indispensable input into the production function.

7. Given any tax rate, all agents choose the same rate of growth and the model admits a growth rate maximizing tax rate.

8. Taking an individual's response to a tax rate into account, the government can solve for the tax rate that will maximize his welfare. The optimal tax rate is individual specific, since agents differ from each other in terms of the initial distribution of labour and capital endowments. For example, for a pure capitalist, i.e. one who owns capital alone and has no labour endowment, the optimal tax rate is equal to the growth maximizing tax rate.

9. The smaller the endowment of capital relative to labour (i.e. the greater the inequality), the larger is the optimal tax rate and lower the growth rate. If the choice of a tax rate is left to majority voting, then greater inequality leads to lower growth. The result has been a source of controversy, since many empirical studies suggest that the relationship between the growth rate and inequality should be positive.

10. Galor and Zeira (1993) analyze the role of wealth distribution through investment in human capital. Their work rests on the premise that levels of skill formation (hence, investment in human capital) have positive implications for growth and that inequalities in inherited wealth in the presence of imperfect capital markets determine individuals' capacities for skill formation.

11. Individuals have the choice to work as unskilled workers in the both periods of their lives and consume the output, after taking care of bequest, in the second period. Alternatively, they can use the bequests received from parents and borrow in an imperfect capital market to acquire skills in the first period and produce in the second period with the help of an efficient technology.

12. A society that starts of with an unequal wealth distribution (as is the case with underdeveloped economies) tends to move towards unequal distribution of income, whereas a society that has an equal distribution of income tends towards equal distribution of incomes.

13. This is the only work presented in this book which uses an overlapping generation set up rather than the dynastic household concept.

Problems

1. Prove, following the Romer (1990) approach, that the Private Economy of the Jones model is capable of a balanced growth equilibrium. Show in particular that $g_A = g_Y = g_C = g_K$.

2. Show that under the Romer (1990) assumption of $\phi = 1$, there is no balance growth equilibrium for the Jones' Private Economy model. What is the economic intuition underlying this result?

3. Derive (8.8). Argue why a change in the productivity parameter a leaves the equilibrium share of human capital unchanged.

4. Solve for the Command Economy balanced growth path in Jones' Command Economy. Derive (8.9).

5. Read Jones (1995).

6. Read Galor and Zeira (1993) with particular attention to Theorem 1 which deals with long run behaviour of income inequalities.

7. Read Aghion et al (1999).

References

Aghion P. and P. Howitt (1992) 'A Model of Growth through Creative Destruction', *Econometrica*, Vol 60: 323–51.

——- (1998) Endogenous Growth Theory, Cambridge, Massachusetts: The MIT Press.

Aghion P., E. Caroli and C. Garca-Penalosa (1999) 'Inequality and Economic Growth: The Perspective of New Growth Theories', *Journal of Economic Literature*, Vol XXXVII: 1615–60.

Alesina A, and D. Rodrik (1994) 'Distributive Politics and Economic Growth', *Quarterly Journal of Economics*, Vol. 109: 465–490.

Arnold, L. G., (1997) 'Stability of the Steady–State Equilibrium in the Uzawa–Lucas Model: A Simple Proof', *Zeitschrift für Wirtschafts- und Sozialwissenschaften*, Vol. 117: 197–207.

——- (2000) 'Stability of the Market Equilibrium in Romer's Model of Endogenous Technical Change', *Journal of Macroeconomics*, Vol. 22: 69–84.

Arrow, K.J. (1962) 'The Economic Implications of Learning by Doing', *Review of Economic Studies*, Vol. 29: 155-73.

Atsumi, H. (1965) 'Neoclassical Growth and the Efficient Programme of Capital Accumulation', *Review of Economic Studies*, Vol. 32: 127–36.

Barro, R. (1990) 'Government Spending in a Simple Model of Endogenous Growth', *Journal of Political Economy*, Vol. 98: S 103–S125.

Barro, R. and X. Sala-i-Martin (1992) 'Public Finance in Models of Economic Growth', *Review of Economic Studies*, Vol. 59: 645–61.

—— (2003) Economic Growth, Second Edition, Cambridge: Massachusetts: The MIT Press.

Bellman, R. (1957) Dynamic Programming, Princeton, NJ: Princeton University Press.

Benveniste, L.M. and J.A. Scheinkman (1979) 'On the Differentiability of the Value Function in Dynamic Models of Economics', *Econometrica*, Vol. 47: 727–32.

Bond, E., Ping Wang and Chong K. Yip (1996) 'A General Two Sector Model of Endogenous Growth with Human and Physical Capital: Balanced Growth and Transitional Dynamics', *Journal of Economic Theory*, Vol. 68: 149–73.

Bond, E., K. Trask and Ping Wang (2003) 'Factor Accumulation and Trade: Dynamic Comparative Adavantage with Endogenous Physical and Human Capital', *International Economic Review*, Vol. 44: 1041–60.

Burmeister, E. and R.A. Dobell (1969) 'Disembodied Technological Change with Several Factors', *Journal of Economic Theory*, Vol. 1: 1–8.

—— (1970) Mathematical Theories of Economic Growth, London: Macmillan.

Cass, D. (1965) 'Optimum Growth in an Aggregative Model of Capital Accumulation', *Review of Economic Studies*, Vol. 32: 233–40.

—— (1966) 'Optimum Growth in an Aggregative Model of Capital Accumulation: A Turnpike Theorem', *Econometrica*, Vol. 34: 33–50.

Chiang, A.C. (1984) Fundamental Methods of Mathematical Economics, Singapore: McGraw-Hill.

—— (1992) Elements of Dynamic Optimisation, New York: McGraw-Hill.

Das, Mausumi (2006) 'Book Review: Growth Theory: Solow and his Modern Exponents', *Indian Economic Review*, Vol. 41: 231–2.

Dasgupta, D. (2001) 'New Growth Theory: A Supply–Demand View in Contemporary Macroeconomics', Chapter 5, 155–205, in A. Bose, D. Ray and A. Sarkar (2001) Contemporary Macroeconomics, New Delhi: Oxford University Press. .

—— (1999) 'Growth vs Wefare in a Model of Nonrival

Infrastructure', *Journal of Development Economics*, Vol. 58: 359–85.

——- (2001) 'Lindahl Pricing, Nonrival Infrastructure, and Endogenous Growth', *Journal of Public Economic Theory*, Vol. 3: 413–30.

——- and S. Marjit (2004) 'Consumption, Quality of Life and Growth', Discussion Paper No. ERU 2002–12, Kolkata Indian Statistical Institute, (Revised).

——- (2004) 'Public Infrastructure and Sustainable Growth in a Small Open Economy with and without Foreign Direct Investment', *Arthabeekshan*, Vol. 14: 11–26.

——- (2005) Growth Theory: Solow and his Modern Exponents, New Delhi, Oxford.

——- (2005) 'Notes on Optimal Control Theory for the Neoclassical Model of Growth', Chapter 4, 39–81, in S. Lahiri and P. Maiti (Eds) (2005) Economic Theory in a Changing World: Policy Modelling for Growth, New Delhi: Oxford University Press.

——- and Koji Shimomura ((2006) 'Public Infrastructure, Employment and Sustainable Growth in a Small Open Economy with and without Foreign Direct Investment', *The Journal of International Trade and Economic Development*, Vol. 15: 257 - 91.

——- (2008) 'Fixed Coefficients, Harrod, Domar and the AK models of Growth: Some Common Misconceptions Explored', *Indian Growth and Development Review*, Vol. 1: 112-18.

De la Croix, David, Philippe Michel (2002) Theory of Economic Growth, Cambridge: Cambridge University Press.

Diamond, P. (1965) 'Disembodied Technical Change in a Two-Sector Model', *Review of Economic Studies*, Vol. XXXII: 161–8.

Dinopoulos, E (1994) 'Schumpeterian Growth Theory: An Overview', *Osaka City University Economic Reveiew*, Vol. 21: 1–21.

——- and F. Sener (2004) 'New Directions in Schumpeterian Growth Theory', in H. Hanusch and A. Pyka (eds), Elgar Companion to Neo-Schumpeterian Economics, Cheltenham: Edward Elgar (2004).

——- and P. Segerstrom (2004) 'A Theory of North-South Trade and Globalization', Mimeographed.

Dixit, A. and J. E. Stiglitz (1977) 'Monopolistic Competition and

Optimum Product Diversity', *American Economic Review*, Vol. 67: 297–308.

Dixit, A.K. (1990) Optimisation in Economic Theory, Second Edition, Oxford: Oxford University Press.

d'Autume, A. and P. Michel (1993) 'Endogenous Growth in Arrow's Learning by Doing Model', *European Economic Review*, Vol. 37: 1175–84.

Dorfman, R., P. A. Samuelson and R. Solow (1958) Linear Programming and Economic Analysis, New York: McGraw-Hill Book Comany, Inc.

Domar, E. (1946) 'Capital Expansion, Rate of Growth and Employment', *Econometrica*, Vol. 14: 137–47.

Drandakis, E.M. and E.S. Phelps (1966) 'A Model of Induced Investment, Growth and Distributiuon', *Quarterly Journal of Economics*, Vol. 76: 823–39.

EPW Research Foundation (2002): National Accounts Statistics of India, 1950–51 to 2000–2001, Mumbai, India.

Ethier, W.J. (1982) 'National and International Returns to Scale in the Modern Theory of International Trade', *American Economic Review* Vol. 72: 389–405.

Feenstra, R. C. (1996) 'Trade and Uneven Growth', *Journal of Development Economics*, Vol. 49: 229–56.

Frankel, M. (1962) 'The Production Function in Allocation and Growth: A Synthesis', *American Economic Review*, Vol. 52, 995–1022.

Futagami, K., Y. Morita and A. Shibata (1993) 'Dynamic Analysis of an Endogenous Growth Model with Public Capital', *Scandinavian Journal of Economics*, Vol. 95, 607–25.

Galor, O. and J. Zeira (1993) 'Income Distribution and Macroeconomics', *Review of Economic Studies*, Vol. 60: 35–52.

Galor, O. (1996) 'Convergence? Inferences from Theoretical Models', *Economic Journal*, Vol. 106: 1056–69.

Galor and Zeira (1993) 'Income Distribution and Macroeconomics', *Review of Economic Studies*, Vol. 60: 35–2.

Grossman, G. M. and E. Helpman (1991a) 'Quality Ladders in the Theory of Growth', *Review of Economic Studies*, Vol. 58, 43–61.

—— (1991b) Innovation and Growth in the World Economy, Cambridge, Massachusetts: MIT Press.

Guha, S, D. Dasgupta and K. Shimomura (2006) 'On the Relationship between the Number of Firms and the Endogenous Growth Rate for a Model with Public Infrastructure', *Contemporary Issues and Ideas in Social Sciences*, http://journal.ciiss.net/index.php/ciiss/issue/view/6.

Halkin, H. (1974) 'Necessary Conditions for Optimal Control Problems with Infinite Horizons', *Econometrica*, Vol. 42: 267–72.

Harrod, R.H. (1939) 'An Essay on Dynamic Theory', *Economic Journal*, Vol. 49: 14–33.

—— (1948) Towards a Dynamic Economics, London: Macmillan.

Hicks, J.R. (1963) The Theory of Wages, London: Macmillan.

Human Development Report (2003), United Nations Development Programme, Oxford: Oxford University Press.

Jones, Charles (1995) 'R and D-Based Models of Economic Growth', *Journal of Political Economy*, Vol. 103: 759–84.

Kaldor, N. (1957) 'A Model of Economic Growth', *Economic Journal*, Vol. 67: 591–623.

King, R.G. and R. Levine (1993) 'Finance, Entrepreneurship and Growth: Theory and Evidence', *Journal of Monetary Economics*, Vol. 32: 513–42.

Koopmans, T.C. (1965) 'On the Concept of Optimal Economic Growth', in The Econometric Approach to Development Planning, Amsterdam: North Holland.

Lewis, W. A. (1954) 'Economic Development with Unlimited Supplies of Labour', *The Manchester School*, Vol. 28: 139-91.

Long, J. B. and C. I. Plosser (1983) 'Real Business Cycles', *Journal of Political Economy*, Vol. 91: 39–69.

Lucas R.E. Jr. (1988) 'On the Mechanism of Economic Development', *Journal of Monetary Economics*, Vol. 1: 3–42.

—— (1990) 'Supply Side Economics: An Analytical Review', *Oxford Economic Papers*, Vol. 42, 293–316.

—— (2002) 'The Industrial Revolution: Past and Future', 109–88, in Robert E. Lucas, Jr. Lectures on Economic Growth, New Delhi:

Oxford University Press. (2002).

Malthus, Thomas R. (1798) 'First Essay on Population', Reprints of Economic Classics, New York: Augustus Kelly, 1965.

Mangasarian, O.L. (1966) 'Sufficient Conditions for the Optimal Control of Non-linear Systems', *SIAM Journal on Control*, Vol. 4: 139–52.

Mino, K. (1996) 'Analysis of a Two-Sector Model of Endogenous Growth with Capital Income Taxation', *International Economic Review*, Vol. 37: 227–51.

Peretto, P. (1998) 'Technological Change and Population Growth', *Journal of Economic Growth*, Vol. 3: 283–311.

Perotti, R. (1993) 'Political Equilibrium, Income Distribution and Growth', *Review of Economic Studies*, Vol. 60: 775–76.

—— (1996) 'Growth, Income Distribution and Democracy: What the data Say?', *Journal of Economic Growth*, Vol. 1: 149–87.

Persson, T. and G. Tabellini (1994) 'Is Inequality Harmful for Growth?', *American Economic Review*, Vol. 84: 600–21.

Phelps, E.S. (1961) 'The Golden Rule of Accumulation: A Fable for Growthmen', *American Economic Review*, Vol. 51, 638–43.

—— (1962) 'The New View of Investment: A Neoclassical Analysis', *Quarterly Journal of Economics*, Vol. 76, 548–67.

—— (1965) 'Second Essay on the Golden Rule of Accumulation', *American Economic Review*, Vol. 55, 739–814.

Pontryagin, L.S., V. G. Boltyanskii, R. V. Gamkrelidze, and E. F. Mishchenko (1962) The Mathematical Theory of Optimal Processes. (Trans. K.N. Trirogoff; ed. L.W. Neustadt) New York: Wiley-Interscience.

Quah, D. (1996) 'Twin Peaks: Growth and Convergence in Models of Distribution Dynamics', *Economic Journal*, Vol. 106: 1045–55.

Ramsey, F. (1928) 'A Mathematical Theory of Saving', *Economic Journal*, Vol. 38: 543–59.

Rebelo, S. (1991) 'Long-Run Policy Analysis and Long-Run Growth', *Journal of Political Economy*, Vol. 99: 501–21.

Ricardo, David (1817) On the Principles of Political Economy and

Taxation, in Pierro Sraffa (ed) The Works and Correspondences of David Ricardo, V 1, Cambridge: Cambridge University Press, 1951.

Rivera-Batiz, L. A. and P.M. Romer (1991) 'Economic Integration and Endogenous Growth', *Quarterly Journal of Economics*, Vol. 106: 531–555.

Robinson, Joan (1938) 'The Classification of Inventions', *Review of Economic Studies*, Vol. 5: 139–42.

Romer, P.M. (1986) 'Increasing Returns and Long Run Growth', *Journal of Political Economy*, Vol. 94: 1002–1037.

——- (1990) 'Endogenous Technical Change', *Journal of Political Economy*, Vol. 98: S71–S102.

——- (1994) 'The Origins of Endogenous Growth', *Journal of Economic Perspectives*, Vol. 8: 3–22.

Schumpeter, J. A. (1934) The Theory of Economic Development, Cambridge: Harvard University Press.

——- (1950) Capitalism, Socialism and Democracy: New York, Harper and Row.

Segerstrom, P., T.C.A. Anant and E. Dinopoulos (1990) 'A Schumpeterian Model of Product Life Cycle', *American Economic Review*, Vol. 80: 1077–92.

Segerstrom, P. (1998) 'Endogenous Growth without Scale Effects', *American Economic Review*, Vol. 88: 1290–1310.

Sheshinski, E. (1967) 'Optimal Accumulation with Learning by Doing', 67–85, in K. Shell (1967) Essays on the Theory of Optimal Economic Growth, Cambridge: MIT Press.

Solow, R.M. (1956) 'A Contribution to the Theory of Economic Growth', *Quarterly Journal of Economics*, Vol. 32: 65–94.

——- (1960) 'Investment and Technical Change', in Arrow, K. J., S. Karlin and P. Suppes (Eds) Mathematical Methods in the Social Sciences, Stanford: Stanford University Press (1960).

——- (2000) Growth Theory: An Exposition, Oxford, Oxford University Press.

Stokey, N. (1996) 'Free Trade, Factor Returns and Factor Accumulation', *Journal of Economic Growth*, Vol. 1: 421–47.

Swan, T. W. (1956) 'Economic Growth and Capital Accumulation', *The Economic Record*, Vol. 332: 334–61.

The India Infrastructure Report (1996) New Delhi: National Council of Applied Economic Rresearch.

Uzawa, H. (1961a) 'Neutral Inventions and the Stability of Growth Equilibrium', *Review of Economic Studies*, Vol. 28: 117–24.

——- (1961b) 'On a Two-Sector Model of Economic Growth: I', *Review of Economic Studies*, Vol. 29: 40–7.

——- (1963) 'On a Two-Sector Model of Economic Growth: II', *Review of Economic Studies*, Vol. 30: 105–18.

——- (1965) 'Optimum Technical Change in an Aggregative Model of Economic Growth', *International Economic Review*, Vol. 6: 19–31.

von Neumann, J. (1945-46) 'A Model of General Economic Equilibrium', *Review of Economic Studies*, Vol. 13: 1–9 (Translated from original German article (1938) by G. Morgenstern).

von Weizäcker, C. C. (1965) 'Existence of Optimal Programmes of Accumulation for an Infinite Time Horizon', *Review of Economic Studies*, Vol. 32: 85–104.

World Bank (1994) World Bank Development Report, Washington DC: 1994.

Young, A. (1993) 'Substitution and Complementarity in Endogenous Innovation', *Quarterly Journal of Economics*, Vol. 108, 775–807.

Xie, D. (1994) 'Divergence in Economic Performance: Transitional Dynamics with Multiple Equilibria', *Journal of Economic Theory*, Vol. 63: 97–112.

Index